S W A N S O N G

A Memoir

Barbara Swanson

ISBN   978-0-9567095-0-9

Copyright © Barbara Swanson 2010

Barbara Swanson asserts the moral right
to be identified as the author of this work.

A catalogue record for this book
is available from the British Library.

Published by Barbara Swanson and
printed in England by Print on Demand-
Worldwide, Peterborough, using paper
from sustainable sources.

To
Grace, Aeone
& Michael

AUTHOR'S NOTE
Some names have been changed.
The dialogue used is either what was
actually said or the memory of
voices which have stayed with me
like echoes from the past.

O N E

There were no stars that night, no moon.
Beneath the darkling sky the city lay,
Its people wakeful
Waiting, waiting
For the death that stalked the skies.
In their midst, a child
Too afraid to sleep, too sad to cry.
That child was me.
My name is Barbara Mary and this is my story.

FLORENCE WAS THE MATRIARCH.   She lived on one side of Fortune Green, a small grassy square in West Hampstead, whilst her married children lived on the other – near enough to bask in her warmth yet far enough away to escape the blast when her fiery temperament, the Aries ram, went on the rampage.

Her youngest daughter Ethel's home was in Agamennon Road where she lived with her husband Toby and two children, my cousins Peter and Judith.   Ethel was plump, good-looking and maternal yet, like her mother, had an inner toughness.   She adored cats nearly as much as children and a succession of them not only lived like kings but were given curiously witty names.   One, a fine mouser, was called Erasmus, whilst her fourteenth was logically named Quatorze.   Just round the corner in a smart mansion flat at the end of Gondar Gardens lived Florence's eldest child, Evelyn.   I loved my Aunty Evelyn.   She wore silky clothes and smart little hats, and her opulent fur coat smelled of perfume.   She was sporty and once, in her teens, had played at Wimbledon. She was married to an accountant, a gentle, timid Jewish man who rejoiced in the name of Sidney

Dickey. Much though she loved him, so mortified was Evelyn by this surname that she tried never to use it, sticking to her maiden name whenever possible. This was something I could not understand.

"But *why* Auntie?" I'd nag when I grew a little older, "*why* don't you like being called 'Mrs Dickey'?"

My father would snigger behind his hand whilst Auntie, glaring myopically through her little round glasses, snapped,

"For God's sake Charlie, *do* shut up."

But I never did get an answer.

My own home was further down Gondar Gardens at number 32 where I lived with my parents, Charles and Grace, big sister Patricia, and my brother, Richard. And that was us, the Davis clan.

I was five when my story begins. It was 1942 and all the world was at war. Hitler's Blitzkrieg had ended - during which London, particularly Docklands and the East End, had been bombarded for 76 consecutive nights - but London was still a dark and dangerous place where air raids were a regular and terrifying occurrence. The great city's streets were scarred by bombsites, buildings reduced to rubble or their shattered remains shored up, sorry skeletons of what had once been homes. Street lamps were no longer lit at dusk and people drove without headlights. Indeed, if convoys of army vehicles had to cross the city, black cabs acted as pilots to lead them through the darkened streets. Windows were criss-crossed with sticky paper to prevent shattered glass blowing inwards and black blinds were drawn each evening to limit the amount of light visible from the sky.

Despite the ever present danger, many evacuated children had been brought back to London and families reunited, my brother, sister and I included. However, the mother we adored was now in hospital, and Patricia, Richard and I were staying with Auntie Ethel in Agamennon Road.

Whilst the nervous Sidney had been called up to become an unlikely soldier, my father and Uncle Toby were exempt from military duty because, as builders, they were in reserved occupations. They were also deemed medically unfit, Charles because he was bronchial and Toby, who was deaf. This does not mean their life was either easy or safe. Both of them volunteered for the ARP (Air Raid Protection) which meant that, having worked all day, they then went out each night patrolling the streets in their allotted area of Hampstead. They were responsible for maintaining the blackout and if someone forgot to pull their blinds, they would thump on the front door, shouting:

"Put that light out! Don't you know there's a war on?"

Once the air-raid sirens sounded, it was their job to get people into shelters as quickly as possible and look after them during and after raids. Every house with a garden had a bunker-like air raid shelter lined and roofed with corrugated iron and half buried in the soil. Other people hid in their cellars although for many the only refuge was either in the long, low reinforced concrete shelters in the streets or the deep safety of the underground train system. Because houses tended to collapse from the roof down, often leaving exterior walls and the outline of rooms standing, there was also a theory - held by the foolhardy few - that it was safe to sit round the edge of a room, backs to the wall and legs facing inwards.

It was tough, dangerous work - putting out fires caused by incendiary bombs, helping to demolish or make safe bomb-damaged buildings, checking air-raid shelters, watching the skies as bombs were released from enemy aircraft and literally running in the direction they fell, administering first aid if professionals were not at hand, even helping to rescue people buried in the rubble of collapsed buildings. It was their own front line and they were every bit as brave as the servicemen fighting on distant battlefields. Working both day and night, my father became so white with exhaustion that my cousins, Judith and Peter, called him 'Uncle Ghost'. Yet, despite their bravery – and because they both looked fit, strong men – they were often accused of cowardice because they had not 'joined up'.

Night after night, with both fathers out on patrol, we children were put to bed only to wake up a couple of hours later to the sound of the air-raid sirens whose eerie, undulating wail soon became synonymous with terror. Up we'd jump, instantly awake, and stumble down the cellar steps to relative safety. There we huddled, listening to the drone of German planes overhead, the heavy stutter of anti-aircraft guns, the whistle and thrump of bombs as they fell, the distant crashes as they exploded - you were safe, it was said, if you could hear the whistle, it was the ones you didn't hear that killed you. My aunt tried to read us stories or encourage us to sing but our attention was elsewhere and our voices usually faded away. When at last the danger was over, the 'all clear' siren would tell us that it was safe to climb out of the cellar and fall wearily into bed.

One night the sirens woke us up as usual. But this time it was different because the warning was hardly over when the onslaught began.

The sounds outside were even more terrifying than usual. And they were right overhead.

"*The cellar*," screamed Auntie Ethel, "*quick, run...*"

Patty snatched Richard from his cot and one after another we half-fell down the steps into the cellar. There we all were - Auntie, Peter, Patty, Barbie, Richard, Judith... Judith? Oh God, Judith wasn't there! Ethel flew up the stairs to the bedroom, swept four-year-old Judith into her arms and turned to run. But as she did so a huge explosion shook the house and a wardrobe fell, trapping them underneath. But somehow my aunt managed to wriggle free and reach the safety of the cellar again, her precious burden in her arms.

Now the barrage of noise was deafening as bricks, tiles and chimney pots crashed to the ground and every window shattered. Down in the cellar we huddled, trembling with fear. Would it ever end? Were we going to die? But at last the 'all clear' sounded and, one by one, we crept upstairs.

Afterwards, as we sat sipping hot drinks, the front door burst open and in ran Charles and Toby followed soon afterwards by Granny and Auntie Evelyn. We were kissed and kissed, enveloped in their arms, half-heard their muttered prayers and felt their tears on our cheeks.

Years later, when we were old enough to understand, my father told us his side of the story. He and Toby were out on patrol that night, walking up a hilly road from which they had a clear view of the surrounding area. Suddenly, the air-raid sirens sounded and almost immediately they heard the drone of approaching enemy aircraft. And then, clearly illuminated in the beam of a searchlight, they saw a plane release a stream of bombs, which to their horror they realised were falling either very near, or on, Agamennon Road. They turned and ran back down the hill but even as they did so they saw house after house in our street collapse, and felt certain they would soon have to dig the remains of their family out of the rubble. By the time they reached the end of the road, masonry was already blocking it and fires had sprung up everywhere as gas mains exploded. But somehow they managed to get through and, to their amazement, saw that our house was one of the few left standing. Next day they discovered that a bomb *had* hit us but had ricocheted off the roof without exploding and buried itself in the back garden. Having made sure we were all safe, the two men went back onto the street to help in the rescue effort.

Opposite us lived a family: Mum, Dad, three teenage boys - the oldest of whom was on leave from the army - and a little girl of six, plus

Granny and Granddad who had a small flat on the top floor. Their house had received a direct hit and was now lying in ruins. As Charles and Toby fought their way through the wreckage they heard a weak cry and in the remains of what had been the hall they found the little girl alive, lying in her dead brother's arms and protected by his body. And in the ruins of the sitting room they found the rest of the family, all of them dead. It seemed clear that they had not had time to get down to the safety of the cellar and had sat, legs out, in the sitting room. And it was also clear that the oldest boy had died saving his little sister's life.

But in the midst of tragedy there were also miracles. Our own survival was one, but perhaps the most extraordinary story was that of an old lady who lived in a flat at the end of the road. She was a very religious woman who had once been a missionary, a sweet and friendly soul who loved children and saved up her minute food ration to make little cakes and biscuits for the neighbourhood's kids. No-one could ever persuade her to take shelter when the air raid siren sounded, because, she said, she knew God would save her. So when on that fateful night a bomb hit her block of flats, she was, as usual, in bed. And God did indeed save her because when the building received a direct hit, she was blown into the street on her bed with her Bible under the pillow, where my father and uncle found her completely unharmed.

The house in Agamennon Road was badly damaged and so the next morning we children were taken out, blindfolded as we left the house to spare us the sight of the devastation in the street. We were taken round the corner to Auntie Evelyn's flat and somehow she managed to squeeze us all in. The night raids continued and, as auntie lived in a flat, we now had to use the public air-raid shelters. As soon as the sirens sounded we were bundled into our dressing gowns and slippers, hurried downstairs and out into the street. This I found terrifying, for now we could see the searchlight beams criss-crossing the night sky whilst the menacing throb of German bombers, the stutter of the British ack-ack guns and the sound of bombs exploding was louder and more frightening than ever. Inside the shelter, however, our fear quickly receded because the chatter and sing-songs and general bonhomie kept everybody's spirits up, both young and old. We were lifted up onto the tiers of bunks that lined the walls and told to go to sleep, but of course we never did. Now and again there would be a tinny *clunk* at the door. "That'll be Mr Davis!" everyone would cry, for our tall father in his ARP tin hat hit his head every time he ducked to enter the shelter and check that all was well.

As the air-raids intensified, it became clear that it was too dangerous for we children to stay in London and it was decided that, whilst 12-year-old Patty would stay in the city with Evelyn, Auntie Ethel would take the four youngest to live in safety in the country. Our Granny and Granddad owned a cottage in Essex and it was here that a whole new phase of our life began.

* * * * * *

Our new home was an old cottage in the village of Langley in Essex. It stood beside the churchyard gates like a gentle sentinel, guarding the place where ancient crosses and lichened angels leant in peaceful benediction over the mossy graves.

Church Cottage was tiny, its little windows peeping out like shy and shining eyes from beneath a thick thatched fringe. A short path led up to the front door and a vegetable garden wound around the side of the house and along the back. Behind us were nothing but fields and open countryside. In one corner of the back garden, behind a rickety fence, lurked a green and murky pond. This, we were warned, was so deep that an unfortunate carthorse had once drowned in it and we were on no account to let Richard, the baby of the family, go near it. Peter, Judith and I, it seemed, were immune to the dangers of a watery death. Inside, the house was just 'two up, two down' with a kitchen and sitting-room on the ground floor and, at the top of a few narrow, winding stairs, two bedrooms.

For our lovely, long-suffering aunt, as for most women, life must have been hard. Now she had four small children to look after instead of two, in a cottage with neither electricity nor gas. Water for cooking and washing came from the farm, which lay behind the church, and had to be pumped up from a well and carried back in buckets. Water for everything else came from the large wooden water butt which stood outside the kitchen door. Every Monday - which, back then, was the traditional washday - she lit a fire under the big copper boiler built into the corner of an outhouse, filling it with buckets of water from the butt. All the larger items were boiled up in this whilst smaller things were washed separately using a large slab of yellow Sunlight soap and a scrubbing brush. In the evening, the damp washing was arranged on a wooden clothes horse around the fire or hauled up to hang like bunting on the old pine rack. There was no ironing board, just a couple of blankets and an old sheet folded on top of the kitchen table. Two heavy metal irons were heated on the trivet over the fire and their temperature gauged by spitting on them - if it sizzled, they were ready.

Auntie cooked on a strange oil-fired contraption with rings above it on which to balance pans, plus a metal oven which could be lifted into place for baking. There was also a black iron range in the sitting room with an oven In Its base and a swivelling trivet on which the kettle stood. There were only two buses a week to the nearby town of Bishops Stortford where she went to buy our meagre wartime rations. In many ways, coping with food shortages was easier in the country than in London. The baker clip-clopped up the lane in his horse and cart a couple of times a week, and our milk came from the farm. As Mrs Carter, the farmer's wife, was measuring it out from the big urn in her dairy, she would sometimes say:

"Tell your auntie I've got a cabbage for her."

We soon learned that this was good news because 'cabbage' was the codeword for gifts of food which, by rights, were destined for government controlled distribution. So the 'cabbage' might be some extra milk, cheese, or on rare occasions a piece of illicitly home-cured bacon. Like everyone else, Auntie grew fruit and vegetables in the garden because everyone was exhorted to 'Dig for Victory'. We were given a brimming spoonful of a treacley compound called Cod Liver Oil and Malt every day - issued free of charge to all children during the war - which many kids hated but I found delicious. Although we never went hungry, we dreamed of the day when the war was over and we could have unobtainable treats like sweeties, butter, ice cream and bananas.

At night the cottage was lit by the soft glow of oil lamps and candles. We were bathed cosily in a tin hipbath placed in front of the fire, the water first heated in a galvanized bucket on the kitchen stove. But going to the loo was anything but cosy, for not only was it in a small shed in the garden - a place where spiders lurked and cold winds whistled through the holes in the walls - but it was also very basic. The seat was made of wood, the pine pale from years of scrubbing, with two round holes worn smooth by countless bottoms. And somewhere beneath this 'thunder box', as it was known, lurked a noxious place into which our offerings fell. The twin-seater arrangement always puzzled me and still does. Who, I wonder, would share their toileting time with someone else? Was it the custom for a husband and wife to go together? Did mothers say 'now then you two, off you go and do your business - and Jack, make sure your brother doesn't throw his teddy down the hole this time'? Or did housewives sometimes go in there for a bit of peace and quiet and a gossip over a cup of tea? There was little or no toilet paper available during the war and so we cut newspaper into convenient squares, threaded these on a string and hooked them up beside the loo. As though this was not enough to give you constipation, an element of danger was soon added to the experience when my aunt bought six hens and a cockerel, who took up residence in the back garden. We named the rooster Henry VIII for obvious reasons. He was a massive bird with a cruel beak, gimlet eyes and a tail like a shimmering waterfall. He was arrogant, he was evil, and we were his target. Now, whenever we ventured out to the lavatory, we carried a stick to beat him off as he sprang from nowhere, ready to attack. Little did he know that we would one day get our revenge, for whilst his six wives' purpose in life was to give us eggs, his fate was to be far more grizzly and one that we would relish on Christmas Day!

Peter, Judith and I were soon enrolled at the village school. Richard, only three-and-a-half, was still too young. But after a while, Auntie became so terrified he would fall into the bottomless pond that she begged the school to take him and he was allowed to join us. To start with we were unhappy because we were not accepted by the other children. Indeed we must have looked and sounded very odd to them. We probably appeared stiff and formal, the three oldest still wearing the uniform from our London convent school: navy gabardine mackintoshes, Peter in a little peaked cap, Judith and I in velour hats with upturned brims, held in place by elastic under our chins. We spoke differently too, our accents no doubt jarring to the country kids with their soft brogues. They were horrible to us.

"Here come the evacuees, here come the evacuees," they jeered whenever we came into view, "Lon-don-ers, Lon-don-ers, you're just horrible Lon-don-ers."

But before long they got tired of this game and there was no more trouble. It was a Church of England school and the headmistress, and teacher of the main class, was a deaconess in holy orders who wore the black habit of a religious - a plain, calf-length black dress with a white collar and a black headdress edged in white. Even though she became a great friend of the family, she was only ever known as The Deaconess. She was a kind, sweet-tempered lady who made each day at school a happy one and who enriched our lives. Although it was headed by this devout woman, the school could not have been more different from our last school, La Sagesse Convent, incongruously located in Golders Green, where nuns in voluminous habits, their pale faces dwarfed by vast, starched wimples, floated like ravens through the gloomy corridors; where reciting ten Hail Mary's or kneeling to repent before the Virgin - of whom there was a figurine in every classroom - were standard punishments for our misdemeanors. Here in Langley, there were just two classes, a small one for the 'infants' and a large one for all the other children up to the age of ten. Instead of city streets, we now looked out over the village green and instead of the background noise of passing traffic, all we could hear was the occasional car, an army lorry or two, and the gentle clip-clop of horses' hooves as they pulled farm carts and tradesmen's traps around the neighbourhood. Our lessons took place in a gentle, almost informal atmosphere. Although I loved lessons, my favourite treat was our 'nature walks' when we explored the surrounding fields and woods, carrying the treasures we found proudly back to school. Birds' nests, whose tiny occupants had long since flown, frogs' spawn which we watched eagerly, waiting for tiny legs and tails to appear, violets and primroses, cowslips and golden celandine, shining conkers, velvety cushions of moss, the sad white skulls of rabbits and mice, remnants of a fox's or a weasel's meal - all in their season found their way back to a place on our nature table or to grace a sunny window ledge.

Now and then we had 'air-raid drill'. Without notice, the Deaconess would suddenly blow three shrill blasts on the silver whistle she wore round her neck and shout "*duck*". At this command, everyone pushed their little chairs aside and scrambled under their desks, giggling, tickling and shoving each other whilst Deaconess patrolled the room demonstrating how to crouch with heads down and arms wrapped round the knees. We evacuees, however, were very nonchalant and superior about air-raid drill. We slipped casually and without fuss under our desks, straight into the correct crouch position. After all, we'd been in the thick of it, we'd been bombed out, we'd seen the real thing. We sometimes boasted about how we'd been bombed but the village children were not impressed. Little did we realise that we were not out of the firing line and that before very long we would once again stare death in the face.

Our parents, too, must have thought this idyllic village was far removed from war. But they were mistaken, for just a few miles away was a big American airbase. Once or twice we saw the airmen when there was a dance on in the rusty, corrugated village hall just down the lane. The village girls and the Land Army girls all streamed in, dressed as prettily as their clothing coupons allowed, black lines drawn carefully up the back of bare legs to simulate the seams on unavailable stockings, the stub-ends of bright red lipsticks shared amongst them. Almost every young, fit British male had been called up so these Yanks in their immaculate uniforms must have seemed even more exotic and alluring to romance starved girls. Once, we children stood on tiptoe to peer through the windows and watched as they jitterbugged their way around the hall, swinging the squealing girls out at arm's length, flinging them over their shoulders, through their legs or holding them far too close, whilst the few local boys stood in gloomy clusters, outgunned. Not for nothing were American serviceman said to be 'oversexed, over-paid and over here'.

But these occasional chances to be young and light hearted were rare breaks from the danger and bravery of their real and terrible task. For on most evenings as dusk fell we watched wave after wave of bombers setting off from the airbase for Germany. We tried to count them as they flew overhead and we always called out 'good luck'. In the morning we saw them returning but there never seemed to be as many coming back as had set off. We often saw stragglers limping home, engines stuttering, propellers stationary, wings or tail fins damaged, or with gaping holes in the fuselage. Once we saw a plane coming in on fire. Moments later, a huge explosion, smoke and flames told its own terrible tale. Now, when I remember those far off days, I think too of the German people who were, as we had been in London, waiting in fear for these nightly bombardments.

There was a German prisoner-of-war camp just outside the village. Now and then on our way home from school we'd see them as they marched through the village in a straggling column. They always seemed to be happy and laughing, singing as they marched in a language we didn't understand. Perhaps they were relieved to be far from the battles that raged in other parts of the world, glad to be alive, knowing they would one day return to their families. Maybe they smiled and called to us because we reminded them of their own kids.

Long lines of Americans from the air base also swung through from time to time, big, healthy and confident. But whether it was the Germans or the Americans, we village children ran along beside them. Auntie Ethel had forbidden us to do so, saying it was 'common', but we took no notice because we knew that, if it was the Yanks, we could call out 'got any gum chum' and, if we were lucky, chewing gum or a piece of chocolate would come flying our way. Bliss for kids starved of sweeties.

Once home from school we'd have tea at the pine table in the kitchen. The moment it was finished we'd gabble: "For-what-we-have-received-may-I-be-truly-thankful-Amen-please-may-I-get-down", then rush into the sitting room, ready for the high point of our evening - Children's Hour. The radio which stood on a shelf beside the fireplace was housed in a shiny mahogany case and powered by a huge, immensely heavy battery. As five o'clock approached, Auntie switched on and we clustered round, waiting for favourites like 'Norman and Henry Bones, the Boy Detectives' and 'The Magic Bed Knob'. We knew that once Children's Hour had finished we must be absolutely quiet whilst Auntie listened to the six o'clock news reporting on the fearful progress of a world at war. And even at that young age we recognized Winston Churchill's deep, inspiring voice as he urged the British people to 'never flinch, never despair, never surrender.'

There was a piano in the sitting room and, to keep four mischievous children occupied, Auntie Ethel taught us songs. Peter was the star of our tiny choir because he had a beautiful treble voice which people used to say was 'better than Gracie Fields'. Our favourites were from a collection entitled 'Safety First' and all had a solemn and important message to impart. With much finger wagging, dramatic shaking of heads and tragic expressions we would lisp:

'A boy stood on the wailway twack
To watch the twains go froo
We'd like to tell you the rest of the tale
 But it's too sad for you
So-o-o-o
Keep away from the wailway twack
 It isn't the place to play
For twains go fast when they go past
 And you might be in the way.'

and:

'Pins and needles, needles and pins
That's where all the twouble begins
Never put needles and pins in your lips
You know what will happen
 If one of them slips.'

We mainly learned these so we could sing for 'the two Daddies', Charles and Toby, who came down for the weekend whenever their petrol allowance let them. Now and then our teacher would ask us to entertain the children at school and once we were even asked to perform at a concert in the village hall. However, our biggest fans seemed to be the elderly ladies who either came to tea or whom we visited. One of these was Mrs Chipperfield, a strange old woman who lived alone in a ramshackle cottage on the outskirts of the village. She was thin and bent with wild grey hair. She wore mud-spattered men's boots and always had a long black apron tied over her filthy clothes. Her companions were a flock of chickens which not only had the run of the garden but had also taken over the house. They were her 'little ones', her children. They strutted round the kitchen, helping themselves to anything edible, fluttering up to sit on the table and chairs, perching in a line on the mantelpiece, laying eggs on the one easy chair - and, of course, poo-ing everywhere. Mrs Chipperfield was never without a hen tucked under her arm, or perched on her knee, clucking and crooning to it in its own language. Why we were taken to visit her I have no idea, but she was always delighted to see us. We, on the other hand, hated it because we didn't like the chickens squawking and flapping, we didn't like the poos, we didn't like the smell and, most of all, we didn't like her kissing us. "One germ, two germs," Richard and Peter would chant in a stage whisper as Judith and I squirmed to avoid her lips. On the way home we got into trouble for our rude behaviour but we didn't care because we were certain she was a witch, and one surely didn't have to be polite to witches. Years later we discovered that poor old Mrs Chipperfield had been struck by lightning and killed as she crossed an open field, an awful but perhaps quite fitting death for a witch.

As summer ended and the corn turned to gold we were allowed to 'help' Mr Carter from Church Farm with his harvest. Out in the fields, his huge shire horse pulled the combine harvester whilst behind it men gathered up the falling sheaths and arranged these 'stooks' into neat lines. After the men came the gleaners - women and children carrying bags into which we scooped any grains of corn on the ground, all of which would be used to feed poultry and livestock during the winter months. At noon, the men stopped work, the horse was given water and his nose bag, whilst we sat in the shade and ate our lunch. Our greatest treat came later, though, when the dried stooks were tossed onto a cart and strong arms lifted us up to balance on the top, high above the ground, for the ride back to the farm. On our scratchy pinnacle we clung to each other, squealing, half afraid we were going to slide off, as the great horse took up the strain and pulled the swaying cart homewards through the gentle evening light.

One evening in the summer of 1943, Peter, Judith and I were out in the back garden with Auntie. Armed with sticks, we were trying to persuade Henry VIII to join his wives in their coop. Richard was already tucked up in bed. Suddenly, above the sound of the cockerel's squawks and our shouts and laughter, we heard an aircraft approaching. By this time, we could identify planes not only by their appearance but also by the sound of their engines. In fact, we even learned to draw their silhouettes. We knew the difference between a Spitfire and a Lancaster Bomber, we knew what an American Liberator looked like, and we certainly knew German bombers when we heard them. But this was different - a sort of phut, phut, phut rather like a motor bike. We looked up and there, low in the sky, heading straight towards us, was a sinister black craft like a small plane with very short wings, a scarlet flame streaming out behind its cylindrical body. This, although we didn't know it, was a doodlebug, a flying bomb, Hitler's top-secret weapon which had recently become a new cause for fear in our war-torn land. Now a doodlebug was heading our way. Suddenly, with a stuttering sound, its engine cut out and it went into a steep almost vertical dive, straight towards us.

"RUN!" screamed Auntie.

I remember running to the cottage and clinging to its stone walls. I remember the black shadow of this evil thing and the whoosh as it descended, skimming the thatched roof with inches to spare and exploding in the next field. The shock and terror of that moment were far worse than the night of the bombing in our London street but once again we survived and our country life continued.

The sad background to what may sound an idyllic life was that, although we did not know it, our darling mother was now terminally ill. Whilst Daddy came down to see us whenever he could, Richard and I saw Mummy only twice during the time we lived in Langley, once when we were taken to visit her in hospital and once, during the first week in April, 1944, when she came to stay at Church Cottage. It was a beautiful spring that year and, each day, my mother lay in a deckchair in the front garden. She was so still, so quiet that birds hopped down and perched on her body. We were so happy to have her back again. We picked her little bunches of primroses and violets. We sang her our best songs. We drew pictures for her. We snuggled into her arms as she read us stories. And we did our best to be good and quiet because, Auntie whispered, "Mummy is very tired."

Every evening before we went to sleep, Auntie helped her up the stairs and she sat on a little stool beside our beds, first Richard and then me, to hear us say our prayers. My birthday, the 15th of April, was fast approaching and one night I said:

"Oh Mummy, I *wish* the time would hurry up and pass so it was my birthday."

16

"My darling," she said, "promise me you will never wish time away."

A couple of weeks later, my father arrived to take her back to hospital. We stood at the front door, my little brother and I, our aunt's arms around us, as our parents walked up the garden path, my father supporting Mummy's frail figure in her apple green coat, her head leaning on his shoulder. He helped her into the low, black car, started the engine and drove slowly away down the lane.

I tore myself from my aunt and ran - down the lane, over the stile, up the meadow behind the cottage until I stood at the top of the hill. From there I could see the road. From there I could see the car winding its way out of the village. And as I watched until it disappeared from view, my heart knew what my child's mind did not - that I would never see her again.

And I was right, for Grace Edith Mary Davis, our beloved mother, died on the 19th May, 1944, six months after her thirty-ninth birthday.

T W O

OH, WE HAD BEEN SUCH a happy family. Our mother Grace was a beautiful woman, slim, elegant, even glamorous. She made not just her own clothes but also her children's. In fact, we were so beautifully dressed that people thought we were better off than we were. Her sense of style was also reflected in our home, where she was not afraid to be innovative and unusual in the way it was decorated. My father too was rather dashing. I can remember him in calf length tweed breeches, called 'plus fours', with long Argyll-patterned socks and highly polished brogues, or smart trousers in Prince of Wales check, for the Prince was *the* style icon of his day. They made a very handsome couple.

They met in rather a romantic way. My father was very musical, indeed he boasted that he could play six instruments. In his late teens he formed a dance band which performed at small events round North London and one evening when they were playing in a church hall in Kilburn, he spotted a beautiful, auburn haired girl amongst the dancers. It was Grace. He and his band had just been offered the chance to play on one of the great Cunard liners which plied the Atlantic at that time, but he and Grace fell so deeply in love that he could not bear to leave her. They were married in December, 1928, when Grace was 23 and Charles a year younger, and three years later my sister Patricia was born.

On the 15th of April, 1937, my father bought a motorbike and sidecar. My mother was otherwise engaged, giving birth to me. When, two weeks later, she walked down the steps of the Middlesex Hospital with me in her arms, she took one look at this new acquisition and said tartly:

"I'm not going home in *that* thing, I'm catching the bus."

And so we did.

My grandparents, Frederick and Florence Davis, were far from pleased when Charles first married Grace for they felt he had married beneath him. Frederick, after all, was a journalist whilst Grace's late father, Albert, had worked on the railways as stoker. And whilst the Davis family lived in middle-class West Hampstead, Grace, her widowed mother and siblings, lived in a semi-basement flat halfway between Paddington and Kilburn. Frederick and Florence conveniently overlooked the fact that their son, who was not as academic as them, was a builder and decorator by trade. What's more, they underestimated their new daughter-in-law's rather wonderful family.

Albert and Elizabeth Jones had eight children, four boys and four girls. All of them had red hair, ranging from my mother's deep auburn to her brother Tommy's flaming copper. Poor they certainly were, for raising a large family on a labourer's pay must have been hard, especially at a time when the country was still struggling to recover from the devastating social and economic effects of World War One and the Great Depression.

And yet, despite their poverty, this was a happy family, as vibrant as the colour of their hair; a musical family where everyone had a beautiful voice and someone was always singing, and a family where, if a child had talent, it was given free rein to blossom. When they grew up, one boy became an Anglican priest, another, a senior army officer, whilst the youngest two joined the RAF and the Navy. Grace and her sister Doris became skilled dressmakers and at the time of her marriage, my mother worked for Singer as a manageress and demonstrator of dressmaking techniques. As for Rose May, she became an opera singer, a member of the world famous Carl Rosa Opera Company. Violet, the youngest, was a waitress - a 'nippy', as they were called - at Lyons Corner House. It was this which so incensed my grandmother.

"A *nippy*?" she exclaimed to my father, "a *nippy?* We can do without a *waitress* in the family, thank you very much."

In fact, her own family's achievements were similar to the Jones's, in that they too progressed from extreme poverty. Florence's great-grandparents, Robert and Ann Radford were greengrocers who lived in the St Pancras area of London. However, they clearly believed in education as their son Christopher, who had once been their errand boy, became a police court reporter and highly respected journalist. Family legend has it that Christopher was a friend of Charles Dickens, helping him in research for his books. As Dickens had also been a court reporter, albeit earlier than Christopher, it is entirely possible that they met.

His son, Robert, also became a reporter and, more remarkably, so did my grandmother Florence, for when she was 14 she joined her father in his profession. He was a 'penny-a-liner' who wrote his stories on sheets of paper sandwiched together with soot - a precursor of carbon paper - and then touted these copies to whatever newspapers seemed most likely to buy them for, literally, one penny per line.

On Florence's first day, she accompanied her father to the Marylebone Coroner's Court. I can imagine her, a tall, well-built girl in an ankle-length black skirt, little button boots, probably a high-necked and frilled white blouse and most definitely a little hat tilted forwards on her head. I can visualise the dark interior of the courtroom and its sombre atmosphere. As the Coroner entered an usher called out "all rise", but as Florence stood, her head was jerked backwards and she let out a piercing shriek - someone behind her had tied the ribbons on her long plaits to the back of the bench. History does not relate what happened next except that the young reporter who carried out this naughty prank was Frederick Percival Davis whom she married five years later.

My grandmother claimed to be the first woman reporter, but we have no way of proving this. What is certain is that, whilst there have been women journalists for hundreds of years, these were usually writers contributing articles to various publications. Florence, on the other hand, was a working reporter with a nose for a story, so perhaps she was, if not the first, at least a trail-blazer. After working with her father, she graduated to a newspaper and had only to hear a horse-drawn fire engine clatter by, its bell clanging, or the sound of a policeman's whistle, to grab her coat and run. The editor, seeing her empty chair, would ask:

"Where's Florence?" And everyone would shout:

"Where's the nearest fire?"

Frederick and Florence were married in 1904. Within ten years, however, their family life, like so many others, was disrupted by the advent of World War One when Frederick marched away to the carnage of battle, leaving behind him a wife and three children. Florence became a working mother when she took over her husband's job on the Marylebone Gazette. Unlike other young men in the family, Frederick survived the war, although he never recovered from his exposure to mustard gas attacks on the Western Front. With his lung function severely impaired, he eventually became an invalid and Florence the family's only breadwinner. With a sick husband to care for and a family to support she realised she could no longer work in a newspaper office. Over the years Frederick had bought a string of cottages and even a farm, all of which were rented out. However, when the family solicitor informed her that the properties were mortgaged, he added:

"It would be very bad for a woman in your position to be saddled with debt. You must get rid of them at once."

And so, instead of providing her with a steady income, she sold all but one cottage in Essex and bought a shop on Fortune Green in West Hampstead. She started by selling paraffin for oil stoves and lamps, gradually adding dried goods such as rice, tea, sugar, dried fruits and flour – a combination of stock which would now be impossible. The shop stood in a rank of three, the other two being a vet's practice and a dairy. Coincidentally, all three were owned by people called Davis and they soon became known as Doggy Davis, Oily Davis and Milky Davis. I adored Granny's shop, with its odd yet strangely comforting aroma of food overlaid with paraffin. Neat bundles of kindling wood were stacked in front of the mahogany counter on which stood a pair of brass scales, a graduated line of weights, a big metal till and a pile of thick blue paper. A flight of deep wooden drawers covered the wall behind the counter, each with a brass handle and a sign showing its contents. There was nothing I liked better than to watch Granny as she served customers, shovelling things up with a small wooden scoop, weighing them, then tipping them into bags which she skillfully folded and twisted from a sheet of the blue paper. I was allowed to 'help' by counting out Oxo cubes from a big glass jar or scooping dog biscuits from a sack behind the counter. Best of all I liked to press the button on the till which pinged out a drawerful of money.

Frederick's health eventually deteriorated so much that he had to go into a nursing home, where he remained for the rest of his life. By now, all three of Florence's children were married, so to generate extra income, she took a lodger, an elderly butcher who rented the top floor of the three-storey building. Andrew Beard was a gentle, quiet man who kept himself to himself. However, I adored him and always insisted on clambering up the stairs so that he could sing to my dolly and me. At the age of three, I came down and announced to the assembled family that Granny was going to marry Mr. Beard. This was seen as screamingly funny, especially as my grandfather was still alive.

In September, 1939, our happy home life ended when, for the second time in twenty-five years, the world erupted into war. My sister, aged eight-and-a-half was evacuated soon after the outbreak of war during 'Operation Pied Piper', the first effort to move children out of danger. A few weeks later, my pregnant mother and I were also evacuated. Unbeknown to either Patricia or my mother, we were all billeted in Bedford and it was not until my father heard from them that he was able to put Grace in touch with her eldest daughter. Just two months later, on her own birthday, Grace gave birth to a son, Richard Godfrey, and soon after that we were moved again to the village of Bedmond in Hertfordshire. Meanwhile, my sister, unhappy and homesick, ran away. Even though the adults of the family had been very kind, their two sons bullied her and, to make matters worse, she had to share a bed with the younger boy, who wet the bed. Somehow, she found her way across the city to our old lodgings in Bedford, only to find that we had gone.

Patricia was not unusual in running away, for hundreds of evacuated children did they same thing. Someone I met years later told me how he and his seven brothers and sisters were all sent to Devon, each billeted with a separate family in different parts of the county. They were all bitterly unhappy, missing not only their parents but each other. Somehow, their eldest sister, aged fourteen, managed to locate each of her siblings and hatched a plot whereby they all ran away on the same day, met at the same station and caught a train back to London and home. Quite apart from the fact that they had no money, this was an organisational triumph.

We settled down in our new billet in Bedmond, a kindly couple allotting us half of their small council house. My mother set up her little dressmaking business and our father visited us whenever he could. The time came for me to start school and I, a nervous little girl, became more and more anxious.

"Don't worry," said Mummy, "the first day will be the worst."

"Well can I go on the second day then?"

Rennie's indigestion tablets appeared in our home. We called them 'Mummy's sweeties' as, she explained, they were not for us but to ease the pains she had in her tummy. But it became clear that there was something wrong with her that a simple anti-acid tablet could not cure and she was sent to hospital for tests.

"Mrs Davis," said the consultant, "you have a carcinoma of the stomach and will need an operation."

My father would tell of how, in their naivety, neither he nor Grace knew what this meant nor yet the gravity of it. For the moment, arrangements had to be made for we three children to be cared for whilst our mother was in hospital. It was decided that Aunty Evelyn would have Patricia, Richard would go to Aunty Ethel, whilst my Great-Aunt Laura volunteered to look after me.

However, shortly before our family was dispersed, something extraordinary happened; I woke up one night to find the bedroom filled with light and a tall, luminous figure, beautiful yet stern, standing on the left of my bed. His eyes seemed to hold my gaze with such power that I could not look away, and yet I was not afraid. Then, without apparent movement, he materialized at the foot of the bed and finally to my right. He stretched his arms towards me and an unseen force pulled my little body into a sitting position. For a timeless moment, he stood there until the same power laid me down, my shining visitor disappeared and I went peacefully back to sleep. Next morning I told my mother that a silver man had been to see me.

"I expect you were dreaming, darling," she said gently.

But I knew I was not and that it had really happened. This visitation has stayed with me throughout my life, as vivid now as it was so long ago. I like to think that the 'silver man' was an angel who, knowing our mother was soon to die, had come to my little brother and me, and that, because the heavy veil of mortal life had not yet blinded me, I was still, in my innocence, able to see him.

Great Aunt Laura, who was known in the family as Aunt Dig, was my grandmother's youngest sister and was a widow who lived in Derbyshire. She took me to her home in Swadlincote by rail, the first time I had travelled on a train. I remember how my initial fear turned to excitement as the whistle blew and the train chugged out of the station, slowly picking up speed until we were racing through the countryside, plumes of steam and smoke streaming back from its funnels as we sped north.

Aunt Dig had a drapery shop with living quarters above it so large that there were two staircases. She had a maid called Ruby Ellen and between them they ensured that I was thoroughly spoiled. Every couple of weeks Aunt Dig opened a trunk full of remnants from which I was allowed to choose any fabric I liked which within a few days she had made into a new dress with a little lace collar and matching knickers. The knickers had a patch pocket at the front in which to put my hanky. Even more wonderful, there was a dairy next door which now and then made a few illicit gallons of that unheard of treat, ice-cream.

Aunt Dig, who was as generously built as my grandmother, every bit as kind but of a gentler temperament, had a unique way of entertaining me when the occasional air-raid took place. Our shelter was the cupboard under the stairs where we crouched - one fat elderly lady and one little girl –

and where, by the light of a guttering candle, she took out her false teeth, wrapped them in a towel and, like a ventriloquist's dummy, entertained me with stories. Only once did she get cross with me and that was when, thrilled by the rhythm, I marched off behind a Salvation Army band and was lost for hours.

After some months, however, it was felt safe enough for me to return to London and so I left this dear soul, never to forget her loving kindness. What I did not know was that she had once been at the centre of a scandal that rocked the family. What was it? Wait and see!

As the months went by, Richard and I were too young to understand that the mother we loved so much was desperately ill and that we would never again be reunited as a family. My sister, however, now aged 14, was living near enough to visit Mummy regularly. She went to see her the day before she died and Grace's last words as she kissed her daughter goodbye were:

"Look after the little ones for me."

Grace died seventeen days after D-Day. Within the span of her lifetime there had been two world wars. The military and civilian casualties from both conflicts totalled over eighty-eighty million, a horrifying figure which conjures up the agony and barbarity of war. As though there had not been enough suffering, the 'flu pandemic which swept the world hard on the heels of the 1918 Armistice, resulted in another fifteen million deaths. Measured against these statistics, the loss of one woman seems insignificant, yet on the day Grace died, the heart of our little family stopped beating.

The sun shone late that year
The summer lingered
In fields beneath the cloudless skies of England
The harvest's home.

On village green
Leather struck willow, children played
Their laughter and the birdsong
Drowned
The menace of the far-off sound
Of jackboots marching over European plains.

In dappled shade, fearful they clung
Lover to lover, mother to son
In sad rehearsal of farewells to come.

Night
And the siren's first, false, terrifying wail
Shrill with foreboding
Prophesying doom:
'Cities will tumble, nations fall
The weak, the innocent, the old
Will, starving, perish

Death
Like some black, chaotic pall
Will stalk the earth,
War, War, Annihilating all.'

Victory
Was it in vain?
The loss, the suffering, the pain?
Peace in our time? Mercy mild?
God and sinners reconciled?

Oh Voyagers
As you speed on towards the Milky Way
Turn your eyes Earthwards one last time
Beam back your vision of us
Tell us what you see
Before you pass forever from this galaxy.

Weep,
For as dawn breaks, a blood red sun
Shines on the hallowed graves
Of those now gone.

T H R E E

IN OCTOBER 1944, just five months after his wife's death, my father married again. His new wife was a nurse whom he'd met during our mother's last days. Our aunts and grandparents were scandalised at what they saw as indecent haste and a lack of respect for her memory. Indeed, they always swore he had been 'carrying on' with her before our mother died. Daddy, however, maintained that he remarried to get his three children back and try to establish a family again. Whatever the truth of the matter, he made a terrible mistake.

On a spring day the following year we returned to our home in London. We were wildly excited as Daddy drove Richard and I back from the Essex countryside to Gondar Gardens. We were going home! We would have our own toys again, our books, our garden; we'd sleep in our own beds. But then came the slow realisation that the one person we most longed for was no longer there. Despite the tears we children had already shed, it was probably the first time the reality of our mother's death had truly hit us. Now, not only did we have no mother, but a woman we quickly began to dislike had taken her place.

Daphne Shepherd was a big, handsome woman. Her sallow skin and her mass of black, wiry hair gave her a coarse, gypsy-ish look. She was 23 when she and Charles married, just nine years older than Patricia, who remembers her despair at having to be a bridesmaid at the wedding.

To start with all went well and, during what was in a sense a honeymoon period, we were glad to be together and glad to have our darling Daddy back again. We also had VE Day to celebrate when, on the 8th May 1945, the war in Europe officially ended. Anticipating this, people had been building a huge bonfire on Fortune Green for days, piling anything flammable on it and perching an effigy of Hitler on the top. All day long people thronged the streets, stringing them with bunting, hauling ancient

27

pianos into the streets for impromptu sing-songs, waving flags, laughing, crying, singing, hugging, cheering. That night we joined the crowds dancing around the bonfire, its flames lighting up the sky, rejoicing that the years of conflict and suffering were at last over. Amidst the celebrations, many wore black armbands, my father included, tokens of a life lost, a soul departed, a hidden grief.

At home, the cracks soon began to appear. Gone was the nice new auntie we had liked so much when Daddy drove her down to the cottage, the kind lady who brought us little gifts and sat us on her knee and kissed our cheeks. In her place was another woman entirely, someone who would dominate our lives for years to come. One by one, everything that had any connection with our mother disappeared. It was as if Grace had vanished without trace. Our memories, our emotions, her very name were all taboo subjects. Only our grandmother spoke about her and then it was just to mutter 'if your mother could see you now' as she inspected the holes in our socks and increasingly scruffy appearance.

I had one precious keepsake, a gold locket my mother had left me, inside which lay her photograph, the only one I had. I kept it in a little green satin box under my pillow and every night before I went to sleep I opened the locket and said goodnight to her. One night a few months after our return I opened the little box only to find that the locket had disappeared. I ran crying into the sitting room to tell Daddy and Daphne what had happened. Daphne jumped up and hustled me back into the bedroom and, for the first time, turned on me. She'd never seen it, she said in a hard whisper, didn't know what I was talking about. I was just a careless little thing and had probably dropped it in the street.

"Now get back to bed and leave us alone. And don't you *dare* bother your father again with this rubbish, you know how tired he gets."

At that moment my fear was born. I never mentioned the locket again but as I grew older and learned that she had taken and sold many other things - including our mother's sapphire and ruby rings intended for my sister and I - I guessed what had happened.

Over the years, I have sometimes thought of Daphne and tried to imagine things from her point of view. Swept off her feet by a charming man - either a widower or soon to be one - she must have fallen madly in love and imagined a glowing and romantic future. Perhaps her parents encouraged the match. Perhaps they thought it would move their only daughter a bit further up the social scale or felt he might offer her more security than someone her own age. Soon Charles introduced her to his children - Patricia, a tall, highly intelligent girl of fourteen with big blue eyes and long flaxen plaits, Richard and I, still at the adorable ages of five and seven, both blue-eyed and blonde-haired like our sister. Did she imagine the happy family we would be and think about the day when she would have children of her own?

The reality was very different. Yes, she got the husband but it came at a price. Charles had already been through so much; the harrowing war years, the exhaustion and trauma of his rescue work, Grace's terrible illness and death, the long separation from his children, not to mention the daily struggle to make a living in our poverty-stricken country. What is more, he had re-married too soon when his grieving could not have been over. Worst still, she soon discovered that Charles did not want more children and so her dreams of motherhood were dashed from the start.

Although many married woman had worked during the war, as soon as the troops returned to 'civvy street', society largely reverted to the custom that, once married, a woman gave up paid work. So Daphne lost her professional status as a nurse and became a housewife looking after a ready-made family. She had been a cosseted only child who had never done things for herself. She had never laundered clothes, never faced the ordeal of shopping for groceries in those days of scarcity, and she certainly couldn't cook, regularly phoning her mother for help. Yes, she got the ready-made home in a desirable part of London, but it was full of memories of the first wife. Of *course* she would have changed furnishings and tried to stamp her own personality on the place. What woman wouldn't? However, one might have thought that, having been in a caring profession, she would have had a kind and compassionate nature. Nothing could have been further from the truth, as we were beginning to find out.

As for we children, the truth was that we did not see Daphne as a substitute for our mother and, unable to articulate our sadness, this probably showed itself in other ways. Perhaps we shrank back when she tried to hug us. Perhaps we cried a lot - Richard and I certainly did. Perhaps we were difficult to deal with, difficult to understand. I was an anxious, nervous little thing and stress-related alopecia had made patches of my hair fall out. My little brother wet the bed in his anxiety whilst Patricia had already shown herself to be a feisty girl who was not afraid of a row or to stand up for herself.

As well as the introduction of this awful stepmother into our lives, other changes were also on the way. In the aftermath of the war, the thousands of bomb-damaged buildings in London meant that builders were

29

at a premium and as a result my father's business was expanding. So it was that at the end of 1945 we moved away from our home in leafy Hampstead to Hendon, where my father had found a property more suitable for his business. In moving, we left behind our much-loved granny, aunts and uncles, and our cousins Judith and Peter, for although our new home was just a few miles away, Granny and the aunts did not like Daphne and so, from then on, we saw the rest of the family but rarely.

Our new home was a tall, ugly house at the end of a run-down rank of shops, opposite a small bus terminal and a noisy pub. On the ground floor was a showroom facing the street, behind this an office and at the back a large area which my father used as a workshop. Upstairs was a kitchen on a half-landing (it was always advisable to rap on the door before going in to give the mice a chance to scatter) a dank, windowless bathroom, a living room and large sitting room. Finally, at the top of the house were the bedrooms. There was no garden. Instead the house backed onto a small industrial unit from which the high-pitched whine of machinery issued every working day.

The house was cold even in summer and at the first sign of winter chilblains returned to our fingers and toes like old friends. Only the living room fire was lit except on special occasions. Otherwise, portable oil stoves were moved around the house as needed. Hot water bottles were a necessity rather than a luxury and these we stuck in our beds before scurrying down to put on our pyjamas in front of the fire. Every winter morning the inside of our bedroom windows were iced over in exquisite patterns which melted slowly to form wet puddles on the lino floors.

But the chill in the air seemed to be due to far more than the weather. It was a creepy place. Whilst I was comfortable on the ground and first floors, the stairs to the bedrooms were scary, especially as they passed a dark half-landing. Here I sometimes glimpsed, or thought I glimpsed, a little black girl and would scoot past as fast as I could, my heart racing. Daphne's two cats also seemed to sense the supernatural on the landing, their hair standing on end as they ran wild-eyed, back down the stairs to safety. Many years later, reminiscing with my sister, we discovered that we had both seen the same child's ghost. An old woman also haunted the place and Patricia remembers me rushing down the stairs one night screaming 'don't let the old lady get me!' The bedrooms were no better. Doors creaked, windows rattled, curtains sometimes billowed, no doubt from the draughts whistling through ill-fitting windows, but to us there were more sinister connotations. Sometimes I woke in the night to see strange shadows silhouetted against the windows or drifting across the room and heard the pitter-patter of feet in the attic above. None of this helped we three children, still deeply affected by our mother's death and now at the mercy of someone who seemed to become more and more like the proverbial wicked stepmother with each day that passed.

Every Wednesday, Daphne's mother came over for the day, catching the bus from Finsbury Park. She and her husband lived in a dingy first floor flat overlooking a steep railway embankment where all conversation had to stop as passing trains hurtled by, rattling the windowpanes. Auntie Renee, as we were told to call her, was a tiny woman from whom all vestige of colour appeared to have drained away. Everything about her was pale from her thinning hair to droopy beige clothes which dwarfed her tiny frame. She had a deformity of the spine which gave her a hunched back and this convinced Richard and I that the poor woman was a witch. After all, we'd met a witch so we knew one when we saw one. She was not strong and only ate white fish - 'a nice bit of plaice' - and anaemic milk puddings. She was a spiritualist and I would surreptitiously flick through the pages of the magazines she brought each week, scaring myself by reading accounts of hauntings and exorcisms, poltergeists and ghouls. She attended a spiritualist church, went to séances and consulted mediums, and I eavesdropped avidly to conversations about which departed souls had 'come through' at last week's meeting, how Mrs So-and-So had had a nasty turn when her dead Nan tapped her on the shoulder, or what the Ouija board had revealed. Strange, therefore, that she never detected the spooky atmosphere in the upper reaches of our house.

Auntie Renee had been a hairdresser in her youth and every so often she cut our hair. I simply dreaded my turn. Before beginning she lit a long wax taper and stood it in a glass on the table beside her. Between snips she took it in her bony fingers and singed the ends of my hair. Then, as an acrid smell of burning filled the air, she cut the singed bits off. This, she said, stopped the ends from splitting. However, I found it absolutely terrifying, certain that my whole head would go up in flames at any moment.

Once a month both Daphne's parents came to Sunday lunch. Richard and I really liked Uncle Jack, her father, who was as big as his wife was small, a bluff, loud, jolly man who had at one time played football for Arsenal. He made and shifted scenery at the Phoenix Theatre in the West End, which gave him a bit of glamour in our eyes. We loved his theatrical stories, especially the one about the actor who had annoyed him and so, when the man had to 'enter stage left' carrying a suitcase, Uncle Jack filled it with bricks. What we liked best about his visits, though, was the large sponge cake he brought for tea. An amazing treat at that time of austerity, it was topped with pineapple chunks, grapes and peaches perched on a thick layer of cream. To Patricia, however, he was not the jolly, avuncular figure he appeared. She never trusted him after he crept into her bedroom and tried to touch her under her nightie.

Daphne, we soon discovered, had a terrible temper and was as unpredictable as a dangerous dog whose mood changes as swiftly as the weather. One moment she was smiling, the next she was in a rage, shouting and lashing out, terrifying me and reducing me to a shaking jelly. One day Richard might be in favour, treated kindly, perhaps given a little extra at meal times, whilst I was yelled at and slapped. But next morning, creeping down to breakfast in fear of the onslaught, I would find the tables had turned and I, for no discernible reason, was 'in' and my brother was 'out'. I particularly hated coming home from school because I never knew what awaited me.

Another nasty twist in her unkindness was that she would sometimes insist that the 'in' child ignored the 'out'. She used this tactic in a particularly spiteful way when Richard, aged eight, returned from a trip to Paris where he had been staying with French friends. Such a holiday was almost unheard of in those days and I was longing to see my little brother and hear all about it. But, as we heard the car draw up, Daphne turned to me and snapped:

"Don't you dare say a word to him, d'you hear?"

The poor child had been seasick on the ferry and arrived looking like a little ghost. Daphne greeted him coldly and, with a shove, sent him straight to his room. I can see his face now, white as milk, and the misery in his eyes as he ran past me up the stairs, remember too my guilt that I did not, dare not, speak to him. Not until bedtime was he able to creep into my bed and tell me about his holiday.

Mealtimes were an ordeal. In the evening Daphne and we three children sat at the table for supper whilst our father - tired after a long day's work - sat in his armchair beside the fire, the radio tuned to the BBC's Home Service. His meal, served on a tray, was always something hot and substantial after his hard day's work, ours cold and unvaryingly awful. We were each allowed three pieces of grey bread and margarine. On the first we had to spread a vile substance called Beetox, some sort of poor relation to Marmite. The second slice was for fish-paste and the third for jam. The order in which this was eaten, indeed whether we ate it, was non-negotiable. Finally, we had a thin slice of whatever dreadful cake Daphne had made.

Richard and I went to Bell Lane Elementary School, just a short walk away from home. The school's claim to fame was that Dennis Compton, the famous cricketer, had been a pupil there, a name we actually knew because our father was mad on cricket and always listened to commentaries on the radio. Despite the strict regime and very formal teaching methods, it was a happy place. For both my brother and I it was an escape from home and the woman we had grown to hate. I liked almost everything about school, particularly history with its tales of long ago, and geography, when, as we turned the pages of our atlases and saw the extent of the British Empire, we took it for granted that we were the greatest nation on earth. I was hopeless at arithmetic and didn't much like 'drill' when, even in the coldest weather, we changed into our plimsolls and went out to the playground to be put through our physical paces. Most of all I loved English and Art. The little stories I wrote were often praised and my teacher sometimes sent me next door to the 'infants' class where I would proudly read aloud to the children.

Pamela Jenkins and Helen Kornblum were my best friends. I admired Pamela because she seemed to be everything I was not. She was small and pretty whilst I was a gangling, skinny child who was constantly told by her stepmother that I had big feet and big ears, I was awkward, clumsy and nothing like as pretty as my cousin Judith. Each night Pamela's hair was twisted up in rags to be curled around her mother's fingers next morning into plump ringlets bunched on each side of her face with ribbon bows. Thanks to Auntie Renee, my hair soon lost its pretty curls and was cut way above my ears into an unbecoming 'pudding basin' style. Most of all, however, I envied Pamela her shoes. They were black patent leather with dainty straps which buttoned around each ankle. Mine, on the other hand, were tough, scuffed lace-ups which, along with all shoes in our household, had black metal studs called 'blakees' hammered in a semi-circle around the toe, and a solid metal half-moon on the heel. Pamela went to tap-dancing classes and would demonstrate as we walked home from school. I, with my metal reinforcements, sounded more like a cart-horse as I clip-clopped along beside her.

I loved going to Pamela's house where her plump little mum was kind and never shouted, and gave us slices of cake, where her Dad and her two big brothers teased us and where we could play with her baby sister.

Above all I loved the laughter that seemed to fill this happy home.

One day I received some important information from Pamela. She had asked Helen Kornblum and me to tea and, as we played in her bedroom, she told us she knew how babies were made. Now this just happened to be a subject of great interest to me because whenever I was asked what I wanted to be when I grew up I always replied 'A Lady With A Baby'. But until now I had never really given much thought as to how, when the time came, I would acquire said baby. So I was all agog as she informed us that, to make a baby, the daddy did a wee-wee on the mummy's tummy. I remember gasping that this really could not be true but she told us importantly that she knew it was because she'd seen her daddy and mummy making her baby sister in this way and, what's more, she thought they were trying to make another one. I was horrified and decided to change my ambitions for the future straight away. I don't know what Helen thought but I seem to remember she turned a trifle pale.

During the freezing winter of 1947 my father became ill with bronchitis. We normally went home for lunch at mid-day but, saying she couldn't cope, Daphne now gave Richard and I sandwiches to eat at school. They had the same filling every day – icy slices of beetroot which my little brother and I ate, shivering, in the school playground. One day a large lady wearing a black astrakhan coat and hat appeared and announced that we were going to have lunch with her. It was Mrs Kornblum, Helen's mum, who must have told her what was happening. Like a plump mother hen, she gathered us up and swept us back to their flat at the smarter end of Bell Lane where every day until Daddy recovered, we sat down with the family while our plates were heaped with food; steaming stews and tiny dumplings, strange but delicious soups, sausages with mystery fillings perched on piles of snowy mashed potato. And as we scraped our plates clean, Mr Kornblum, who was smiley and fat, and wore a striped suit, cried:

"Haf some more, haf some more, go on Mother, gif 'em more!"

And then there were the puddings - oh, we had reached the promised land; warmth, kindness and lots and lots of food!

We told Daddy and Daphne what had happened and they seemed pleased. So one day some weeks later when Daddy was well and back at work, I decided to ask Helen home to play after school. I had never dared bring anyone home before but felt sure she would be welcomed after her family's kindness to us. I rang the bell and Daphne opened the door. She looked from me to Helen and her face filled with disgust. Smiling nervously I said,

"This is my friend Helen, she's come to pl..." But before I could finish the sentence, she shouted,

"You're not coming into *my* house, you filthy little Jew," and, grabbing me by the arm she hauled me in and slammed the door. I hardly felt the pain as she boxed my ears and pushed me stumbling up the stairs ahead of her. For though I cried, I couldn't understand what had just happened. What was a Jew? Why had she called Helen filthy, when I knew she wasn't? And why was Daphne rude and cruel when Helen's family had been so kind to my brother and me? I felt bitterly ashamed and wondered how I would ever be able to face my friend again. But the miracle was that Helen never once referred to what had happened and her own lovely family continued to welcome me into their home.

We were constantly accused of stealing, even though there was precious little to take. Picking a few currants from a cake was stealing. Taking half a stale biscuit was stealing. Once I 'stole' four grapes from a bunch we had bought Daphne for her birthday. Her discovery of this crime resulted in days of punishment for all three of us until I plucked up the courage to confess.

One day Daphne gave me sixpence and sent me to buy some vegetables. In the inevitable queue at the greengrocers I found myself standing behind a very old lady I had often seen before. She was a strange-looking woman whose head hung forward onto her chest and who, winter or summer, always wore the same long black coat and shapeless hat. I was sure that, like Auntie Renee and Mrs Chipperfield, she too was a witch. So I did not at all like standing behind her as the queue inched slowly forwards. Suddenly I noticed that her large black handbag was hanging open. What an opportunity! It was not often, after all, one had the chance to find out what witches have in their bags. I peered in nosily. Any toads? Any dead rats? Any spells written in vampire's blood? But then something happened which arguably filled me with more terror than if she had turned round and changed me into a mouse - I dropped my sixpence into her bag. Horrified, I stared into it. I could see the coin but did not dare reach in and take it for fear she would notice. At last I decided to give it a try, but just as my hand hovered she moved her arm, the bag shifted and the coin slipped out of sight. I realised I had only two options and I didn't like either: should I ask the old lady to give it back or go home and face Daphne's wrath? Which was worse? But between the Witch and the Wicked Stepmother, there really was no contest. - fear of the latter won hands down. So, taking a deep breath, I tapped the witch on the shoulder and told her what had happened.

"Done what?" she croaked in a surprisingly loud voice, "you done what? Dropped yer what? 'Ere, this kid's sayin' she's dropped 'er tanner in me bag. That's a good'un innit? Try ter cheat an old woman out of 'er money. I never 'eard such a fing." Everyone in the queue turned and stared at me. With a burning face, I walked out.

I trailed miserably back up the road as slowly as possible, putting off the moment when I would have to tell Daphne what had happened. Of course, she didn't believe me and whacked me repeatedly round the head, even shutting me in the broom cupboard as she tried to force me to tell her what I had spent the sixpence on, or where I had hidden it. Finally, she sent me to my room in disgrace, shrieking that she didn't know what would become of me.

"You'll find yourself in Borstal if you go on like this, my girl," she yelled as I ran sobbing up the stairs. Borstal - the detention centre for bad boys and girls - the very name was used to instill fear into wayward children, of which I was obviously one. Before I went to bed, supperless, she called me down and announced that as she could do nothing more with me she was going to the school in the morning to tell the headmaster.

"Perhaps *he* can think of a punishment that'll stop you becoming a habitual thief. Me, I wash my hands of you."

My father sat in his armchair, studiously immersed in his newspaper, taking care not to get involved. That night I could not sleep and lay in bed dreading the morning, sobbing quietly for my mother, begging her in a way I now knew was futile to come back from heaven.

The next day, whilst my class was hard at work, the door opened and in came the headmaster, a lofty figure I had never spoken to. Only naughty children were sent to him and I was never naughty. So when he asked to see Barbara Davis I knew Daphne has carried out her threat. Outside in the hall he said, "come with me" and, spindly legs trembling, I followed him into his office.

"This won't take long,'" he said, settling himself behind his desk and looking at me over his glasses in what I felt was a kindly way considering the reason for my presence, "your mother has been to see me this morning. She says you steal and tell lies all the time and she can't do anything with you. She told me something about a sixpence you were given to buy vegetables, for example. Is any of this true?"

I was too nervous to speak so I just shook my head.

"You're quite sure?"

Trying not to cry I managed to stutter that yes it was true, I was a thief because I had stolen some cake and four grapes but that I only told lies when I was frightened. And then I explained about the witch at the greengrocers. He nodded understandingly.

"Now there's something else I want to ask you, Barbara. Is she your real mother?" I shook my head again.

"And is she kind to you?"

I burst into tears, which must have told him all he needed to know for he got up and handed me a hanky and told me to wipe my eyes. He told me he believed me and said that if I was ever frightened or if anything bad happened at home, either to my little brother, my sister, or me I was to come and tell him. Then, taking my hand, he led me out to the school secretary's office, who sat me down and gave me a glass of milk. Of course, I never did tell him what was going on at home because I was much too scared of the repercussions. Whether he and Daphne spoke again I do not know, but when I got home that night, trembling with fear, I found that I was 'in' and all had been either forgiven or forgotten.

Strangely, whilst my sister remembers our stepmother's appalling temper, she doesn't recall the cruel and spiteful treatment meted out to Richard and me. This, we now think, is because she was much older than us as well as being tough enough - as forthright as her grandmother - not to be cowed by Daphne, as we were. In addition, she only spent three years under the same roof as her stepmother. Certainly, there were plenty of rows between them, but even though she was far from happy, she was able to stand up for herself.

What of my father? Why did he appear to ignore what was going on right under his nose? He was essentially a weak man and, whilst his love for his children was never in doubt, he was no match for the woman he'd married in such haste and so chose to close his eyes to what was happening. At the same time, he did his best for us in other ways, taking us swimming, bringing home little treats and, now and then, things that he found in the bombed-out houses his firm was re-building. Once he found an entire clockwork train set and built a track for it all round our playroom.

My escape was in drawing, reading and bed. My nose was never out of a book and being sent to bed early was never a punishment. As soon as I was tucked under the blankets I felt safe - safe to inhabit my nightly world of make-belief that, to me, was completely real, and safe to think about my mother, talk to her in my head and try to conjure up her face, which was fast fading from my memory.

I also found solace in music. Daddy was a talented musician and, even though his dance-band days were long gone, he still bought the sheet music of the latest hits every week and hammered them out on the piano that stood in our enormous, chilly sitting-room. His taste in music was on the light side when he married Daphne. But, if nothing else, she brought the family one special gift - a love of classical music and opera. She had a large collection of records and our house was often filled with the glorious music. This influenced my father's choice of piano music and he began to play the classics. I was enthralled when a friend came over now and again and together they would play pieces for four hands.   I longed to learn the piano. My sister was already having violin lessons and her practice made our little Cairn terrier, Jeannie, point her nose up to the ceiling and howl, whether in ecstasy or agony I'm not quite sure. But at last it was my turn and I was dispatched to Mrs Miller who lived just down the road in a house that smelled of cats and nicotine. She was a chain smoker, the cigarette perpetually glued to her lower lip bouncing and spraying ash as she spoke. Lessons took place in her 'front room' which was dominated by an ancient, out-of-tune piano with yellowing keys.   She was fat, blowsy and immeasurably kind, and from the moment she put the first piece of music in front of me I was hooked. She sat close beside me, her smoker's cough accompanying my efforts like rumbling thunder. When I struggled she leaned over to demonstrate, brushing away the ash that dropped from her ciggy onto the keys and all but enveloping me in her overflowing cleavage. Every week I practiced like mad and great was my joy when one piece was ticked off and we turned the page to something new. No-one had to nag me to practice at home because playing the piano became a beacon of happiness in a life which was often difficult. My timid nature disappeared when I sat at a piano and I never needed to be coaxed to play for visitors or take my latest piece with me when we visited relatives and friends. When Mrs Yates decided she could teach me no more I was moved on to a Mrs Walker, where lessons were very different. Soon I was learning scales and arpeggios, and struggling over books of complicated musical theory. She was nothing like the cosy Mrs Yates, being brisk and strict, and not above giving me a sharp rap over the knuckles with a ruler if my mistakes tried her patience too far. But she forced me on, playing harder and harder pieces and getting me through my grade exams.   However, although I became a competent pianist, that was all and the true musical genes from both my father's and my mother's side were to be inherited by my own and my sister's yet undreamed of children.

My brother and I had a yearly treat which was the best escape of all from our hated stepmother – a country holiday. Frederick, the grandfather I never knew, had died in 1943. The following spring my prophesy at the age of three - which had made everyone laugh so much - came true when Granny married her lodger, dear, gentle, Andrew Beard. Soon afterwards they moved to Gloucestershire where they bought 'Hillcrest', a cottage in Cromhall, the village where Andrew Beard was born. Although the move to Gloucestershire meant our much-loved grandmother was no longer nearby, its positive effect was that Richard and I, Judith and Peter, now spent every summer with Granny and our new grandfather.

One might have thought our stepmother would have been glad of six weeks respite from the children she appeared to dislike so much, but it seemed to make her even crosser. I can remember how angry she was before our first holiday in 1945 and the way she nagged us, on and on and on. What was it about her we couldn't bear? Why were we so eager to get away? Well, if we wouldn't tell her, no doubt we'd enjoy telling our grandmother. She'd planned all sorts of lovely treats for the holidays - the zoo, the circus - and we were ungrateful little wretches. We knew she was lying about the treats but even so she made us feel guilty. The tirade went on until the last moment when she stuffed our clothes into a suitcase then sulked upstairs as Daddy put us in the back of the car. Then off we drove, the anxiety in my little body draining away the further we got from London.

As soon as we arrived, Daddy carried our suitcase up the narrow stairs and after a while Granny went to unpack it. Within minutes she came stomping down again, her irate voice preceding her:

"For goodness sake, you should *see* their clothes! I swear they haven't been washed for months. The *filth*! And *vests*, where are your *vests*? Not a vest in sight. What does that stepmother of yours suggest you wear instead, paper bags? Charlie, the minute you get back, just you tell that wretched woman to put their vests in the post *immediately*, d'you hear me? And suggest she tries washing them first, just by way of a change. What Grace would say if she could see her children now, I dread to think..." Then, seeing our woebegone faces, she collected herself:

"Now come on you two, it's not your fault. Let's see what's for tea. And I think I know a boy and girl who'd love a glass of Tizer."

Straight away all was well, for Granny's bark was always worse than her bite and, unlike Daphne, we knew she loved us.

As one entered 'Hillcrest', a smell of beeswax and baking wafted like a welcome from the little house. Everything glowed, from the furniture and brass to the fire which, in my memory, always crackled in the black-leaded hearth. Along the mantelpiece stood Granny's treasured collection of Royal Doulton shire horses and Toby jugs whilst in the chintz armchairs on each side of the fire sat my grandparents, for all the world like Tweedledum and Tweedledee. For even though Andrew was twenty years older than his bride, physically they were a perfect match; large people whose stomachs proved they loved their grub.

Florence, our formidable grandmother, was big in every sense of the word. She not only had a big body but a personality to match. Like a naval battleship she was iron clad and indomitable, her ample torso strapped into massive boned corsets which, when pinned up on the washing-line, were a sight to behold, with laces and straps, hooks and suspenders adorning the flesh-coloured fabric. .

"Oh drat," she exclaimed one day, clutching her side, "I've broken one of my blessed bones."

Later, when my cousin Judith and I met the Vicar in the lane and he enquired after Granny's health, we announced importantly that she had broken her *blessed* bone."Dear me, I'm sorry to hear that," he exclaimed and hurried round to see how she was, no doubt wondering where exactly in the body this hallowed bone was located. Why, we wondered when we got home, was she so cross?

The four of us quickly made friends in the village. Chief amongst these were Roy Drew, whose family were relatives of Granddad's and who owned a nearby farm, and Ann and David Holpin. We were all about the same age ranging from Peter, Ann and I, who were eight, Judith and David, seven, and five-year-old Richard – whom the family had nicknamed 'Little Dicky Doughnut'.

Every morning we 'helped' Granny whilst she cleaned the cottage, an activity which mainly involved dusting whilst Granny, on hands and knees, large flowered bottom in the air, wielded her dustpan and brush to the constant cry of:

"The *filth*, the *filth*, and I only did it yesterday!"

Then we set off to meet our friends. Up on the Drew's farm the seven of us rampaged through the yards, prodding the cattle with sticks, feeding the chickens and searching for eggs in the coops and hedgerows, climbing ladders high into the haylofts and hurling ourselves down onto lower levels, riding on the back of wagons behind Roy's easy-going Dad, feeding the great cart horses with apples and carrots, helping herd the cows down the pastures into the milking parlour and chopping up mangle worzels for them in machines like giant mincers. We rarely went into the farmhouse for fear of meeting Roy's granny who was fifty times fiercer than ours. Old Mrs Drew was a tiny ramrod of a woman who ruled the household with a steely grip, browbeating her timid daughter-in-law into submitting to her every whim. I later heard that it took two women to hold the old lady down when her end came. She thrashed about her bed for three days and nights, raging, cursing God, and swearing that she would - not - die.

Ann and David's mother could not have been more different than our horrible stepmother. Mrs Holpin was an angel; gentle, smiling, always welcoming and patient beyond belief. They lived at the bottom of a steep lane and their neat villa had a big garden with an orchard beyond where we ran and shouted, played, laughed and squabbled throughout the holidays. Yet not once did that dear woman get exasperated with this constant invasion. Their house lay beside what had once been a stately home but was now an open prison and we often ventured down to the lake which lay in the grounds. One day we decided to make a raft from a wooden sledge. We dragged it down to the lake, balanced it on the bank and, despite his protests, forced Richard to climb aboard for the maiden voyage. I'm sorry to report that both ship and passenger sank. Panic-stricken, we grabbed Dicky Doughnut and hauled him out, dripping, howling and covered in duckweed. But let me make this clear - our panic was not so much because we had nearly drowned my little brother as terror at the thought of Granny's wrath. We dawdled home, dragging the snivelling child behind us, trying to think up excuses for his sodden state. Then Peter had a brainwave, an idea so brilliant we were sure Granny would believe it. We burst into the cottage, pushing the dripping, shivering Richard ahead of us.

"Granny, Granny," we cried, "come quickly, a cow's done a wee-wee on Richard!"

Our Granny's anger was like a summer storm, brief and noisy but followed by the sun. And there was much more sunshine than rain. She was a magnificent cook. Whilst Judith and Peter were used to well-cooked food, with Daphne rattling the pans, we were not. And even though rationing was still in force it seemed to be non-existent at 'Hillcrest'. This was partly due to largesse from the Drew's farm – extra milk, butter, eggs, plus cuts from the home-cured bacon which hung on hooks from beams in their kitchen. Granddad, the former butcher, still made sausages – the best I have ever tasted - and pig's-head brawn. This may sound revolting by today's standards but it was a delectable treat of tender morsels quivering in savoury aspic jelly.

The hour or two before bed were a special time. Sometimes Granddad performed magic tricks, making coins disappear, producing silk handkerchiefs from thin air and puzzling us with playing cards. Granny organised spelling bees and taught us tongue-twisters and poems. No evening was complete, though, without stories of her childhood in late-Victorian London. She told of naughty boys who jumped up and hung behind the horse-drawn hansom cabs and elegant carriages that clattered through the crowded cobbled streets, and how passers-by shouted 'whip behind governor'. We flinched as we imagined that thin leather strap curling back to flick the urchins' legs. We were enthralled when Florence told us how, when she was eight years old, she and thousands of other school-children lined the streets of London for Queen Victoria's Diamond Jubilee.

"It was a boiling hot day," she recounted, "and we had to wait for so long that some of the children fainted. And then, when the procession finally came along, I was so disappointed because the Queen was a tiny old lady and I'd expected a beautiful, fairytale one. We were all given a currant bun and a bottle of milk but the bun was stale and the milk was sour." Ugh, sour milk - that's the bit we liked best.

We particularly loved hearing about school where she was very, very naughty and her teachers, who were called 'governesses', were very, very strict. Most of her stories were funny and she would often stop in the middle to gasp:

"Oh, I can't tell you for laughing," whilst we waited breathlessly for her to finish, even though we knew every word of every story by heart. We loved the one about her and her best friend Polly Catchpole going into a bookshop and asking:

"If you please, how much are the threepenny Bibles?"

And we'd all shout the shop's assistant's answer:

"Sixpence, nine pence and a shilling!"

Granny also asked us some rather odd questions:

"How can your sister be your mother-in-law? How can your aunt be your great-aunt? How can your father-in-law be your brother-in-law?"

These we could never work out and she would laugh and say:

"Oh, I'll explain one day."

The village Flower Show always took place during the holidays and we would be busy for days before, preparing our entries, Granny with her preserves, home-made wine and cakes, Granddad with vegetables, whilst Judith and I made 'a dolly on a clothes peg' or 'a garden on a plate'. The boys were not interested, being far too busy delving down the side of armchairs and under beds in search of lost pennies and suddenly becoming super-helpful in the hope of extra pocket money to spend at the show.

On the great day we had to contain our impatience as we stood amongst the crowd of respectful villagers whilst the vicar introduced the local dignitary who had come to open the show.

"If he speaks to you," whispered Granny, "for goodness sake be polite because he's an Hon."

"What's an 'Hon'?"

"Sssshhhhh."

After the Hon had stopped droning, Granny and Granddad hurried into the marquee to see if they had won any prizes but we children were more interested in the sideshows. There were coconut shies and lucky dips, raffles and races, a fancy-dress parade, a dog show, a tug-of war, and of course there was a fortune teller.

"I think she's a gypsy," I whispered as we peered into her murky booth. Looking at her nut brown face I felt a bit scared because I'd read all about the Raggle Taggle Gypsies who stole children. But Ann said she was sure it was only Miss Evans from the choir.

But what I loved most was the line of faded wooden swing boats where, for a penny, one could pull on a plush rope and swish to and fro, higher and higher until it seemed one could fly like a bird, up, up into the shining summer sky.

Every Saturday night, Granny washed our hair ready for Sunday School the next day. I looked forward to Sunday School because, even though Jesus had never answered my constant prayers for Mummy to come back, I still believed in Him and loved the Bible stories and hymns.

"*Jesus wants us for a sunbeam*," we sang. Perhaps, I used to think, my mummy's a sunbeam now.

Judith's mother had been a hairdresser so her hair was always properly shampooed, but for me this pampering was a real treat and a world away from Daphne who never did more than give our hair a cursory wash with a bar of Sunlight soap. The final touch came next morning when Granny removed the bendy pipe-cleaners she'd wound into our hair and brushed it into curls, finishing off our coiffures with huge satin bows.

At the end of the holidays there was one last treat – a trip to the seaside at Weston-super-Mare. Granny always made Cornish pasties for our picnic, their succulent fillings nestled in an envelope of golden, buttery pastry. Then, wearing our knitted swimsuits under our clothes and carrying our buckets and spades, we clambered onto the bus ready for a wonderful day of donkey rides, sea and sandcastles.

Those summers were a magical time when the sun always seemed to shine and each day was happier than the last. And living in the present as children do, thoughts of life with Daphne faded from my mind until they seemed like a bad and distant dream. But at last the day came when Daddy came to fetch us and, with sinking hearts, we returned to the gloomy house in London and the gloomy life within.

Daphne was by no means always a tyrant and it would be wrong to suggest that our lives were one long nightmare. And, of course, as time went by, we developed coping strategies. We knew when to avoid her, how to suck up to her, what pleased her, what made her angry. The mood in the country was also lighter. By 1946 people were beginning to put the war years behind them, and even though the general austerity had not lifted, there was a feeling that it was time to enjoy life again. Our own lives improved dramatically when Daddy bought a couple of ex-army tents and we started to go camping every weekend.

My father had been an early member of the Boy Scout Movement founded by Robert Baden-Powell in 1907, so camping was close to his heart. He found a beautiful spot in Hertfordshire called Tyler's Causeway where Richard and I ran wild with the new friends we made, making woodland camps, climbing trees, paddling in streams, swimming in the lake – it was heaven. If you couldn't swim, the dads, mine included, made sure their kids learned the fast way by tying a rope round our waists and throwing us in. In the evenings the men lit a big bonfire and we all gathered round, singing songs until the moon sailed high and the night owls went a'hunting.

Throughout the following winter, having decided we should go up-market in the camping world, my clever father spent every spare moment building a caravan. I liked to sit on the bench in his workshop, watching as he measured and hammered and sawed, pinning the curls of wood he planed onto my head like ringlets and watching as the caravan miraculously took shape. When it was finished the whole family came over for the official launch, which I was chosen to perform:

"I name this caravan Venturer," I said in my squeaky little voice, "may God bless her and may we all have a lovely time in her."

Patty did not like camping and usually stayed with Auntie Evelyn on the weekends we were away, but by the age of 16 she was considered old enough to stay at home on her own. One Sunday evening we returned to find that she had gone and with her a suitcase full of clothes. She had run away.

Hurray, I meanly thought, now I can have her room, and was surprised by the furore that ensued as the police were notified and frantic phone calls flashed between relatives and friends. But days passed and there was no sign of her.

Down in Gloucestershire the following week Granny was waiting in a Bristol bus station for her bus home to Cromhall. As she glanced at the left luggage shelves behind the counter, what should she spy but an unusual green suitcase, which she was sure was Patty's. Granny, explaining the situation, asked the attendant if should could open it and sure enough it was full of her granddaughter's clothes. So there she sat for hours and hours until eventually in came the erring girl. And - shock, horror - she was with a man, her boyfriend Paul. I've always thought it was unkind and unnecessary to call the police, but, as they were already involved, she did and poor Patty was carted off to the police station. My father drove down overnight from London to collect her and bring her back in disgrace.

This was the beginning of the end for my sister. She not only hated her stepmother but her relationship with her father was at rock bottom, not least because, when she won a coveted place to Hornsey School of Art, he wouldn't let her go and said she had to leave school and get a job. Added to this was the unpleasant fact that Daphne was using Patricia's name in an illicit affair, thus getting my sister into all sorts of trouble. So, at the age of 17, she walked out. For a while she lived in a YWCA hostel until Auntie Evelyn and Uncle Siddie persuaded her to move in with them. Soon after that my father took the extraordinary step of allowing them to adopt her legally and in their care she blossomed - loved, respected and her artistic talents encouraged.

It was 1948 and the time was fast approaching when I had to sit the Scholarship Exam, introduced in 1944 to determine whether children were more suited to grammar school, secondary modern or a technical college education. As the scheme was in its infancy, there was still great kudos attached to being selected for a grammar school. At Bell Lane School we were drilled rigorously in all the subjects we would have to take but even so the exam itself was daunting. Weeks passed until at last the headmaster came into our form room to announce the results. There were only about ten names on the list and he had almost reached the end before he said 'Barbara Davis'. I'd done it! I raced home and ran up the stairs shouting:

"I've passed! I've passed!"

My father was thrilled although, as my sister was already at a grammar school, he had taken it for granted that I would be successful too. Strangely enough, Daphne seemed disproportionately proud and appeared to bask in reflected glory. She bought me little presents, spoiling me at the expense of poor Richard, and every day when I got home from school would tell me who had congratulated her or, which pleased her immensely, that none of the neighbour's children had passed. When I went out with her she dropped the news neatly into conversations with perfect strangers in queues and bus stops. An assistant at the Home & Colonial Stores gave me a biscuit and told Daphne she should be proud of her clever daughter, adding, "...and, oh my goodness, doesn't she look like you?" Daphne smilingly agreed although even I knew nothing could have been further from the truth. Despite her pride, however, she still managed one last spiteful act just before I left Bell Lane School.

Our school had a strong musical tradition and in my final year I became a member of the choir. That summer we entered a music festival in the borough and spent hours rehearsing with our inspirational choirmaster. The song he chose for us was adapted from John o' Gaunt's speech in Shakespeare's 'King Richard II':

'This royal throne of kings, this sceptred isle,
This earth of majesty, this seat of Mars
This other Eden, demi-paradise
This fortress built by Nature for purpose
Against infection and the hand of war.
This blessed plot, this earth, this realm, this England
We highly dedicate oh Lord to thee.'

At assembly on the day before the festival, we trooped onto the stage and as we sang to the school, our high, clear voices weaving the descants into a silver tapestry, my heart swelled with the beauty of it. The headmaster wished us luck and said he was sure we would bring honour to our school.

'Now, three cheers for our wonderful choir!'

Oh, I thought I would burst with pride! Before we left school, our choir master told us to be at Hendon Central Station at 9.30 the next morning:

"...and don't be late."

I was ready early, excited and quite certain our school was going to win a prize. At nine o'clock I put on my coat and called out "goodbye" as I ran down the stairs to the front door. Daphne appeared from the kitchen.

"Hey you, come back here", she shouted, "where d'you think you're going?"

"To the station, it's the music festival today".

"Oh no you're not," she said, delving in her purse. "Here, go and get me two pounds of dog meat."

"But I can't…I'll miss the train," I stammered.

"Just do as you're told" she said, "and don't you dare come back without it."

The Dog Meat Shop, where horsemeat was sold as pet food, was just down the road from our house. It was a disgusting place. Great sides of stinking meat, dyed green to deter human consumption, hung from hooks and dripped congealing blood onto the sawdust below. I hated going there to buy food for our little dog, Jeannie.   Daphne must have hated it too because she made sure either Richard or I took this chore off her hands as often as possible. I ran as fast as I could to the shop, hoping against hope that, as it was early, there would not be a queue. But there was, and I knew I had to stand in it. By the time I'd taken the dog meat home and run to the station, the choir had gone. And, just as she had intended, I missed the festival.

That September, dressed in my new uniform, shiny leather satchel swinging on my back, I set off for my first day at Copthall County School for Girls, two bus rides away. I had hardly been able to sleep for the excitement of moving to my 'big school'. But from the moment I got there I was unhappy because, as it was out of our area, I knew no-one and was too shy to make new friends. I had never felt more isolated and alone. Every evening I came home crying, every evening Daddy said things would soon get better and I must just persevere.   If only I had known that this ordeal would soon be over.

F O U R

A YEAR AFTER GRANNY moved to Gloucestershire, Auntie Ethel, Uncle Toby and our two cousins followed. Auntie Evelyn and Siddie had long had a dream of owning a village shop so when, a couple of years later, they received a telegram from Granny saying 'come at once, Padfield's for sale', they caught the milk train and had bought the village store in Cromhall before the day was out.

Then, in the summer of 1949, we also left London. My father's health had deteriorated; the work of rebuilding bomb-damaged buildings was proving too much for him, his bronchial problems were increasing and his doctor urged a move to the country and fresh air. So the decision was made to join the family exodus to Gloucestershire. An old friend agreed to buy Dad's busy little building firm and, although the deal had not been finalised, had given him a cash deposit. So it was that, on a summer day in 1948, we left for a new life far away from Hendon and the haunted house.

"We're rich!" shouted Daddy as we drove away with the caravan behind us, "here, catch!" To our amazement, he threw two pound notes over his shoulder, a vast sum which convinced my brother and me that we were wealthy at last.

However, very soon after our arrival in the West Country, things began to go wrong. With the money from the sale of his London firm my father had planned to buy a house and start up a new, if smaller, building business, but when after a few weeks the balance had not been paid, he began to get worried. He rang and wrote letters to his friend, as did his solicitor, but there was always an excuse. He made several trips up to London but the 'friend' was always conveniently unavailable. Finally, having realised he had been well and truly conned, the affair went to court, but even so, the money was never recovered. Meanwhile, the money was fast disappearing. We had been living in a rented cottage but by Christmas that year, when it became clear he could no longer afford the rent, my father bought a second, caravan – battered, leaky and old - and here we lived throughout the following winter. All of us, not just Daddy, succumbed to bronchitis as well as constant coughs and colds. And far from once again being boss of his own business, he now found himself doing the occasional odd job wherever he could find it.

The following spring he at last managed to get a permanent, if lowly, job as maintenance man on a country estate, the huge benefit of which was that a house went with it.

I don't quite know what we imagined we'd find as we drove down a long track, our car juddering over the muddy, rutted surface. A tumbledown house? A dilapidated cottage? But as the lane came to a sudden end, there, perched on the side of a valley so beautiful it made one's heart turn over, stood a perfect little farmhouse, its golden limestone walls aglow, the afternoon sun twinkling on its latticed windows. Although outwardly so beautiful, there was plenty wrong with the place: the paintwork was peeling, the ceilings looked precarious and the floorboards not much better, damp penetrated the walls in ominous patches, there was one cold tap in the kitchen, no gas, no electricity, and the only lavatory was outside at an inconvenient distance from the house. It was also a lonely spot, a mile from the little village of Alderley. And yet none of this seemed to matter, for 'Whitehall', as it was called, could not have been more different from our grim, eerie home in London. This house was interesting, even eccentric. It seemed to have been wedged into the hillside so that every room was linked to the next with a few steps up or down. Light poured in from every window whilst oak beams, crooked stairs and sloping floors added to its charm and spoke of its history. Out-buildings clustered round the back of the farm – barns, a pig sty, a circular granary on tall stone stilts - and a big orchard of apple and pear trees tumbled down the hill to a fast-flowing trout stream at the bottom of the valley. And that was it; no grimy streets, no traffic, no fog, no shops, no people, no scars of war; naught but the verdant meadows, air sweet with the smell of wild flowers and skylarks singing above the high hills.

The estate was owned by Squire Hale, a man in his sixties who was both a gentleman and a gentle man. He cared not only for his land but for every tree, every bird, every living creature on it; he cared not only for the people who worked for him but for their families. Entering this small, paternalistic society must have felt like a haven to my father after all that had gone before. Now he had found quiet, easy work, out in the fresh air much of the time, which meant that his health quickly improved. And, as an added bonus, he now had a rather beautiful home.

One might have thought such born-and-bred Londoners would have hated the remote spot in which we now lived. But, rescued from the claustrophobia of the caravans, we loved it, even my brother and I with not a friend in sight. Daphne, in particular, had never seemed happier, striding around big-bottomed in ex-Land Army jodhpurs, apparently relishing her new role as a country woman. And, of course, a cheerful Daphne meant Richard and I were less often the butt of her temper. Everyone lent a hand with the decorating and when that was finished, the cultivation of the huge, overgrown kitchen garden. As well as vegetables, Daddy grew his own pipe tobacco. Row after row of the huge plants were soon springing up and, when the time came, we picked the leaves and strung them up to hang like bats from beams in the barn. Once dry, we formed a little assembly line, painting them with a solution of black treacle, tying them into neat wads which Daddy compacted under a vice. Then, months later when the sticky wads had dried, he sliced them into thin strands ready to smoke. We acquired three beautiful, amber-eyed goats - Blossom, Betsy and Bertha - which we quickly learned to milk and which, staked on very long chains, were also the perfect lawn-mowers for the orchard. This was the best life had been since our mother's death.

On arriving in the Cotswolds, Richard and I had started school in Wotton-under-Edge, our nearest town, although because he had not passed the scholarship exam, we were not at the same establishments. However, both schools were historically interesting. Richard went to The British School in Bear Street, founded in 1837 by Isaac Pitman who had developed a phonetic system of shorthand, 'Stenographic Soundhand', to help children who found reading and pronunciation difficult. A modest man, he had it published without fuss or fanfare, never anticipating that it would become the most widely used system in the world and would eventually earn him a knighthood.

I joined my cousins Judith and Peter at Katherine Lady Berkeley's School. Founded in 1384, it was the earliest known grammar school foundation in the country. There were about 350 pupils in 1949, small by today's standards, and I loved it from the start, not least because my summer holiday friend, Ann Holpin, was in my class. Ann already had a 'best friend', Eleanor Cornoch, a farmer's daughter, but luckily for me a girl called Pat Jackson was best-friendless. She could not have been more perfect as a pal because she, too, loved art. The four of us became inseparable.

The school was run on the formal lines that were then the norm and by and large we were well taught. Each day started with Assembly when the headmaster - who, having survived the battlefields of the Somme had become deeply religious - intoned long prayers and impassioned passages from the Bible. As light relief, we sang the hymns as rowdily as possible before marching out and dispersing for the day's classes. Our teachers were a motley crew, ranging from the inspired to the truly awful. Only our geography teacher fell into the latter category, her mind-numbingly boring lessons rendering one almost comatose. I took in so little of what she taught that, at O-level, my paper's main feature was a beautifully executed picture of a man climbing a coconut tree. I failed.

Mr Logan, our Latin master, must have been in his forties at the time. He was red-faced, thick-necked and overweight. His suits were too tight, the fabric straining over his slightly stained crotch, the waistband cutting into his paunch. He had a sarcastic wit. It was a time when, for girls, autograph books were in vogue. They had padded covers and pages tinted in pastel shades on which friends, relatives and, of course, teachers wrote amusing or cringingly sentimental entries. (Granny's entry in my album read: 'Be good, sweet maid, and let who will be clever'. Thanks Gran). Mr Logan was known for the wit of his entries so I asked him to write something for me. His offering was blunt and to the point: 'Barbara Davis has a voice like a Mavis; you can hear her call from here to Whitehall'. I was deeply offended.

A bull of a man, his temperament was as unpredictable as his bovine equivalent. His roar if our *amo, amas, amat* was incorrect had us all ducking as pieces of chalk flew round the classroom, reaching their intended victims with unerring accuracy. He waged a running battle with Mrs Macpherson, the Domestic Science teacher whose classroom was directly above his, but this doughty Scot was every bit his match. To amuse ourselves during cookery lessons we poured hot water through gaps in the floorboard onto his head, waited for the roar then scattered, giggling, to our places, knowing we were immune from prosecution because Mrs Mac always defended 'my gerrls' from the enemy below.

But there was something even more unpleasant about Mr Logan. If a girl's work did not come up to standard, if we talked too much in class or handed in our homework late, the punishment would be to write a few hundred lines. But if a boy was in trouble he was called to the front of the class and told to bend over Mr Logan's knee, who would then insert his fat hand down the back of the unfortunate boy's trousers, pull the material taut and then smack his bottom - not particularly hard, but in a leisurely way and with a faint smirk on his face. At the end of the punishment the boy would get up, unhurt but embarrassed, and sidle back to his seat. We would snigger about this but his victims never complained and it somehow didn't seem to be a big deal. At that time my friends and I had never even heard the word 'homosexual' and it was not until a school reunion many years later that I learned what was in retrospect quite obvious; that Mr Logan had a preference for school boys.

In fact, there was a trio of gay men amongst our teachers, another of whom was the aptly named Mr Organ, our music master. He was Mr Logan's opposite in every respect. A sweet, sensitive man whose hair flopped in a Byronic wave over his brow, the poor soul should never have crossed the threshold of a classroom. For, oh, how we looked forward to music lessons when we could let rip with extremes of bad behaviour as Mr Organ, his voice becoming ever more shrill, begged us to sing 'Nymphs and Shepherds' with a teensy bit more delicacy.

The third was Mr Minnett, the English master. He was my favourite teacher, doubtless because I shone at English and so was always in his good books. His great gift was not only to instill in us the building blocks of our language but also to inspire us with his own passion for literature, poetry, and the beauty of the written word.

As time went by, Daphne's enthusiasm for country life slowly evaporated and this had a predictable effect on her mood. Whilst she never returned to the worst of her wicked stepmother ways, she was a difficult woman to live with, bad tempered, always unpredictable, still on occasion as scary and unkind as ever. One day I left my school shoes on the bus and was so frightened of her reaction that I actually stood by the side of the road trying to pluck up the courage to step in front of a car. I didn't intend to end it all but thought that, if I was seriously injured, she couldn't be angry with me. But the moment passed and I had to go home and face the music. Whilst her wrath was predictable and in a way deserved, her punishment was not. She decreed that, as the shoes had been lost due to my carelessness and had not simply worn out, no replacement pair would be bought. Instead, my 'sentence' was to wear Wellington boots to school, which, whatever the weather, I did for months on end. Richard and I therefore remained as wary of her as ever. But on a summer's afternoon in

52

1951 when we came dawdling down the lane after school we were not prepared for what was about to happen.

We were late because we'd made a detour into a field of cows and amused ourselves by poking their bony bums with sticks and watching them gallop away. We'd spotted a particularly large cow and given it an extra hard prod. It let out a bellow and, as it turned, we realised our mistake - it was a bull! We ran for it, satchels thumping up and down on our backs and, with the bull thundering behind, threw ourselves over the gate just in time - whew! So we were out of breath and giggling as we approached the house. Daphne came hurrying out to meet us.

"You're late," she snapped, "got my cigarettes?"

I clapped my hand to my mouth - oh no, I'd forgotten them.

"I'm really sorry - I nearly missed the bus and I didn't have time…"

As though someone had lit a blue touch-paper, she exploded. She grabbed a garden broom and lunged, beating me round the head, the shoulders, the back, anywhere she could reach. I ran away, down the path and along the track into the kitchen garden, with her hot on my heels. Up and down we raced, trampling rows of lettuce and carrots, toppling canes of runner beans and tomatoes to the ground, whilst she rained blows on me whenever she got near enough, screaming, screaming, abuse spewing from her mouth in a poisonous stream, her neck corded with rage.

All of a sudden, something seemed to burst in my head. What on earth was I doing? Why was I letting this vile creature treat me like this? I wheeled round, wrenched the broom from her and started to scream even louder than her.

"That's it, I've had enough! Don't you *dare* hit me again! Don't you *dare* shout at me! You've always been cruel to us and I hate you, hate you, HATE YOU!"

I flung the broom away, turned and ran back to the house, shrieking over my shoulder:

"… and I'm telling Daddy as soon as he gets home!"

Then I rushed upstairs to my bedroom and locked the door before I collapsed sobbing on the bed.

After a while there was a gentle knock on the door.

"Barbie, are you all right dear? Come out and we'll…"

"Go away!" I yelled.

Half an hour later she was back.

"Look, I've put a cup of tea on the floor here and a nice piece of buttered toast.'"

This time I kept quiet. For several minutes I could hear her breathing on the other side of the door but then, once again, she retreated. Suddenly, as I lay there, the most amazing thought popped into my head - the balance of power had shifted. Now *I* was in control. It felt good.

She had one more go: *"Please come out,"* she wheedled in a whiney voice I'd never heard before, "I'm *so* sorry, really I am. And please don't tell your father..."

Behind my locked door I smiled grimly. I stayed put until I heard Daddy's car coming down the lane and then went down to find her, wreathed in smiles with supper on the table. Lucky for you none of my bruises show, I thought as, giving her a defiant stare, I sauntered over to the table and helped myself to a slice of ham.

I never did tell my father what had happened. But then, as he appeared to have been blind to all that had gone on over the past seven years, there didn't seem much point.

After that, our relationship changed and an unexpected if uneasy friendship developed. We went for walks together, we chatted amicably as I helped her cook or wash-up and she even seemed interested in my teenage hopes and dreams. She was equally nice to Richard. Why hadn't I stood up for myself before, I thought? Nevertheless, my brother and I both continued to tiptoe round her, afraid that this pleasant bubble might burst. Then, one afternoon, as we sat beside the stream at the bottom of the orchard, she asked me if I could keep a secret.

"Of course," I said, wondering what on earth she was going to tell me.

"I'm leaving your father," she said, "I'm going back to London."

I was absolutely stunned, not quite knowing if I should look pleased or upset, or what I was supposed to say. But she went on talking: she was fed up with Daddy, he was a misery, he was too old for her, always moaning, always pretending to be ill. And she was fed up with this isolated country life, she had no friends, she hardly saw a soul day in day out and she missed her parents terribly.

"I'm a Londoner," she said, "I'm sick to death of country people. They're so slow, so boring. And anyway, I'm only 30 and I want a bit of life."

As I listened my teenage self-obsession lifted briefly and I suddenly understood how lonely her life must be, living in the middle of nowhere, effectively cut-off from the world. Suddenly and unexpectedly, I felt sorry for her. She swore me to secrecy and that was that. Not another word was mentioned and, as the weeks went by, I sometimes wondered if she'd just said it because she'd had another row with Dad. I put it out of my mind.

One wet November afternoon three months later, as the school bus pulled in to Alderley, who should be waiting for Richard and I but Daddy. This was strange because it was too early for him to have stopped work and, what's more, he was on foot. His face was grim. What on earth had happened?

"Where's the car?" we asked as we got off the bus.

"Broken down, gear box I shouldn't wonder" he said, "I've had to leave it up at the farm. Wretched thing - it's going to cost a packet to repair."

Oh, so that was why he looked so fed up. We set off down the lane to Whitehall, none of us speaking, heads bent against the driving rain. But eventually he broke the silence.

"I've got something to tell you," he said, his voice breaking, "Daphne's left me."

Then, in a torrent of understandable self-pity he bemoaned his terrible luck: he'd been through a war and if we thought that'd been easy we were wrong, and he'd lost his wife and he'd had to be mother and father to us, and now Daphne had gone and what had he ever done except try to make her life as happy as he could, why had she walked out on him and how on earth were we going to manage without her and his chest was playing up again and the car was broken and God knows where the money would come from to mend the damned thing and we wouldn't be short of money in the first place if his so-called friend hadn't swindled him and now all he was was an odd job man when he'd had his own company in London and, and, and...

Richard and I linked arms with him as we squelched through the mud and tried to say cheerful things, assuring him we'd manage just fine without her. But my mind was in turmoil. I was full of guilt because now I felt I had been wrong to keep quiet and should have warned Daddy that she planned to go. And I felt so sorry for him. He was clearly terribly upset and he truly had been through so much. And, who knows, perhaps he actually loved Daphne. But at the same time, great waves of relief kept breaking through. She'd gone! She'd gone! Oh my God, she'd really gone!

When we got home, Richard and I bustled round whilst Daddy sat slumped in his armchair. Richard lit a fire whilst I rustled up something to eat and instead of sitting at the table as we usually did we balanced our plates on our knees in front of the fire. After supper, Daddy lit his pipe then poured us all a whole glass of cider. Richard and I glanced at each other - things were definitely looking up as we were never normally allowed more than an inch or two of this lethal offering from our orchard. Richard said his friend Dave's dad always warmed their cider up with a poker when the weather turned cold. So Dad stuck the poker in the fire until it was red hot then plunged it, hissing and sizzling, into our tankards, making the golden liquid seethe and foam. We emptied our glasses and decided it would be a good plan to have another, which tasted even better.

Dad began to cheer up. Well, he said, she'd been a pain in the neck, always arguing, lazy as they come, a terrible housewife, a terrible cook, smoked like a darn chimney, and he'd had his suspicions when he came home and found her in the barn with Gus the cowman. What were they up to, eh? Come to think of it, he really couldn't stand the woman. What a good thing she'd gone.

Not a word about the way she'd treated his children, but we didn't care, we were happy, happy, happy! Dad poured out some more scrumpy...

All I remember about the end of that evening is waking up to find the fire out and Richard and Daddy slumped in their chairs, fast asleep. Dad was snoring.

$F\ I\ V\ E$

AND SO, AFTER SEVEN LONG YEARS, life without Daphne began. Looking back I can see that on the scale of wicked stepmothers she didn't rate that highly. Although she was unkind, bad-tempered and unpredictable enough to make me a nervous and eager-to-please person for many years thereafter, she was not a villain and did what was probably the best she could, given the circumstances. Strangely, my brother and I never discussed the Daphne years and told neither family nor friends about the way she had treated us. We neither knew nor cared what happened to her after she left, although I have learned that she returned to Hendon, remarried in 1954 and the following year gave birth to a daughter in January and a son in December.

Now, however, Daddy, Richard and I rejoiced that she had gone and that a new regime was beginning. And I was in charge. For a start, I had the heady experience of controlling the Order Book, the notebook in which our weekly grocery list was written. I began to slip in delicacies like wafer biscuits, tins of pineapple and condensed milk, gradually adding sachets of Silvikrin shampoo and little bottles of Amami setting lotion, sheer luxury for a teenage girl. Dad didn't seem to notice and the power was intoxicating.

Richard celebrated his new-found freedom by creating a secret smoking den in a disused pig sty, equipping it with bales of hay arranged to make a comfy, if inflammable, armchair, with bottles of cider, pipe, tobacco and matches nicked from his Dad. We wondered why he kept coming into the house rather green around the gills but it was not until he set fire to the sty that his secret was uncovered. He also took to going off for hours on end. We'd see him striding purposefully up the lane or over the hills but when asked where he'd been, he'd just grunt 'nowhere'. But this liberty suited my independent, friendly brother and we could see him blossom.

The three of us discussed how we were going to manage the

cooking. It was tricky because we were out all day and didn't want to spend hours preparing supper when we got home. Added to which, we couldn't cook. Then Richard and Daddy had a good idea – rabbits.

"What?" I asked.

"Leave it to us," they said.

They made some enquiries and drove off one day to see a man in a nearby village, returning with a pair of cream ferrets, beautiful, smelly, sinuous creatures with pink eyes and vicious teeth. The boys named them Arfer-Mo and 'Ere-a-Tick. But I doubt if the rabbits got the joke, for soon they were being driven out of their burrows where Richard and Dad waited to dispatch them, a thought which now horrifies me but which pleased us mightily back then. My part of the deal was to gut and skin the rabbits, and chop the meat into joints. We dug out a huge saucepan and into this capacious pot went the rabbit together with onions, carrots, potatoes, Oxo cubes, water, even a good slug of cider, which was then left to cook on the anthracite stove which stood in the scullery. The result was a succulent stew, hot and ready to eat when we came home each evening. After supper we simply added this and that to the pot - more vegetables, baked beans, rice or another rabbit if the men had been hunting. Throughout that winter we came home to a hot meal until, by the following spring, I had gradually started making the dishes learned in my school cookery lessons, which my two loyal boys ate, however awful.

Daphne had been anything but house-proud but now, without even her rudimentary efforts and bad-tempered constraints, things gradually got out of hand. Beds were never made, clothes littered the floors, dishes stood in the sink unwashed. We all marched into the house scattering mud from our Wellington boots, whilst the slightest ray of sunshine edging its way through the windows revealed the thickening layers of dust. I knew things had gone too far when my father emptied a sack of anthracite into the bath because, he said, it would be much easier to stoke the boiler than if it was outside in the bunker. So the holiday period had to end and every weekend I tried to clean the place, sometimes with help from Daddy and Richard if they responded to my nagging.

The rest of the family was delighted by Daphne's departure, particularly Granny.

"Thank God *I'll* be able to do your washing now," she said, "heaven only knows *how* that woman could let you go out looking like tramps."

"Tramps?" objected my father, "I say Mum, that's a bit rich, we didn't look that bad..."

"No, Charlie, I *said* tramps and I *mean* tramps. What the neighbours must have thought I can't imagine."

"But Granny, we haven't *got* any neighbours," Richard said with perfect logic.

"That's beside the point, and we'll have less cheek from you my lad, *if* you don't mind. No, from now on you bring your washing over here once a week and that's that, alright?"

Well, I for one was not going to argue. Neither did I feel guilty about giving Granny extra work because she had a washing machine. It was a massive green enamel contraption which made a noise like a tank, vibrating wildly and spewing clouds of steam into the kitchen. But it was her pride and joy, particularly as she was one of the few people in the village to own such a thing. So every Sunday we piled our laundry into a bag and set off for Granny's, speculating on the way about what we'd have for lunch. Would it be roast beef this week, or pork with loads of crispy crackling or – unbelievable treat – a chicken? And what had she made for pud?

But before this feast, we knew we had to endure what quickly became a ritual humiliation when, as soon as we arrived, Granny pounced eagerly on the laundry bag and dragged out each offending item.

"Just look at your shirt collars, Richard, the *filth*! I bet your neck hasn't seen a flannel all week. Let me see. Yes, just as I thought - black. Go on, go and wash it immediately - and don't forget your ears. Only two sheets? Who hasn't changed their bed I'd like to know? And *look* at the *size* of this *hole*! Is this your sock Barbara? Can't you spell d-a-r-n? How you can hold your head up with your foot hanging out I just *do not know*. Honestly, Charlie, you should be ashamed. I don't think you give two hoots what your children look like when they go out in the morning. Suppose they have an accident, eh? That's what I want to know. Just think about it for a minute. They're in the ambulance, their clothes are being cut off and what's underneath? Filthy grey vests. Then what, eh?"

"Oh, for goodness sake, Mum."

"Don't you 'for goodness sake me', d'you hear? And another thing...."

The fact was that, thanks to her, we all looked cleaner and smarter than we had for years. So whilst she ranted we squirmed a bit and grinned sheepishly at each other whilst Granddad in his armchair by the fire shook with silent laughter. In any case, it was soon over and she'd be off on another tack.

"Have I told you about old Mrs Duffy? Oh my giddy aunt, you won't believe this. She came to WI last week with her hat on back to front and...oh, I can't tell you for laughing...."

After lunch Granddad always asked me to play the piano. He loved the old folk songs like 'My Darling Clementine', 'The Skye Boat Song' and 'Scarborough Fair', and sang along in his quavery voice. His favourites were the sad, sentimental ones and when we got to verses like:

'Nita, Juanita
Ask thy soul if we should part
Nita, Juanita
Lean thou on my heart'

a tear or two would trickle down his dear old cheeks.

By now he was in his eighties and so we were not surprised when he fell ill and lay in bed for weeks, growing steadily weaker. His condition grew worse and we hurried over to see him, tiptoeing solemnly up the stairs behind Granny - and there he was, eyes closed, face much thinner, nose now like a beak. The room was silent but for his jagged breathing and I remember feeling very frightened at the thought that perhaps our darling Granddad was going to die. Suddenly the sound of a shot-gun broke the stillness as a nearby farmer took a pot-shot at a rabbit. The old man in the bed stirred.

"Another bugger gone," he muttered.

A few seconds later he sat up in bed and asked for a cup of tea. He lived to be 97.

"Now come on, try and guess," said Granny after lunch one day, "how can your sister be your mother-in-law as well?"

It was those old riddles she'd been setting us for years. We were bored with them. "Oh, give up! Come on Granny, why can't you tell us?" I begged, and so at last she did:

She and Frederick Davis married in 1904. Her father-in-law, Charles, was a jeweller and clock-maker, an upright citizen of Nailsworth in Gloucestershire. A deeply religious man who was a lay preacher at the local Methodist church, he was widowed in 1912 when Rebecca, his wife of many years and mother of their seven sons, died. Just five years later, however, something happened which provoked a scandal within the family and doubtless within the local community when, in 1917 at the age of 62, Charles married again. His bride was none other than Granny's young sister, Laura (my beloved Aunt Dig; she of the entertaining false teeth) who was just 17 years old.

"So now do you see?" asked Granny as she ended her explanation of this family mystery. Suddenly, all became clear, for with this marriage, her sister suddenly became her mother-in-law, her children's aunt their grandmother, her husband's father his brother-in-law...the weird combinations were endless. But even though the riddle had been explained I did not consider the wider issues. Only very recently has my second cousin, John – now in his 90's - told me that the marriage was seen as so shocking that the younger members of the family were never told and it was not until many years later that he discovered he had a grandmother who was 23 years younger than him. Even though this was a perfectly valid marriage, one can imagine the scandal in the town, the whispers and unkind gossip, the sniggers, the winks and nods amongst the worthy congregation of the Methodist church. Perhaps it was enough to drive them away, for Charles and Laura moved to Swadlincote in Derbyshire, where he opened another clock-making and jewellers shop. Unlikely though it seemed, this was a very happy marriage which produced a baby girl, Mary, in 1923, and ended with Charles' death in 1934.

There is one other unsolved mystery on this side of the family involving my grandfather's brother, Arthur. As a young man he went out to India and became a successful tea-planter. Here, members of his immediate family recount, he shot and killed someone in the prestigious Calcuttta Club, left swiftly for the docks and sailed away to South Africa, where he became a fruit farmer and lived out the rest of his life, apparently un-pursued by the law. What had happened? I like to imagine that he had a duel over a beautiful woman, shot his rival then fled the country, leaving a bleeding corpse and the girl in this love triangle bereft of either suitor. Sadly, we shall never know.

My school friends and I began to be interested in boys and lived in hope that we would soon be asked 'to go for a walk', this being the euphemism used when asking for a date. Eleanor had no trouble attracting boys, not surprising as she was blonde, buxom and pretty, and, unlike the rest of us, already had bosoms - large ones. I so longed for someone to ask me to 'go for a walk' but no-one ever did. Why not? Why did none of the boys at school like me? Was it because I was too tall or too ugly or a Londoner or what? In fact, I really didn't like the boys in my class and secretly, if groundlessly, felt vastly superior to them. But even so, they could at least *ask*. It wasn't *fair*. Then one day, scuffing moodily down the lane on the way home, I had a brilliant idea. I would invent a boyfriend! Then, in a further flash of inspiration, I decided to base him on one of the farmhands in the village, whose name was Ron. That night I lay in bed, plotting.

At school the next day I casually mentioned the new guy who had come to work at Home Farm. He was six foot tall, I said, with dark wavy hair and beautiful brown eyes. In fact, totally gorgeous.

"And," I said giggling bashfully, "he winked at me when I was waiting for the bus this morning."

As the days went by, my tale unfolded: Ron had wolf whistled when I walked by; Ron had said hello when I got off the bus; Ron had asked me to help round up the cows; Ron had held my hand as we came back with said cows. Then the great day came when Ron had - yes - formally asked me to go for a walk...

"Oh, and by the way, he's 20," I added.

This last, I felt, was a master stroke as none of us knew any boys older than 17 and they were superior sixth formers who wouldn't dream of speaking to us.

I began to embellish the details. Ron was a student at Cirencester Agricultural College. Ron's father was very wealthy. Ron had taken me for a drive in his sports car... Every day, my friends pressed me for details and my reports became more and more colourful. In fact, I even believed them myself because for me - a girl who, ever since my mother's death and throughout the Daphne years, had found an escape from sad realities in my land of make-belief - this came very easily. To me, Ron *was* real and everything I invented about him felt true.

Valentine's Day was fast approaching and we all began to speculate on how many cards we would receive. I, of course, boasted that Ron would probably buy me red roses. I got home from school on the 14th of February to find a large envelope waiting for me. I could hardly believe my eyes. Could it possibly be a Valentine's card? But who on earth was it from? I ripped open the envelope and pulled out a pink, rose-strewn card. 'To my darling Barbara,' it read, 'you are my Valentine, all my love, Ron.'

I decided then and there to kill myself. Either that or run away. At the very least I was never, ever going back to school. Because it didn't take a genius to guess that my so-called friends had sent it and I knew I could never face them again. I felt sick. I couldn't eat my supper. I hardly slept, tossing and turning all night as I imagined how they must have laughed behind my back all these weeks, how they must have sniggered when they bought the card and posted it. The next morning I pretended to be ill. I'd got a temperature, I moaned, and wanted to stay in bed. Daddy pressed his hand to my forehead.

"There's nothing wrong with you," said the world's leading hypochondriac, "and no, you're not staying at home. Get a move on or you'll miss the bus."

So I had no choice but to face the music. My friends asked if I'd had a Valentine card and I stared at the ground, my face burning. But, strangely, after a bit of giggling and smug looks at each other, they said nothing else. Stranger still, Ron disappeared without trace. But my guilt and mortification, and indeed my sense of loss, loomed over me like a sad shadow for weeks to come.

However, a few months later, something happened which made me recover instantly - I met a real live boy and, yes, he asked me to go for a walk! What's more he was not only darkly handsome and older than me but he actually went to boarding school. How exotic was that? His name was Bruce. His mother, a sweet lady married to a German ex-prisoner-of-war, had proudly told me about him, the son from her first marriage, and as soon as he came home for the Easter holidays, she made sure we met. He was a lovely boy, friendly, easy-going and full of fun. We got along fine, chatting and laughing as though we had known each other for ages. We did indeed go for walks, taking their dogs for miles along the country lanes and up over the hills.

Then one day he asked me to go to the pictures with him the following Saturday. Head in a whirl, I walked home. On the one hand I was utterly thrilled to be invited out on a real date, on the other I knew I'd have to ask Dad if I could go. How could I possibly face the embarrassment of that? He was not at all pleased when I mentioned it but, post-Daphne, I was no longer the cowed wimp I had been and I persisted. The next day was Sunday. We arrived at my grandmother's and after her usual rant about the state of the laundry, Dad followed her into the kitchen as she prepared lunch. I strained my ears to hear what he was muttering but soon had no doubt as Granny's strident tones rang out:

"...go to the *cinema*? I trust you said no, Charlie. You didn't? Are you mad? The girl's fifteen. And he's what? You don't know? Well you should know. Old enough for a bit of hanky panky, I'll be bound. Just think about that for a minute..."

Hanky panky? Oh for goodness sake. I could feel my face getting redder and redder. Granny came in bearing the joint and, shooting accusing glances in my direction, started to carve...

"You may well blush, miss..." she said ominously, sinking her knife into the meat.

As we drove back to Alderley, Dad told me I wasn't allowed to go. I was, he said, far too young. We argued and argued all the way home and finally, his 'anything for a quiet life' philosophy won and he capitulated, although, borrowing his mother's phrase, he qualified this by insisting that there be:

"no hanky panky, do you understand?"

Grown-ups! Honestly!

We saw a film called 'Scaramouche' and afterwards trundled back from Dursley on the bus. As it neared our stop and started to slow down, what should I see but my father's car parked on the other side of the road. Oh no, I would *die* if my Dad met me after my first date. But Bruce had seen too.

"Quick", he said, grabbing my hand and we jumped off the bus before it stopped and disappeared into the darkness. He walked me slowly home, gave me my first dizzying kiss then left me at the gate. It was very late. Daddy was still up and he was hopping mad. He'd waited at the bus stop for over an hour he yelled. He'd been worried sick. Where'd we been? What'd we been up to?

"Oh," I said innocently, "we got off at the wrong stop, you must have missed us." Then I raced up to bed to dream about that kiss.

Despite Dad's disapproval, I continued to see Bruce until the holidays ended and he went back to school. My friends, understandably, looked sceptical when I started talking about this wonderful new boyfriend, but this time I was armed with a photograph his mother had given me and then, a week or so later, with the first of quite a few letters. But then came a bombshell - he wrote to say he had met someone else and so it was over between us. I was devastated and at school that day I read and re-read the letter in case, in some miraculous way, it turned out to be a bad dream. Suddenly, as I was reading it for the umpteenth time, a boy I particularly hated snatched it and ran off, holding it above his head as I tried to get it back. Then, in a loud, dramatic voice, he read it out to the whole jeering class. Once again, I wanted to die.

A couple of years later, I heard that Bruce, that lovely boy, had joined the army and been sent to Cyprus where, as he walked down a road in Nicosia, he was shot in the spine and paralysed for life.

I had one more invitation to 'go for a walk'. It was from a very nice boy who handed me a note on our way out of church one Sunday. Scrawled in pencil on a scrap of paper it read:

"Wood you lick to go owt for a wark with me?"

Well, he could have had an Irishman's blarney and a film-star's looks but I knew I would never go out with someone who couldn't spell!

It would be several years before true romance came my way again. But next time it was to be the hammer-blow of real love that, as the best romantic novels always say, would 'change my life forever'.

Sam Minnett, the English master, also produced the school plays and I discovered a love of, and small talent for, acting. During my final term at school he announced that we would be performing The Antigone of Sophocles on Speech Day and that he wanted me to play Antigone, with my classmate Helen taking the part of Ismene, Antigone's sister. As I had only had minor roles before, I was stunned. I was also scared stiff, quite sure I could neither learn all the lines nor literally take centre stage in this epic tragedy.

But towards the end of July, Speech Day came and with it the moment of truth. The audience assembled and prizes were duly given out. The Headmaster and the Chairman of the Governors droned on for a while before resuming their seats alongside other local worthies, with my father, grandmother and aunts in the row behind.

Backstage, we waited, trying to quell last-minute nerves. The opening scene was to be dramatic and we had rehearsed it over and over again: with the ominous tones of Holst's Planet Suite setting the mood, the curtain would rise on a dark, empty stage. Antigone would appear alone at the top of a flight of shallow stairs, lit by a single spotlight, in her arms a funeral urn. Slowly, she would descend the steps and stand centre stage until the music died away. Then, holding the urn aloft, she would intone her first tragic lines…

Now the curtain has risen and it's the real thing. Antigone is ready. The first notes of music ring out. But, hang on, instead of Holst, Rosemary Clooney's jolly voice singing 'This Ole House' blares forth. This startles our heroine who trips up on the edge of her toga, drops the metal urn, (which clangs and clatters into the front row) hurtles down the steps and across the stage, before disappearing through the opposite wings. The audience titters. The curtain comes down. Pause. Then Mr Minnet's head appears round the curtain:

"Sorry about that, folks, minor setback. Oh, could you pass me

65

that urn madam…?"

After a few moments of hissed recriminations, calming of nerves and changing of music, we begin again. And somehow we pull it off. As we take our curtain calls, my relatives overhear the Chairman of the Governors, the Headmaster and Lady Somebody-or-Other extolling my performance and marvelling at my recovery after the false start.

"Honestly," said Dad as we drove home, "you should have heard them! One of them even said you should go to drama school!"

It was the first time since I passed the Scholarship Exam that I had ever known him proud of me and as a reward he bought me a second-hand bike for five shillings.

I was now thoroughly stage-struck. When I told my big sister of this ambition, she urged me to leave home and join a repertory company as an assistant stage manager, which would, she assured me, quickly lead to acting roles. Of course I didn't, but becoming an actress now figured in my dreams as well as the more realistic ambition of going to art school.

Following Daphne's defection, our Father wasted no time in getting out and enjoying himself. He joined the local Gramophone Society where members played and discussed classical music, he joined a Rifle Club, and new friends came over to play billiards with him at Whitehall. He seemed as happy as a lark.

Squire Hale's estate secretary was a lady called Miss Pearce. She was a sturdy little person in her early forties who strode around in unbecoming tweeds, stout lace-up shoes and ugly hats with pheasant feathers in their brims, all of which disguised the fact that she was really rather pretty. Richard and I liked her. She was kind and friendly, and always stopped to give us lifts as she hurtled round the countryside in a battered Jeep. My father, however, in his all or nothing way, couldn't stand her.

"Who does she think she is?" he'd demand, "talking to me in that snooty voice, anyone would think *she* owned the estate and not the Squire."

So he was irate when he returned from the Rifle Club one evening because: "that dreadful woman has joined. Well, I can tell you here and now, I'm leaving if she starts all her condescending claptrap. Anyway," he added contemptuously, "she looks more like a man than a woman."

Imagine our surprise, then, when we found her Jeep parked outside the house as we returned from school some months later and Miss Pearce having tea with Daddy. Far from hating her as he had always professed to do, he was at his most charming, plying her with biscuits and topping up her cup. Clearly, he'd changed his mind about her and I was glad because she really was so nice.

She didn't visit us again for a while although Daddy began to drop her name into the conversation more and more: Miss Pearce was a bit of a crack shot; Miss Pearce had been in the ATS during the war; Miss Pearce had joined the Gramophone Society; Miss Pearce said this; Miss Pearce said that. Then one Saturday, she arrived to pick him up to go to shooting and, as they left, Dad said he might be late getting back. Next morning, I awoke to the smell of frying bacon - and who should be cooking the breakfast but Miss Pearce. After she left Daddy said

"Whatever you do, don't tell a soul she stayed the night."

Why not, I thought, what's wrong with her staying the night? Then the truth hit me. Oh *no*, Miss Pearce and my Dad...*ughhh!* Surely it couldn't be true? But it was, and Ellen Pearce became a fixture in my father's life. We were sworn to secrecy because, he said, he was still a married man and it would affect his divorce if anyone found out.

Then one day my father fell off a ladder and broke several ribs, an accident which was to bring our life at Whitehall to an abrupt halt. Following his fall, he developed bronchitis and was out of action for a long time, lying in bed at Granny's and emitting low moans of distress when asked how he felt. Meanwhile, Richard and I stayed with Auntie Ethel, Uncle Toby and our two cousins in their rather grand home, Jubilee House. I loved being there, sharing a big room with Judith, more of a sister than a cousin, lying in bed together under her satin eiderdown as we whispered and giggled our girlish secrets.

At about the same time, Ellen – Tiggy as we had nicknamed her – became very ill and returned to her parents' farm in Berkshire. Ellen Pearce and her four sisters and brother had led an idyllic childhood. She knew everything there was to know about nature and country life: every tree and flower, every bird and wild animal, weather sign and cloud formation; the rotation of crops; at what phase of the moon to plant and harvest vegetables. The children roamed the Berkshire Downs where once, as they paddled in a stream, they heard tinkling laughter and looking up, saw a faun – half boy, half goat – sitting in the branches of a tree.

Ellen became a nanny when she left home, gravitating to estate management later. But the highpoint of her life came when war was declared and she, a shy country girl, joined the ATS (Auxiliary Territorial Service) and achieved her greatest ambition, which was to drive. In late

1945, her unit followed the victorious Allied Armies as they crossed Europe into Germany. Her tales of this time were harrowing, heartrending. Driving a lorry full of soldiers, she was part of a convoy which rumbled through ruined villages, deserted towns and the devastated shells of once-great cities. Abandoned and burnt-out vehicles littered their route and thousands of pitiful refugees, ragged and starving, trudged the lonely roads to nowhere. Although forbidden to pick up these starving survivors, she and her fellow drivers often did and she always saved part of her food ration for this purpose. Most horrifying of all, she later visited Auschwitz and realised that the terrible rumours they had heard were all true.

Ellen, our Tiggy, was utterly honest, down-to-earth, sensible, blunt and unsentimental. Love, she said, was just a figment of the imagination. She had never had a boyfriend until she joined the army and, tragically, he had been killed during the evacuation of Dunkirk. But when she was in Germany she met a soldier called Jimmy and they became very close. Indeed, he wrote home to his wife for permission to carry on this friendship.

"Of course, nothing wrong ever happened", Tiggy told us in her earnest fashion.

"Didn't he even kiss you?" we asked.

"Good heavens no!" she exclaimed, horrified, "we just - well, now and then we'd just have a jolly good wrestle...what, what? Why are you all laughing?"

Tiggy and my father were married in January, 1953. My grandmother and aunts did nothing to help the start of their married life, refusing to attend the ceremony, saying they had already been to two of my father's weddings and didn't intend to go to a third. Neither did the happy couple receive any presents from the groom's side of the family. However, their predictions that it would never last proved wrong for this was a loving if unlikely partnership which would last until my father's death almost thirty years later.

As my father recovered from his illness, he began to feel the need for easier work and got a job as a night patrol officer at Leyhill Open Prison. We moved in to married quarters, an ugly, prefabricated bungalow, one of rows and rows of identical homes within the prison's grounds. Our new life could not have been more different. We had lived in a beautiful but isolated country house and Tiggy in the nearby village. Now we found ourselves in an ugly little bungalow and were surrounded by people. Tiggy, as she told me later, was desperately unhappy. She hated everything about it. She had nothing in common with her neighbours, however pleasant, and what is more she felt trapped. She had lost the freedom she had enjoyed as a single woman. She had had such an adventurous life, free to come and go, and do what she liked, but now, aged 41, she was - that awful phrase - 'just a housewife'. She felt like a caged bird.

A typically self-centred teenager, I was oblivious to her feelings and to start with resented another woman coming in and taking over. But as the weight of household responsibilities was lifted from my shoulders, I soon changed my mind. She was kind to Richard and I, she never lost her temper, cooking and cleaning and caring for us in every possible way. And even more remarkably, she made my father happy and was able to cope with his sometimes petulant ways.

Unlike Tiggy, Richard and I were delighted with this new life. We were only a couple of miles from Cromhall where our grandparents lived and where Auntie Evelyn and Uncle Siddie ran the village shop. I got a Saturday job, helping my aunt in the second shop she had so enterprisingly opened to cater for the prison staff and their families. We were not only near old friends Ann and David Holpin, but also made new ones.

God had always played a big part in my life, from our earliest days when Mummy or Auntie Ethel heard us say our bedtime prayers before tucking us in for the night (a gentle ritual which stopped once Daphne entered the scene). We had always said grace before and after meals and Richard and I had always gone to Sunday School. Now I joined the local bell ringers, creeping through the still, flower-scented church to climb the belfry stairs and start the rhythmic, hypnotic task of bringing the bells to life and allowing them to sing.

Perhaps predictably, my father detested his new job. It was not only lonely and terribly boring but because he had always been self-employed he did not take kindly to the discipline of the prison service. His position was lowly; he was a nobody. However, he stuck it out for over a year when his luck suddenly changed. He found a beautiful little house which, because of its very low ceilings, was deemed uninhabitable and scheduled for demolition. Charles bought Nind House for the princely sum of £400 and, clever man that he was, excavated the earth foundations by a foot and succeeded in reversing the demolition order. Soon he had converted the place into a lovely home whilst Tiggy got to work in the beautiful garden which was bordered by a fast-flowing trout stream. My father also bought a former farm building and here he set up a carpentry and joinery business, specialising in the production of farm-related items like five-bar gates and cattle troughs. Soon local farmers were queuing up to have things made and for the first time since we left London, money was no longer an all-consuming worry.

Richard and I, of course, once again found ourselves living in isolated surroundings far away from the friends and social life we had been enjoying. But this did not bother me for long because my school days were coming to an end.

Despite the lack of interest or encouragement at home, I had somehow passed seven O levels and had hoped to stay on in the sixth form to study Art and English. I put aside as unrealistic my dreams of becoming an actress and decided I wanted either to go to art school or become a journalist like my grandmother. I wrote to the Western Daily Press hoping they might take me on as a cub reporter. The editor replied saying he would be glad to discuss it once I had finished my A-Levels. But despite my pleas and letters from the school urging him to change his mind, my father was adamant that he could not afford to keep me any longer. I must do a secretarial course so that I could earn my living as soon as possible. Both Ann and Eleanor were leaving to start their nursing training in Bristol and even though I wasn't interested in nursing, I suggested I do that instead. But Dad had made up his mind. There was a job going in Boots or I could learn shorthand and typing, "take your pick."

There was nothing unusual in his decision for it was only the minority of students who went on to take A-levels at that time, let alone continue to higher education. So, whilst my friend Pat stayed at school and eventually went to art school, I did not. For the next ten months, I travelled into Bristol every day to attend a commercial college where I learned to touch type and write Pitman's shorthand as fast and as accurately as possible. I hated every moment. The girls in my class were sophisticated city girls who wore smart clothes and went out to coffee bars every lunch time. I, on the other hand, brought sandwiches from home and had two shillings a week pocket money. I had two sets of clothes which I alternated each day, and I still stomped around in the terrible size seven black lace-up school clodhoppers. I didn't just feel like a country bumpkin, I looked like one and, if truth be known, I just didn't fit in.

One day, as the bus was trundling through Cromhall, a flamboyant figure with red hair and an equally dazzling red skirt stepped into the road, waving madly for it to stop. She climbed aboard, a bird-of-paradise let loose amidst a flock of dowdy sparrows. It was my sister Patty!

70

"Darling, darling!" she cried, setting all the sparrows a-twitter, "I'm back! Quick, get off the bus!"

She had been living in Paris for the past couple of years, doing secretarial work to earn her living but spending every spare moment involved in the great passion of her life – the ballet. She became involved with the Marquis de Cuevas' ballet, the last privately owned ballet company in the world, and was allowed to sit and sketch the dancers not only during rehearsals but from the wings during performances.

It all sounded impossibly glamorous and I couldn't wait to hear all about it now that she was back – staying with her adoptive parents, of course. I was speechless with admiration at her appearance, particularly her clothes, which she made herself, having inherited our mother's sewing genius. Granny, however, was outraged by the red hair:

"*Dyed hair*? Huh, only floozies dye their hair. Whatever next, eh? Perfume, I'll be bound, one pong to cover another I say, a sure sign someone hasn't washed."

Patty, I am sure, could see what a dowdy little thing her sister was and gave me all sorts of tips on how to look stylish on very little – or in my case no - money.

"But how d'you know if you've got style?" I asked.

"You don't," was her reply, "you've either got it or you haven't."

I found this very worrying. I so wanted to be enviably smart but now, even if I achieved this, how would I know I had?

The day after she returned to Paris, I opened my wardrobe to find that she had left almost all her clothes for me. Suddenly, instead of being the dull and ugly duckling, I had five different outfits to wear to college, including the wonderful swirling red skirt and a pair of cut-off jeans. Not one girl of my acquaintance had a pair of jeans and now I found I was the trend-setter. She even left me a pair of espadrilles with wide red ribbons to criss-cross up ones legs. And, oh, how sweet it was when the girls at college asked me where I'd bought these clothes to be able to say airily:

"Oh, my sister brought them back from Paris for me."

In July, the boredom and drudgery of the college course ended and it was time to be tipped out into the world of work. The college arranged job interviews for its leavers and my first was with a large insurance company. I quailed at the sight of the huge room full of girls typing away furiously whilst a dragon-like woman patrolled the room keeping order. No, no, this was not for me.

Then I was asked if I would like to apply for the position of secretary to the Agent for the Conservative Member of Parliament for South Gloucestershire. It sounded very grand and important so of course I agreed. My father and Tiggy were absolutely thrilled - a job with the *Conservative* party! How wonderful! They began to bombard me with instructions for my interview: smile, but not too much, don't mumble; sound confident; think of intelligent questions to ask about the job; make sure I know something about the MP concerned. Then they turned to what I should wear.

"I know what I'm going to wear," I said, "my red dirndl skirt Patty gave me and my black ..."

"Your *dirndl skirt?*" Tiggy gasped, "you can't go to an interview in a *dirndl skirt.*"

She could not have sounded more shocked if I'd suggested going in my bra and pants. But then, to my dismay, she announced, indeed insisted, that I wear one of her suits - which at that time were called 'costumes' - saying it was vital I make a good impression. And the one she had in mind was her prized, grey-striped 'Hebe Sports' which she had bought before the war. I was appalled. Like all young girls in the early 50's I was used to wearing full, calf-length skirts with a couple of stiff petticoats rustling beneath it, the waist fastened with a wide elasticated belt.

"Oh, I couldn't possibly wear that," I cried.

But Tiggy insisted I try it on. I looked ridiculous, a beanpole of a girl wearing a short, middle-aged woman's clothes. The jacket was too big, its padded shoulders had gone out of fashion years ago and the frumpy skirt just about covered my knees and hung round my hips. I argued and argued but it was two against one and I lost. Oh well, I thought as I lay in bed the night before the interview, I'll just smuggle something else out of the house and change at the bus station. But at breakfast, my father announced that he was going to drive me. So, clad in the ghastly suit, and having sulked all the way, I arrived at a shabby double-fronted house on the outskirts of Bristol to be interviewed by the agent herself, a Miss Young. Creased with embarrassment I walked in to her office, tugging the skirt down over my knees to make it look longer. She stood up and shook hands. It was at this point I decided there definitely *was* a God because Miss Young, a thin, anxious looking woman *d'un certain age,* was wearing a 'costume' equally horrible and of the same style and vintage as the dreadful Hebe Sports. Did I just imagine it or did she look at me with approval? Four other girls from college had also applied and so I was astonished when I received a letter a few days later offering me the job. My salary was to be three pounds ten shillings a week. A fortune!

Before I left home to go out into the world, both my father and grandmother gave me some sound advice.

"Never wear make-up," said Dad, "or people will think you're fast." I nodded, thinking of the Pond's lipstick in my bag.

"...and never, *ever* go to Mecca Dancing."

"Why not?" I asked, but he just answered, "never you mind, just don't go."

"Of course not, Daddy," I said earnestly, wondering where it was and how you got there.

As for Granny, her advice was as unexpected as it was thought-provoking. We were on our way back from Dursley where we had gone to buy me a bra and where, in a loud voice, she had asked the shop assistant to: "measure this young woman for a bust bodice".

"I want to warn you about something before you move to Bristol," she said as the bus rattled along the country lanes.

"Oh, what's that, Granny?"

"Never use Tampax or when you get married your husband will think you're not a virgin."

And so, a couple of weeks later, armed with this wisdom, I sallied forth into the world of work. I arrived for my first day, brimming with confidence because I was now an independent, fully fledged adult. I'd got a wonderful job and on Friday I would receive my very first pay packet, which meant that on Saturday I could buy that pretty pair of shoes I'd seen in Saxone.

I walked in. Off the wide entrance hall were two doors, the one on the left was Miss Young's office whilst on the right was mine. I met Ann, the filing clerk, settled in behind my desk then, picking up my notepad and pencil, walked across the hall to get my orders from Miss Young. She was warm and welcoming and after dictating a few letters sent me off to type them. But as I was leaving her office she called out urgently:

"Don't shut my d..."

But, too late, I'd already shut her door and - oh no - had locked her in.

"The lock's broken!" she shouted, "you'll have to call a locksmith!" Mortified, I rushed into my office. Her voice wafted after me:

"...and don't shut *your* door." But I had.

And so, within an hour of starting my very first day as a working woman, I had locked myself and my boss in our respective offices, where we stayed for the next couple of hours. Following this debacle I fully expected to be sacked, but my terrible debut was forgotten and I began to find out what the job entailed.

Miss Young was a strange woman. She seemed old to me but was probably about 40. She had spent all her life in Kenya and had been caught up in the Kikuyu uprisings of the early 1950's when her home had been set on fire and her legs terribly burned. A nervy, shrill person, she was clearly still traumatised by the horror of what had happened. Often, if I entered her office without knocking, I would catch her with her skirt pulled up, looking at the hideous scars which disfigured her thighs.

And what of the job? Far from being part of an exciting political nerve centre, I soon discovered that, although there was proper constituency work to be done, I was also a dogsbody for a ghastly collection of women, hair tightly permed, broad hipped, magenta lipped, who would sweep in, superciliously demanding that I type and duplicate vital notices for their next little fund-raising event, which they insisted be done immediately. Their husbands were even worse, just as condescending but not beyond pinching my bottom as they passed. As for The Member, as Miss Young in hushed and reverential tones referred to the local MP, we hardly ever saw him, although when he did honour us with a visit, Miss Young disappeared to be replaced by Uriah Heep. She practically genuflected as he wafted in, radiating the pseudo-sincerity of the practiced politician. They would disappear into Miss Young's office, undisturbed except when I served them coffee. Then after a couple of hours he would whisk his simpering agent off for lunch before disappearing back to Westminster.

About four months after starting the job, Miss Young asked me to work late to finish an important report.

"It'll only take an hour", she said.

However, as fast as I typed a page she amended it and I had to do it again, all on an ancient manual typewriter. I began to feel anxious when I looked out of the window and noticed that it was getting not just dark but foggy. At 8.30pm I said I needed to go or I would miss my bus. But she would not hear of it and on we ploughed until at last we finished and I found myself walking out into the freezing November night and an impenetrable 'pea-souper' fog. I made my way to the bus stop only to find that, due to the fog, the buses had stopped running. There was nothing for it but to walk the six or seven miles home. Stumbling through the fog I quickly lost my bearings, turning back the way I'd come, bumping into lamp-posts, terrified because I was alone and had no idea where I was in the almost deserted city streets. When a figure loomed out of the fog now and again or a car pulled up beside me and a stranger offered me a lift, I was sure I was about to be abducted and scuttled away down side streets. By the time I reached home it was two o'clock in the morning and I was in a state of collapse. The next morning, I awoke with a high temperature, feeling very unwell. That afternoon, a telegram arrived from Miss Young asking for an immediate explanation for my absence. My dear landlady had no telephone so she walked down the road to a phone box and rang the office. She told Miss Young what had happened and did not mince her words about the thoughtlessness of letting a young girl walk home late at night in freezing fog.

"Well," replied Miss Young, "you can tell her from me that if she isn't back in three days she's sacked."

I didn't wait for her to sack me but wrote a letter of resignation then and there. My father and Tiggy were aghast when I told them, not as one might have thought about my ordeal but because I had left the job.

"You won't get a *reference*," said my father, "and without a reference you'll *never* get another job. And don't expect *me* to support you if you're out of work, because I won't."

Then another, even worse thought occurred to him.

"...and I hope you realise," he wailed despairingly, "you'll *never* get another job working for the *Conservative* party."

Thank God for that, I thought. But he had unnerved me. Would I ever get another job? How would I live? How would I pay the rent? I could see I'd have to accept any job I was offered, even sitting in a terrible typing pool all day.

First thing on Monday morning I went to the Labour Exchange in Bristol and was interviewed by a kindly man who didn't seem at all worried by my lack references. Thumbing through a file of details he pulled out a sheet of paper.

"I have a feeling this might just suit you. The Lord Mayor of Bristol's office is looking for a secretary. They've interviewed no end of girls but can't seem to find anyone they like. Are you interested?"

Within half an hour I found myself in a small, smoke-filled room in the Council House, chatting happily away to a strange old lady called Miss Herbert-Thomas, who crouched behind her desk like an amiable toad, chain smoking and plying me with questions, not about my qualifications but about me. What was I interested in? Who were my favourite artists? The

75

pre-Raphaelites? Bit girly don't you think? You've played Antigone? Quite a feat at your age. You're good at English? Excellent, everyone should be able to read and write the Queen's English. Did I like history? Thank goodness for that...

A pretty middle-aged lady with red-gold hair served us with coffee and biscuits, joining in the conversation now and then.

"Well now, lass," said Miss Herbert-Thomas, after we'd talked for ages and I had all-but forgotten my reason for being there, "why did you leave your last job?"

Here we go, I thought, I won't have a chance once she hears this. But her lips thinned and she tutted when I told her about the marathon walk home in the fog and anyway, she said, the job sounded so *fearfully* boring.

"Wouldn't you rather work here?"

I could hardly believe it - the job was mine! What's more, my wages were to be £4.10.0 a week, a rise of fifteen shillings! I couldn't wait to ring home that evening to tell them the news. So much for no reference, no job, I thought smugly. Dad was delighted. 'My daughter in politics' was now 'my daughter, the Lord Mayor of Bristol's secretary'. His pride could remain intact.

I decided to move into a YWCA hostel, a handsome four-storey Georgian house in Clifton, an airy affluent part of the city within walking distance of my new office. I took the cheapest option which was to share with five other girls in a big dormitory on the ground floor, our iron bedsteads lining the walls like a hospital ward. Others, with bigger pay packets or richer parents, had rooms for two or three on the hallowed upper floors. I slipped easily into this communal way of life, relishing the feminine atmosphere. Suddenly, I had new friends to add to my school friends who were working in Bristol. I joined the huge central library, an Aladdin's cave to a bookworm like me, and also went to evening classes at the art school. My friends and I joined ballroom dancing classes, went to the cinema or sat late in coffee bars, eyeing the medical students from the university. We even went to Mecca Dancing now and again and, after my father's dire warnings, I found this rather tawdry place a distinct disappointment. On sunny evenings we walked over the Downs to Isambard Kingdom Brunel's awe-inspiring suspension bridge and peered over the edge. It was a much favoured suicide spot although one Victorian lady, intent on ending it all, had floated gently down, saved by her crinoline to face her problems all over again.

The hostel was run by Miss Walker, who, whilst kind and easy-going to her female residents, turned into a dragon when faced by the enemy - men. She hated all men with an almost vindictive passion, which was strange as she wore masculine clothes and her hair was cut in a severe short-back-and-sides. She lurked, chain-smoking in her office by the front door, well positioned to guard 'my girls' as she called us, against the foe, leaping out to confront any male who crossed the threshold. Even the postman was seen as a threat to our virginity and as for the milkman – well, you know what they say about them? Only the bravest boyfriends dared to wait for their dates in the hall, shifting uneasily from foot to foot and trying to avoid her accusing glare.

The hostel's laundry was in the basement and one winter evening I went down to do some ironing. Suddenly I heard a tap-tap-tap on the window and, looking up, saw a man's face pressed to the glass. He was pointing in what appeared to be some urgency towards his nether regions. What I saw gave me such a shock that I dropped the iron on my pink pyjamas and bolted for the stairs. I burst into Miss Walker's office, expecting her, I suppose, to deal calmly with the situation. But she panicked. Help, help: the enemy were without! She dialled 999. She raced into the hall shouting "Quick, lock all the doors!" She lumbered up the stairs, bellowing "emergency! emergency!" shepherding her bewildered charges into the sitting room. Then she stationed herself by the front door to await the squad cars. I, as the star witness, had to stay locked in her office until the police arrived and then, red-faced, tell them exactly what I had seen, although never having viewed this particular part of the male anatomy, my evidence was not terribly reliable. After they had searched the place and found no intruder, the police left and Miss Walker organised hot cocoa for everyone as, she said, it was good for shock. I, of course, was a bit of a celebrity for a few days. And the iron had burned right through my pink pyjamas and ruined them.

The highlight of the week was the Friday night dance at the Grand Spa Hotel. We spent hours getting ready, curling our hair with Kirby grips and applying our make-up. As I drew slanting black lines at the side of my eyes and dampened my cloggy block of mascara, I was glad Dad couldn't see me. But that didn't stop me reaching for my Italian Pink lippy, Woolworth's best. Our bras were stiff and high and cone-shaped, and over our knickers we wore elasticated roll-ons whether we were wearing stockings or the more fashionable bobby socks. Then it was on with several stiff, paper nylon petticoats, the dress with the circular skirt and the

77

flatty shoes, and we were almost ready. It just remained for a thick black belt to be hauled in until ones waist was as small as possible consistent with breathing.

In the ballroom, girls waited in giggling clusters on one side of the floor in the hope that a boy - any boy - would cross the divide and ask us to dance. Even when the dullest, spottiest youth propelled me round the floor, treading on my toes during the quickstep, I was relieved not to be a wallflower. And as I gazed at the blonde singer in her satin gown, the handsome band-leader, the sax player who winked when I caught his eye, the crowd of young people who, despite our home-made frocks and shabby suits, looked beautiful under the glitter ball, I felt sophisticated and, at seventeen, truly a woman of the world.

My new job was wonderful. The Lord Mayor's office seemed like the hub at the centre of this great city, involved with everything of importance that happened and I, albeit as a very small cog in the wheel, had a part to play. I found myself helping to organise everything relating to the Lord Mayor's official life – invitations, seating plans, menus, transport, dress code, press relations, even orders of precedent and protocol. People from every walk of life called on the Lord Mayor, many of them famous. It was wonderful to witness the pageantry of things like the Opening of the Assizes when the Lord Mayor, preceded by his Swordbearer holding the great gold sword of state, processed with the judges and aldermen into the law courts, all dressed in formal regalia and incongruously holding small posies of aromatic flowers and herbs. This was a tradition dating from the time of the Great Plague when it was thought the herbs were a protection against this most deadly of diseases. As the old nursery rhyme went:
Ring-a-ring-a-roses
A pocket full of posies
Atishoo, atishoo
We all fall down.
I was told I would need an evening dress for a forthcoming event and panicked because I didn't have one and certainly couldn't afford one.
I wrote to my sister for advice.

'I will make you a dress', she replied, 'fill in your measurements on this chart and tell me what you want.'

Oh, I knew exactly what I wanted. Could it please be made of pale pink satin with a sort of low neck with frills round it and little straps with bows on and a sort of crinoline skirt and, and, and... When a parcel arrived from Paris a few weeks later, I ripped it open to find a dress in shining, dove grey taffeta with a modest heart-shaped neckline and gently flaring skirt. As a nod to my request for pink there was a long petticoat edged with bright pink tulle and a pink shawl scalloped in the silver grey. Nothing could have been more perfect for a young girl's first evening gown and I felt like a princess when the night came to wear it. Big sister to the rescue once again!

In 1955, the council offices were moved to a new building on College Green, opposite the cathedral. The new Council House was a gracefully curved building bordered by a moat, beautiful both inside and out, and architecturally innovative. The Lord Mayor's department had a grand suite of offices on the ground floor whilst the more mundane departments were upstairs.

The Queen was asked to perform the opening ceremony and, to our great excitement, she agreed. This was an era when the royal family were revered, their popularity enhanced by their decision to stay in the London throughout World War II, when Elizabeth's parents had played a highly-visible role in boosting morale, particularly during the Blitz. Elizabeth's coronation had taken place only three years before and now, aged 27, she was at the height of her beauty with the added advantage of a dashing naval-officer husband, Prince Philip. Her visit to Bristol would therefore be a huge occasion. I longed to tell my friends and family but we were warned that this must remain a closely guarded secret and throughout the months of planning and liaison with Buckingham Palace, nobody found out.

A full dress rehearsal took place just before the royal visit and I was asked to act as stand-in for the Queen during this run-through. For a whole day I purred around in the back of a Daimler, was greeted by fanfares of trumpeters, inspected guards of honour, shook hands with endless lines of dignitaries and waved to passers-by whilst the highest and mightiest saluted and curtseyed, bowed and kow-towed before me. The reality was that I was a mere minion, largely ignored by the grandees as clip-boards were ticked and stop-watches clicked, but I enjoyed every moment of my imaginary royalty. The local newspapers covered the rehearsal and next day there I was in a photograph on the front page, captioned: 'Queen for a day was Miss Barbara Davis who stood in for Her Majesty during yesterday's rehearsal.' My father was beside himself with pride and the yellowing cutting lived in his bureau for years after the event.

Then came the day itself when thousands upon thousands of

cheering people lined the streets and a huge crowd surged forward as the young Queen stepped out onto the balcony of the Council House, a tiny, exquisite creature with the allure of a movie star and the complexion of a wild rose.

Just to lower the tone, I can report that the Queen's lady-in-waiting placed a cover of soft white leather over the lavatory seat in the bathroom assigned for Her Majesty's use and removed it at the end of the visit. As soon as the royal party left, I sprinted up the corridor and into the loo to ensure that I sat on it immediately after Her Majesty Queen Elizabeth II. A small claim to fame, but mine own.

One foggy November in 1955 a Royal Naval ship, HMS Tyne, arrived on an official visit and, as always, various events were organised to entertain the ship's company. I was given tickets to a concert of light classics and took my friend Liz with me. We thoroughly enjoyed the evening, not so much because of the music but because we were surrounded by sailors. Afterwards, the streets were full of these jolly jacks in their bell-bottom trousers, their caps set at jaunty angles, whistling and calling out cheekily at every girl who passed. Arm-in-arm, Liz and I made our way back towards the city centre. Suddenly, a group of five sailors stopped us and one of them, courteous and well spoken, asked if we knew which bus they should catch to Avonmouth Docks. Liz and I looked at each other doubtfully and shook our heads.

"So sorry," we said, "we've no idea."

As we watched them stride away and disappear round a corner, Liz said:

"You know, we should have told them to go to the bus station in the Centre."

"Well, it's too late now," I said, stopping to look in a shop window, "they've gone."

But Liz's social conscience was playing up.

"Honestly, Barbara, your office has been helping to organise their ship's visit, I can't believe you don't want to help them. Come on," she said, grabbing my arm, "let's see if we can catch them."

Charles and Grace on their wedding day in 1928

Charles, Jessie (Florence's sister), Grace, Florence and Ethel

Proud parents - Grace and Charles with baby Patricia in 1931

Elegant Evelyn pushing baby Patty's pram, 1931

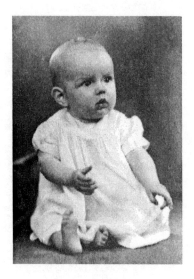

Barbara aged 3 months

Barbara aged 18 months

'Little Dicky Doughnut'
Richard at 2 years,1941

'The Evacuees' outside Langley Church, Essex, 1942.
Back row l to r:
Patricia, Uncle Toby, Barbara and Peter.
Front row l to r: Richard and Judith.

Three sad children who have been to see
their mother in hospital, 1943.

Barbara, Patricia and Richard, 1944.
We may look happy but we weren't.

Barbara, Pat Jackson, Eleanor Cornoch and Ann Holpin.
Four best friends having fun at the fair

Patricia in Paris, circa 1954.

John and Barbara's wedding, 27th March, 1957

Proud Mother.   Barbara with baby Mary–Louise Grace.

Victoria's christening, Aug, 1959

The girls at Nind House, Gloucestershire, with
their grandparents ,Charles and Tiggy, 1959

With Auntie Sarah at the seaside, 1960

Singapore, 1961

Outside the Officers' Flats
Malayan Naval Barracks

'Let's Twist Again'. An Arabian Nights
party to celebrate John's 25th birthday,
Singapore, 1962

A chilly return to England. The girls with Grandmama and Sarah
at The King George V Docks, 1st November, 1963

S I X

I WATCHED THE SAILOR until I could see him no more.

"Well, goodbye Barbara," he had said before he left, "I really hope we'll meet again one day."

Then he shook my hand, snapped to attention and saluted before turning and walking briskly away down the hill. And that was all. No promises, no kisses, we hadn't even held hands, yet as I gazed after him I knew that this was it – I had fallen in love.

Three days had passed since Liz and I ran after those sailors in the street. We had spent an hour or so with them in a café, five boys aged 17 and 18, all of them selected from the lower deck for officer training. Four of them seemed fun, flirty, vying with each other to impress us with their tales of naval life. But the fifth said hardly a word and yet I was acutely aware of him staring at me from big hazel eyes fringed with thick lashes. We said goodbye to them in the city centre, Liz jumped on her bus and I set off for the hostel. Soon I heard footsteps hurrying after me. It was the silent one.

"I wonder if I could see you home," he said, "you shouldn't really be walking on your own in this fog."

We had parted at the top of the hill and I wished him 'bon voyage', knowing that HMS Tyne was sailing on the morning tide. But the fog was our friend because the next day it was as impenetrable as ever and that evening he called me to say the ship had been unable to sail. An hour or so later I found myself walking down the road with Able Seaman John Jeremy Watson, impeccable in his naval uniform – the bell bottom trousers with seven horizontal folds pressed into them denoting the seven seas, the wide white collar with four folds symbolizing the four winds, the sailor hat set square on his head. This time he was no longer silent and we talked as though we had always known each other, he told me stories about life on the lower deck and the places he had visited, we talked about our families, our school days, the books we both loved, music, films, even our spiritual beliefs. He was also witty and terribly funny — a huge plus for someone who liked laughing as much as me. As though all this were not enough, he was by far the most handsome boy I had ever met. At the end of the evening we said goodbye again, only for the ship to be delayed for a third day; fate and the weather gave us yet another wonderful evening together.

And now he had gone. I waited on tenterhooks for him to call or write, rushing in from work in case there was a letter, afraid to go out in case he rang. Weeks passed, Christmas came and went, but I didn't hear from him again. Although the rational part of my brain told me to get over this fleeting encounter, I simply could not forget him. I stopped going out - no more Friday night dances, no more evenings with friends, no more fun, I just stayed in and pined. My appetite disappeared, I lost weight, I couldn't sleep. My friends told me I was stupid. Did I really think he even remembered me after just two dates? My father and Tiggy were equally forthright. Hadn't I heard about sailors with a girl in every port? - the last sort of person I should be interested in. And Granny, who'd been 'informed', said she'd never heard such rubbish in her *life* and look at me, skin and bone, *ridiculous.* I even told myself I was mad. I ran his last sentence over and over in my mind: "....I really hope we'll meet again one day." He hadn't said he'd ring me. He hadn't said he'd write. Perhaps everyone was right and I really *should* forget him. But it was no good, my heart was aching.

Four months passed and then the unbelievable happened - I came home from work to find a postcard waiting for me. It was from him. HMS Tyne was in Amsterdam, from where he'd written: 'Dearest Barbara, the ship returns to Portsmouth next week and, if you haven't forgotten me already, I hope we'll see each other again soon. Love, John'. I was ecstatic – forgotten him? Why, there had been hardly a moment when I wasn't thinking of him. But more to the point, he had not forgotten me! I read and re-read the postcard – '*Dearest* Barbara...*Love*, John'. Oh-my-God!

And so it was that on a chilly Saturday not long afterwards I waited on Temple Meads station as the Portsmouth train pulled in. I saw him at once as he stepped down onto the platform, tall, lean, even more handsome than I remembered, glancing this way and that as he tried to spot me. Suddenly I found myself shaking, legs trembling, heart beating so fast I could hardly breathe. Too nervous to move, I hid behind a pillar and tried to compose myself. Minute after minute passed until, peeping out, I saw him hovering by the entrance and, afraid he'd walk away, took a deep breath and stepped out. He saw me. He came striding towards me. He dropped his holdall and suddenly I was in his arms.

By Sunday evening when I waved goodbye, trying not to cry as his train slid away, I knew I had not been wrong to wait, to pine. I knew for sure that he *was* the one. Not only was I madly in love with him but now I knew he loved me in return. Somewhere in my subconscious I knew that destiny had brought us together and that from now on our lives would be inextricably linked. But if I had also known that this was to be the first of many, many partings, the beginning of a life which would include not just this great love but the most searing heartbreak, I might have ended it then and there. Of course I did not and so gave myself up to the joy and enchantment of first love.

John was now shore-based in Portsmouth where he was completing courses in seamanship. We wrote to each other every day and once a fortnight he travelled to Bristol for another blissful weekend together. We ate in cheap cafés, explored Bristol's museums and art galleries, rode on country buses to the seaside and walked for miles over the Downs or along the banks of the River Avon. One evening we went to see Macbeth at the Bristol Old Vic, witnessing an electrifying performance by a young actor called Peter O'Toole. And all the time we were getting to know each other better. He had been educated at Ardingly College in Sussex where his teachers had high hopes of an academic career for him, but when his parents' marriage ended, John had taken it upon himself to leave school at the age of sixteen and enlist in the Royal Navy.

Joining the Navy on the lower deck had not been an easy option. He had found himself amongst boys from less privileged walks of life and had had to stand up for himself, overcome the ridicule about the way he spoke by – as he put it – 'talking common' and showing that he was as tough as they were. In fact, he said, many of the young boys were so homesick they cried themselves to sleep. They hated the food and found the discipline almost unendurable. John, on the other hand, the 'posh' boy they despised, had experienced all this and worse at boarding school. He knew all about homesickness, he had endured the bullying and the 'fagging' system, and in any case found naval food far better than anything served up at school. It was easy for him to be – and appear to be – stronger than most of the others, and gradually he earned their respect and friendship.

One day that summer we decided the time had come for him to meet my family. Richard, now aged sixteen and absolutely desperate for his eighteenth birthday so that he could start his National Service, was thrilled to meet a real serviceman and they made friends straight away. John and Tiggy also got on well, especially as he was genuinely interested in her wartime experiences. His manners were impeccable; he stood up when she came into the room, helped clear the table and wash the dishes, looked round the garden and made a fuss of her beloved dachshunds. We were summoned to Cromhall for tea and my grandparents, too, fell under his spell. Granny even whispered to me almost girlishly that he looked like Gregory Peck, one of the most handsome film stars of that era.

My father, however, could hardly bring himself to speak and was so curt and disagreeable that his behaviour mortified me. When I went home the following weekend I told him how ashamed he'd made me feel. Tiggy agreed. Yes, she said, she'd felt ashamed too, how refreshing it was to meet a young man with such beautiful manners and Dad should have taken a leaf out of his book instead of being so rude. Daddy was absolutely incensed. What did we mean, rude? Didn't speak to him? What was he supposed to speak *about*, eh? What did we think he had in common with that...that...*Prince Charming* I'd brought home? Public school? Huh, so what? And he'd told me about sailors and their bad reputations so don't say I hadn't been warned. Who did I think I was anyway, Miss High and Mighty all of a sudden, too good for the local boys?

We had a huge row. I walked out. The truth was that John, so well educated and, although only 18, quite sophisticated, made my father feel inferior. He also carried an understandable chip on his shoulder because he had not seen active service during the war. Add to that a father's natural jealousy of anyone showing too much interest in his daughter and there you have a potent and rather unpleasant mix. Of course we patched up our quarrel but I made it clear that whatever he thought, nothing would make me change my mind about John. And if he was unwelcome, well I would simply have to stop coming home. That seemed to do the trick, for the real fear of losing me ensured that we papered over the cracks and my father tried to be a little more welcoming to John from then on.

What they did not know, of course, was that he had asked me to marry him. We had decided to keep this to ourselves (although I immediately told my friends!) and wait to become officially engaged until he left for officer training in Scotland. Then, when he became a Sub Lieutenant, we would get married. My mind whirled with the romance of it all; wedding bells, bridesmaids, confetti, a guard of honour with naval swords; it was all so beyond my dreams and expectations that I sometimes wondered if I – who had spent so much time fantasising – would suddenly wake up to find I had imagined it all. But then I would return to my daydreams and waft away on a pale pink cloud to that land called 'happy ever after'.

Soon it was my turn to meet John's family who lived in Hinchley Wood, a pleasant suburb of Esher, Surrey. His mother, Audrey Watson, was a strikingly handsome, shapely woman whose jet black plaits were looped charmingly over the top of her head like a Tyrolean milkmaid, although there all similarities ended for it was clear that here was someone with a strong, determined character who, whilst charming, was used to being obeyed.

Audrey's father, Frederick Prosser, had been a Plymouth-based naval Petty Officer, a gentle, infinitely kind man, whilst her mother Lily was the beautiful, rather spoilt daughter of a wholesale fruiterer. Audrey, her sister Frances and little brother Freddie had a happy childhood despite their father's frequent absences at sea. When she left school she became a governess, working for a wealthy Torquay family, the Toswills, who quickly came to treasure her when they discovered her magical way with children, and it was here that the first seeds of an ambitious plan were sown; that one day she would open a school of her own..

By 1940 she was married with two young children and when her husband, Anthony Watson, a young artesian well engineer, joined the Royal Engineers and was posted to North Africa, she took the children down to Devon to live with her parents for the duration of the war. Here, rather like my own close encounter with a doodlebug, John and his younger sister Sarah had their own narrow escape. They were walking down a lane with their grandmother when the pilot of a German aircraft, returning from a daylight raid on Plymouth, spotted them – oh, great, he must have thought, a woman and two children, let's get 'em - dived low and strafed the lane with bullets. With great presence of mind, their grandmother Lily threw the children into a ditch and herself on top of them, thus saving their lives.

Meanwhile Lt. Anthony Watson had been captured by the Italian army and shipped back to a prison camp in Italy. However, when the Italians signed an Armistice with the Germans in 1943, the gates of the camp were opened.

"You can all leave," they were told.

But before they could do so, German troops arrived and the men were loaded onto trains bound for Germany. With great daring, Anthony and a number of his companions threw themselves from the train and were free for two and a half months. He was only sixteen miles from Allied lines when he was recaptured and this time was sent to a Prisoner of War camp in Germany where he spent the rest of the war.

In 1948 Audrey decided that now was the time to open the school she had always dreamed of. She and Anthony bought a large, graceful house whose airy rooms would make perfect classrooms, little realising that the neighbourhood was the perfect location. Hinchley Wood was an area which attracted young families, the fathers up-and-coming professionals who, as they advanced in their careers, moved to even more affluent areas whilst yet another young family settled in behind them. Thus, Audrey found she had a captive market and with room for no more than a hundred children, she soon had to establish a waiting list. An ardent fan of Rupert Brooke, she named her school Grantchester House and a portrait of the poet hung in the hall and even had a clock in the hall, stopped at ten to three!

Successful though the school was, things were not going well in her private life. Anthony's job took him abroad for months at a time and in 1956 their marriage ended when he left her for a Christian missionary he had met in Ghana.

At this first meeting I could not have foreseen that Audrey Watson was to become not only a kind, compassionate mother-figure and friend to me but also a difficult, controlling, unpredictable woman. As for Sarah, John's sixteen-year-old sister, she was a sweet, quiet girl, hiding her intelligence, her musical and artistic abilities, behind a shy exterior.

On this first meeting, they could not have been more welcoming and at the end of the weekend I returned to Bristol feeling happier than ever.

It was the end of February 1957 and all was not well in the house of Barbara, for my period was late and I began to suspect that I might be pregnant. The 1950's were a strange time. Whilst my friends and I would giggle and whisper about that last frontier of love, and held in awe those who had 'gone all the way', to become pregnant out of wedlock was quite another matter - a disaster which often led to disgrace. Such double standards meant that, if a 'shotgun wedding' did not take place and a girl was left to give birth and bring up her baby on her own, she was shunned, shamed and her illegitimate child labelled a bastard. To avoid such public disgrace, girls were often sent to isolated maternity homes to give birth, the secret perpetuated by saying they had gone away to work. It was more usual for them to be badly, even cruelly, treated in these places than to find compassion and kindness. The majority of these young mothers then faced the agony of giving up their babies for adoption, never to see them again. Now I, who until a few short months ago had been an innocent, realised that I could well be about to join their number.

Our courtship had started in an old fashioned way, governed not only by the morality of the time but also - on my part - by all the romances I'd read, all the films I'd seen, where the girl remained pure and chaste with just the 'kiss at the end', followed swiftly by the wedding day. But these unwritten moral rules do not allow for emotion, nor for a boy and girl passionately in love. Now I knew I had to be practical and deal with the situation. I wrote and told John who, however shocked he might have felt, was loving and supportive. He told me to go and see a doctor.

The doctor was a kindly middle-aged man. He asked me to go behind a screen to undress so that he could examine me. I started taking my clothes off but - buttons, zips, hooks - all seemed to defeat my shaking fingers. Time passed. Now and then the doctor called out:

"Are you nearly ready?"

Tick, tick, tick…

"You need only remove your undergarments, you know."

Tick, tick, tick, tick…

Eventually, in a slightly impatient voice, he called;

"I hope you're ready, because I'm coming in."

He could not quite hide his look of surprise as he rounded the screen and saw me cowering on the couch, starkers. His examination only took him a few minutes and when I was once again sitting opposite him, he said:

"Well, you're about two months pregnant, Miss Davis. Have you made any plans or can I give you the names of some organisations that can help you?"

"No thank you," I said in as confident a voice as I could muster, "my fiancé and I can make all the arrangements."

I left the surgery and suddenly found myself running wildly down the street, utterly filled with joy – I was going to have a baby! John, me and our own little baby! It seemed like the most beautiful outcome from our love, the most perfect step forward in our relationship. It was not until I got back to the hostel that reality set in. John rang me and I told him the news.

"Well, we'll have to tell our parents," he said.

The following weekend he went home to Esher and I to Nind House. By now my elation had worn off and sitting on the sofa between Daddy and Tiggy, I was so fraught I could not speak.

"Come on now, what's the matter? Just tell us." said Tiggy, tightening her arm around my shoulder.

"Yes," said Dad, "there's nothing so bad that we can't sort it out."

Somehow I managed to blurt out my news: "I'm pregnant."

For a moment there was a stunned silence and then my father said:

"Well, we'll just have to get you married, won't we?"

My precious 'little' brother hugged me and, with an embarrassed laugh, said:

"Don't worry, the kid'll be okay with me as an uncle!"

My grandmother was told the news and I was summoned to Cromhall. I did not relish the prospect of facing the formidable Florence but she was equally kind, equally wonderful, as was dear old Granddad. That evening my father rang John's mother and informed her that as her son had seduced his daughter (I squirmed as I listened from behind the hall door) it was now his duty to marry me. And I gather she in turn informed him that her son would not dream of doing anything but the honourable thing. Then she asked to speak to me.

"Can't you *skip?*" she asked in a voice so tense one felt she would crack at any moment. In retrospect I can imagine how she felt, for this must have seemed like the end of all her dreams for her son. She had struggled to send him to public school, expecting him to go on to a fine academic career at Oxford or Cambridge, only for him to join the Navy. She had redefined her hopes for him, sure that he would become an officer. Now this ambition was to be hampered by a wife and child.

Throughout that weekend I spoke to John only briefly. Everything now seemed to have been taken out of our hands and we were swept away by the decisions being made on our behalf. He came home with me the following weekend. Other than a session behind closed doors with my father, from which John emerged not just white but green, all went well and I was grateful to my father for his unexpected civility. But then, despite his sometimes difficult nature, there was no-one finer, no-one kinder, no-one stronger than my Dad in the face of an emergency.

The next morning John and I went to see the Vicar to ask for the banns to be called, a date for the wedding was set and, well, that was that.

In just a few short days it had all been arranged. And the party line was to be that, as John was shortly being posted to Scotland for his officer training, we had decided to get married so that I could go with him. As for the baby, due in October, it was suggested that, to save embarrassment, its arrival should not be announced until Christmas when it could be called a honeymoon baby. What, keep my baby's birth a secret?

"No," I said, "I'm not doing *that*."

We were married on the 27th March, 1957. I wore a simple flower-sprigged dress, a circlet of white blossom in my hair and carried a little posy of lilies-of-the-valley, my mother's favourite flowers. No fairytale wedding gown, no bridesmaids, no church packed with guests, no peel of bells. And yet for all its simplicity, the beauty of the ancient wedding vows, our youth and the transparency of our love were perhaps what shone through. Afterwards we had a small reception and then left for a honeymoon weekend in Stratford-upon-Avon. We were both nineteen years old.

In July that year I joined John in Scotland where he had been posted to start his officer training. We found a flat in Morningside, a prosperous area overlooking the Braid Hills. The house belonged to an old lady who had had a stroke and now lived on the ground floor with Gwen, her nurse-companion. Two middle-aged sisters, the Miss Ingles, lived on the first floor and we were soon installed under the eaves at the very top. Our new home was just a sitting room, a bedroom and a tiny kitchen with a shared bathroom on the floor below, but light flooded the rooms and the furnishings, although faded, were charming. Even though the other inhabitants reminded us of Agatha Christie characters, we felt immediately at home. The ladies of the house could not have been more welcoming, particularly to John in whose presence they became quite coy.

The drawback was that in order to get to Temeraire, his shore-based college in South Queensferry, he had to catch a bus at six every morning. But he never complained and I got used to getting up with him at 5.15am and, in my new role as a perfect wife, making him a big cooked breakfast before he left.

I quickly found work as a temp in a whisky distillery. It was in the Grassmarket area of Edinburgh which at that time was a dark, menacing place, crouched in the shadow of Edinburgh Castle, the haunt of drug addicts and down-and-outs drinking methylated spirits. I was the only woman working in the Dickensian office with its battered desks and bleary windows, and decided as I entered that this, my first day, would also be my last. But the men there proved to be so kind and thoughtful that I stayed until six weeks before my baby was due.

One of my tasks was to take dictation from the chairman, Old Mr Campbell. He was over 90 and sat slumped behind a huge mahogany desk in a huge mahogany office, his tiny skull emerging tortoise-like from a starched collar. Often, as he dictated, his head would sink slowly onto his chest, his voice would falter and finally stop. It was hard to know whether he was merely composing the next sentence, having forty winks or had passed away to distilleries in higher realms. If the silence became too lengthy, I coughed or shuffled my chair until, with a start, he would wake up and bark "Cowdenbeath!" or "Partick Thistle!" and continue where he'd left off. And when the Castle cannon was fired at noon, Mr Campbell – who had heard this every day for the past seventy years – leapt from his chair as though shot, exclaiming:

"Och, och, what the devil...?" before pulling a gold hunter watch from his waistcoat pocket and exclaiming: "it canna be midday already! Away wi' you lass and stop wasting ma time."

Every evening when the office closed, one of the clerks, ever courteous, escorted me through the Grassmarket to the safety of Prince's Street where I caught a bus back to the genteel heights of Morningside.

Amongst the other Upper Yardmen in John's year were the four sailors I had met on that fateful, foggy night in Bristol. And so, when John and I arrived for a Ladies' Night Mess dinner, I was not only excited to be attending my first event as a naval wife but also looking forward to meeting these boys again. We were all sipping our pre-dinner drinks when one of them said:

"I can't wait to hear your speech, Barbara."

"My speech?"

"Yes, it's a naval tradition. If a member of the Mess has been married in the past six months, his bride makes the speech on Ladies' Night."

"But I..." I turned to John, "this isn't true, is it?"

"Well of course it is," he said, "I told you weeks ago. Oh, for goodness sake, don't tell me you haven't prepared anything?"

"No I...but I can't... I couldn't possibly..."

But at that moment dinner was announced and we all trooped into the dining-room where I sat throughout the meal, unable to take in my surroundings, toying with my food, whilst my mind churned miserably over possible phrases: Ladies and gentlemen, it gives me great pleasure to... no....ladies and gentlemen, as the bride of...no...as the youngest wife it...no... my husband and I...no... I would like to say...I want to say...may I say...I really must say...no, no, no, no, NO!

I felt sick. I knew I couldn't do it and what's more I was about to let my new husband down in a very public way. At last the dinner came to an end and the commanding officer stood up and rapped on the table. My mouth went dry. This was it

"Well now everyone," he began, "just a few words from me before I hand you over to Commander Stephens..."

Across the table I saw John and his mates tittering and suddenly the penny dropped - I had been set up. But there was no time for recriminations for soon the commanding officer's wife was ushering the ladies away to an ante-room whilst the men enjoyed their port. As we sipped our coffee, she wandered over to me and, after a moment or two of small talk, looked pointedly at my burgeoning stomach and said:

"When exactly is your baby due? October? Really? I'd heard you were only married in March."

Ouch.

As soon as we were settled in our new flat, I registered with a doctor and he in turn set about finding a bed for me in a maternity unit. I called to see him a week later only to learn that, as it was now so late in my pregnancy, the only available beds were in the Eastern General Hospital, which he warned me was in a very rough area down near the docks, or the Salvation Army Home for Unmarried Mothers. Flashing my wedding ring proudly, I said I would prefer the hospital, although it crossed my mind that, but for John's making an honest woman of me, I would have been eligible for the latter.

One of our neighbours was a vet's wife called Giselle, who – probably realising what a naïve little thing I was – took me under her wing. To her horror she learned that I had had no pre-natal check-ups and that, other than 'what goes in must come out', had little or no understanding of the mechanics of childbirth and knew nothing at all about relaxation techniques. I did tell her that John and I had been to see a film called 'The Birth of a Baby' but that he had fainted during the first reel and, after first aid, I had had to take him home. She was unimpressed with this excuse and gave me a crash course in the basics, which, as it was now almost the end of September, was all we had time for. As she was walking down the road a week later, who should she spot but me standing at the bus stop holding a little suitcase.

"Where are you off to?" she asked.

"To the hospital," I said, "I've got these funny pains in my tummy and I think the baby's coming."

"And you're going on the bus?" she said, aghast, "oh no you don't my girl." And grabbing the suitcase, she hurried me back to her house, into her car and set off at top speed for Leith.

Within half an hour of being admitted I found myself yearning for the Salvation Army Home for Unmarried Mothers. It could not, I told myself, be anything like as awful as this hellhole. The place seemed to be full of worn-out women having their umpteenth child, calling down curses on the heads of the bastards who'd got them up the duff again, on the doctors, the nurses and anyone else they could think of. It was God, however, who got the worst of it, as He was blamed for every terrible event in their miserable lives up to this, the worst point of all. I scurried to the lavatories hoping to find some peace, but they were filthy, clogged with loo paper and disintegrating fag ends, the floors awash. But help was at hand when the ward sister, no doubt seeing my youth and apprehension, said quietly:

"Nurse, move this wee lassie to number four."

I was bundled away down the corridor and – oh joy! - into a room of my own. Even this had its drawbacks, chief among which were the two mice who lived in the bedside cabinet. But for the moment it was a peaceful sanctuary in which to await my baby's birth. Peaceful maybe but also very lonely. For hour after hour I lay there with only a nurse coming in now and then to check my progress. No one to hold my hand. No pain relief. No-one to reassure me that this agony was normal. But at last I was wheeled on a trolley, groaning loudly, towards the delivery room. The night sister shot out of her door as we passed.

"Stop that noise at once," she snapped, "people are trying to sleep."

"Who's having this bloody baby, you or me?" I snarled between contractions. That shut her up.

Finally, in the early hours of 2nd October, 1957, my baby girl was born. The nurses gasped as they delivered her for they had never seen a baby with eyes so big and beautiful.

Then they laid her in my arms. Here she was at last, my precious one, my daughter. And in that moment the sheer power of mother-love

106

overwhelmed me. I knew then that I would love her, nurture her, protect her, do everything in my power to make her life happy until my dying day. And, oh, I wished with all my heart that my own mother could have lived to see this tiny soul, her granddaughter Mary-Louise Grace.

The next day John came to see us and was thrilled with his baby girl. However, our happiness received a fearful jolt when a senior doctor came in to see me. With him were his houseman and the ward sister. Their faces were grave.

"I'm afraid I have some bad news for you, Mrs Watson," said the doctor, "your baby has a heart murmur."

I stared at him in uncomprehending silence as he hurried on:

"But don't be too worried. We think it may be a small abnormality which normally rights itself within about six weeks. And we will, of course, be keeping a close check on her. Have you any questions?"

I shook my head, so shocked I was unable to speak, and the little group left. I lay there, stunned. A heart murmur? One of those blue babies you read about in the newspaper? But she was beautiful, she looked so healthy and wasn't the slightest bit blue. It couldn't be true. I began to cry and hardly stopped for days. Please, please God, I begged over and over again, don't let there be anything wrong with my baby. Nurses reassured me, telling me these little heart murmurs in newborns were quite common, until by the time we left hospital I began to feel that perhaps all would be well.

And so we returned to the flat in Morningside, where the ladies of the house and several neighbours gathered to welcome us home, twittering like kindly birds at the beauty of our bonnie wee lass. Next morning I put my brand new baby in her brand new pram and wheeled her proudly down the hill to the little rank of shops. All the shopkeepers came out to admire her and when I'd finished my 'errands', as they called them in Scotland, I walked slowly home. Oh, how wonderful it felt to be me! I laughed to myself as I realised I had achieved that childhood ambition and was now 'a lady with a baby'. I'd nearly reached home when I had the feeling I'd forgotten something. Handbag? No, got that. Bread? Butter? Carrots? Apples? Yes, got them too. Talcum powder for the baby? The baby, where was the baby? Ohmygawd, I'd forgotten her! I turned and raced back down the hill and there she was where I'd left her, fast asleep in her pram outside the chemist's. Remorse, remorse and *mea culpa*! There was clearly more to this mothering lark than met the eye.

However, I need not have worried about my inexperience as help was at hand in the form of Gwen, old Mrs Pickering's companion. She was a giant of a woman, built like a prop forward and, in her blue nurse's uniform, the sleeves rolled up to reveal arms like hams, she looked like a drag act. Her black hair, now flecked with grey, was cut in an unbecoming bob and many a whisker adorned hor upper lip. But within this ugly frame dwelt a gentle soul, feminine, kind and imbued with a deep well of compassion. I doubt whether any man had ever glanced her way and yet here was a woman who would have made the most loving wife, the most devoted mother. But God and genetics had got the outward package wrong and marriage was never to be. Instead, she had channelled all her love into other people's children and later the old folk she nursed in their dying days. Now the unbelievable had happened; there was a baby in the house with a mother who hadn't a clue how to look after her!!

My mother-in-law had sent me a book on childcare by a New Zealander called Dr Dick Truby King whose methods she recommended I follow. He was seen as a medical visionary whose work, started in the late 1930's, had a profound effect on infant health and welfare, unseen anywhere else in the world. However, I felt at odds with much of his philosophy. I did not like the thought that, between four-hourly feeds, babies should be left to cry. Nor that they should never be fed or lifted at night. And how many mothers, I wonder, followed this rule: that 'unless you want your baby to grow into a lily-livered, weak-willed adult', it should *never, ever* be kissed or cuddled, although he did concede that '...if you must, a kiss on the forehead when you say goodnight and a handshake in the morning will suffice.' A further charming tip from Dr Truby King was to gather sphagnum moss and strew it in the baby's nappy where its absorbent qualities would soak up urine.

But Gwen and I had other ideas. On my first morning home she thundered breathlessly up the stairs and my crash course in baby-care began. She started with the bath, showing me exactly how to dip ones elbow in the water to test the temperature, how to hold the slippery little body safely, how to wash her. Then, on a lap the size of a table top, she towelled and creamed and powdered before pinning first the Harrington's gauze square and then the terry-towelling nappy deftly into place, both mercifully free from moss with its attendant creepy-crawlies. One aspect with which I, and most mothers at that time, agreed was the importance of fresh air. As soon as the baby was bathed and fed, she was put outside in the garden, tucked into her pram whatever the weather. And every afternoon, she was pushed out for a walk for at least an hour.

At the end of November I took my baby back to the hospital, confident that all would now be well. But the heart murmur was still present and she was referred to a specialist at another hospital. He too thought it was something relatively minor. "Come back in three months," he said.

This was encouraging news and enabled me to put my nagging fears to the back of my mind. After all, she was thriving, feeding well, putting on weight and achieving all the little milestones at the right time. But when we returned three months later he sounded less optimistic. He was not quite sure what was wrong, he said cautiously, but it certainly was not what he'd originally thought. It would be easier to see what was going on when she was a bit older and once again I left with another "come back in three months" and an increasing sense of unease.

I had a wonderful friend in my health visitor, Marjorie, who popped in several times a week and was constantly reassuring. She, too, advised me to put it out of my mind and just get on with enjoying my baby. She had an amazing way of cheering me up with her sense of humour and her fund of stories. Once, she told me, she was visiting a mother of five in the East End of London. As they stood chatting at the front door, a little boy ran out:

"Mum, Mum," he said, pulling at her skirt. She ignored him.

"Mum, Mum, Mum."

"Geroff," she said, shoving him away irritably. But he wasn't giving in.

"Mum," he whined, "Mum, Mum, Muuuum."

"You'll get a clip round yer ear if you don't shurrup."

"But Mum, I wanna tell you sumpin'."

"Oh, what *is* it?" she snapped at last.

"Our Tommy's lightin' bitsa paper an' settin' fire to baby's hair."

The woman took a long puff on her fag, inhaled deeply, tapped off the ash and sighed,

"Oo'd 'ave boys?"

It was not an era when men took much part in childrearing and John was no exception. However, he perfected one skill, which was that when the baby screamed with evening colic, he would swing her backwards and forwards in her carry-cot until she fell asleep, whilst reading a book held in his other hand. In any case, he often stayed at Temeraire as the long bus journey was beginning to get him down.

That winter I caught 'flu which turned to pleurisy. I was very ill and my doctor, who called every day, decided I should be admitted to hospital. However four of our neighbours had other ideas and persuaded him that they could not only nurse me but would also take the baby into their homes for four-hour shifts around the clock. I had never met such kindness. The only person who was not kind was John, who seemed exasperated by the whole thing. Indeed, he said he was "sick of seeing you lying there In a welter of self-pity," words which pierced my heart. He went back to Temeraire and didn't return until I recovered.

We had met a family, the Griffiths, who lived in slightly bohemian poverty in a beautiful, down-at-heel Georgian mansion just outside South Queensferry. Mr Griffiths, a professor of music, was a quiet man in sharp contrast to his wife, who was small, wiry and very forceful. They had a son and two daughters, one a little younger than me. They were extremely kind and hospitable, and their home had become an open house for the naval cadets at Temeraire. Mrs Griffiths, on realising the length of John's journey each day, was appalled:

"This is ridiculous," she said, "you must come and live here with us. We've got a caravan in the garden you can have."

We were thrilled as not only would this save John the long journey and bus fares but also the rent we were paying on the flat. Within weeks we had made the move. But we were in for a shock when Mrs Griffiths told us the cost of renting the caravan, which was a whole pound more than the flat. Furthermore, one of my 'duties', she informed me, would be to help her with the hundreds of deep-litter chickens she kept in large sheds. On my first morning I found myself marching to and fro, a chicken in each hand held upside down by their scaly feet, arching up and pecking me as we transferred them. No, I told her at the end of the morning, I'll help you in other ways but I'm not doing *that* again.

There were other downsides to the new arrangement, one of which was that John found a drinking buddy in a petty officer who rented a cottage on the estate. Every evening they sat in the garden knocking back whisky and this new, semi-sodden husband became someone I did not like at all, especially when his drunken snores mingled with my teething baby's howls and the noise ricocheted off the tin walls of our little caravan. But soon we moved into the main house and became part of the family. It was here we learned to enjoy the Scottish way of life. Christmas, we discovered, was a non-event in Scotland where celebrations all focussed on Hogmanay. We ate haggis, we went first footing, a crowd of us piling into cars to visit friends, exchanging our lump of coal for a 'wee dram', we even learned to like the bagpipes. At Temeraire's Hogmanay Ball, however, we discovered that, even though Scottish dancing is the greatest fun, no-one will laugh if you lose your step in the figure of eight or go wrong during the reel. Wherever we went, baby Lou-Lou, as we called her, came too. She was passed round dinner tables; dangled from knees; tossed from cadet to cadet like a squealing rugby ball; 'little-piggied', 'round-the-gardened'; kissed, cuddled and tickled. Yet however boisterous the horse-play she never lost her baby cool, laughing, hiccupping and cooing until I carried her away to bed.

My sister had beaten me in the baby stakes as she had had a daughter, Lydia, three months before Mary-Louise was born. Patricia had met and married a man called Jim Shallcross who, as well as being a silk screen printer, was also a gifted artist. They were now living in London.

For my brother Richard, meanwhile, National Service had come at last. He joined the Royal Military Police and was so thrilled with his new uniform that he wore it as often as possible, even when off duty. He quickly learned the trick of putting a short length of wooden ruler in his cap so as to force the peak down over his nose, thus giving him – the gentlest, sweetest of boys who took his Granny out for a drive every Sunday – a truly threatening appearance. He liked nothing better than to march up and down outside railway or bus stations, looking fierce. After basic training he was sent to join his regiment in Malaya where a bitter guerrilla war was being fought between Commonwealth armed forces and Malayan nationalists.

Looking at my baby, so bonnie and rosy cheeked, I felt convinced there was nothing the matter with her until, one day the following summer, I found her slumped forward in her pram, blue-faced. Even though her colour swiftly returned, it was at that moment I faced the truth; that there was something seriously wrong. A few days later we returned to see the specialist and I told him what had happened. He, in turn, amended his diagnosis and told me she had a hole in her heart. It was, he said, rather serious. Nothing could be done at this stage and her condition would simply have to be monitored as time went by. He was going to refer her to The Hospital for Sick Children in London's Great Ormond Street. As he spoke, a terrible fear gripped me. From her birth until today, the diagnosis had become steadily worse. And now we were to go to Great Ormond Street which I knew was a place where only the sickest children were treated. Oh, what was to become of my darling?

That August we had another surprise, but this time a happy one. I was pregnant again and another baby would be born the following April.

We were overjoyed even though a little bit worried about money. We wrote to tell John's mother the good news and received her reply by return of post: 'Dear John and Barbara, It is of absolutely no interest to me if you intend to breed like rabbits. Mother.'

Rabbits, eh? Oh well, two down and hundreds to go but, hey, it was a start.

A few weeks later we snuggled into our bunks onboard the night sleeper as it sped south, taking our baby, now 11 months old, to England for the first time. This was an exciting time for John who was now a fully-fledged Sub Lieutenant. He was very ambitious and ever since I'd met him had been studying for advancement in the Royal Navy. Ahead of him lay many more courses and examinations, but he was on the way.

Mary-Louise was nearly a year old when her grandmother and I took her to Great Ormond Street Hospital for the first time. She was a beautiful, outwardly healthy child who, after that one attack of cyanosis, had had no further symptoms. But here we were, walking past the giant teddy at the threshold of the most famous children's hospital in the world. After a battery of tests, we were ushered in to see the cardiologist, Dr Richard Bonham Carter who, with Mr David Waterson, was pioneering heart surgery in babies and children. He did not beat about the bush.

"Mrs Watson," he said, "your daughter has a very complex congenital condition called Fallot's Tetralogy which involves four different defects within the heart. She's actually doing very well but you will find that as she becomes more active and more is expected of her heart, her condition will get worse. We can't correct these defects through surgery but we may need to carry out palliative surgery at some point. For the moment she is coping well and I would like to see her again in six months. My advice to you is to take her home and let her lead as normal a life as possible."

So that was that. At last we knew the truth; our child had something so seriously wrong that even these pre-eminent cardiologists could not cure her. What now lay ahead? Was she going to be an invalid? Would she spend endless months in hospital? Would she suffer? And, one finally dared to ask, would she die before she reached adulthood? It was the worst, the most shocking, the most devastating news. What is more, it made one feel powerless, an emotion with which I am sure every parent of a sick child will empathise. For a parent's overwhelming urge is to protect ones child, an instinct which now seemed futile in the face of something of this gravity. I wished with every fibre of my being that I could

112

take on the suffering, that something could be wrong with me instead of my little one.

However, such emotions cannot – and perhaps should not - be sustained and so we tried to take Dr Bonham Carter's advice and return to a normal life. In this we were supported by our family and friends, chief amongst who were John's mother and sister. Following the 'breeding like rabbits' letter, I had come to realise I did not have the easiest of mothers-in-law but now, in the face of trouble, she was steadfast in her support and overflowing with love for this, her first grandchild. John's reaction was strange. He seemed unable to articulate his feelings or even to discuss the ramifications of Dr Bonham Carter's findings. It was as though the truth was insupportable and so he put it out of his mind.

By the spring of 1959, we had moved into our own home, a tiny bungalow in Waterlooville, near Portsmouth, bought (for £1,750) and furnished with the help of both sets of parents. And on the 22nd of April that year, I found myself hurtling along in an ambulance en route for a nursing home in nearby Liss. Less than two hours later, with the nurses shouting "don't push, don't push!" as they struggled into their aprons, our second baby was born, a tiny girl weighing not much more than six pounds. Once more, as I held her in my arms, I experienced that same extraordinary surge of love. She was as beautiful as her sister, with delicate, doll-like features and as her big, solemn eyes met mine I had the strangest feeling that I knew her already.

"Hello, tiny soul, here you are at last."

Once again I vowed that I would love her with all my being. I prayed that, unlike her sister, there was nothing wrong with her and I asked any attendant fairy godmothers and guardian angels to grant her a life of happiness and fulfilment. Outside, spring had clothed the trees in vivid buds and the wayside banks were awash with flowers of palest yellow. And so we named her Victoria Primrose.

John was as thrilled as I was with his new daughter. Visitors, flowers and cards arrived and I had the happiest of feelings that our little family was now complete. For the next two weeks I shared a room with another naval wife, Tricia, who had given birth to a boy called Hereward. She was one of the funniest people I have ever met and her stories kept me in constant fits of laughter. One day during her pregnancy, she told me, she had decided to give her four-year-old a crash course on the birds and the bees:

"...so you see, darling, the baby is in Mummy's tummy and soon

113

he'll be born and then you'll be able to hold him and...."

"But Mummy," the child asked, "how does the baby get out?"

Tricia decided this was all a bit too technical. "Oh, the doctor sees to all that," she replied vaguely.

"Oh he's in there too is he?"

Victoria was only five months old when John joined HMS Loch Fada, which was to be deployed to the Persian Gulf for a year. When the day came for him to leave us, I felt devastated. We had been so happy in our little home, for as well as being the romantic suitor of our Bristol days he also proved to be a bit of a homebody. Although he was working hard on courses in various naval shore establishments, we still had time for cosy evenings, reading our books, having friends to supper, listening to plays on the radio or watching the flickering black and white television we'd hired from Radio Rentals. He had even made my life easier by buying that huge luxury, a Colston twin-tub washing machine. Oh, the bliss when boiling baby's nappies in a galvanized bucket became a thing of the past. John loved the tasty suppers I made, played happily with the little ones, and our love for each other seemed, if that were possible, to have deepened.

Now his bag was packed and he was on the point of leaving. I clung to him, sobbing, and he held me tight, promising to write every day just as we had in Bristol. Then he kissed the babies and was gone. I picked them up and held them to me, the pain of parting like a knife in my heart. A whole year on our own? How on earth did one begin to cope with that? Suddenly, the door flew open and John dashed back in.

"Forgotten my cigarettes," he said, picked up the packet and ran out. His face had been aglow and suddenly I realised that, for him, this was what the years of training had been about; he was going to sea as a naval officer who, junior though he was, had an important role to play on this deployment. For him, a big adventure was about to begin.

A few days later, as we were having lunch, Lou-Lou began to cry:

"Oh darling," I said, "what's the matter?"

"My Daddy won't have no meats and puddins on ship Loch Fada," she sobbed.

The year that followed was as bleak as the bland housing development in Waterlooville. Row after row of identical bungalows, net curtains a-twitch, lined the streets. There was no focus to the place, no sense of community, nothing to make you feel you 'belonged'. I got to know one or two neighbours but really missed my family, my Gloucestershire friends and the wonderful people we'd met in Scotland. I lived for their visits and even found myself hankering now and then for my old life as a single girl. For I was lonely and my heart ached for my husband. I was upset, too, for far from writing every day, I was lucky if I got a letter once a month. So this at last was the reality of a naval wife's life – a happy marriage, a contented family, disrupted when the man of the house departed and was away for months or years on end.

However, my little girls were the be-all and end-all of my life and I immersed myself in their upbringing. Lou-Lou was now two years old and, realising she was a bright little soul, I felt it was high time she learned to read. So, armed with a Janet & John book and some home-made flash cards, we began. Why, I wondered, did she find it hard? And why did a neighbour, a primary school teacher, look askance at what I was doing? The fact remains that, by the age of three, she adored books and the word games we played. The only signs that she had a bad heart were two blue lines near her mouth and a tendency to squat after exertion. She even sailed through a frightening attack of bronchial-pneumonia when she had spent a couple of days in hospital cocooned in an oxygen tent. Victoria, sweet tiny mite, was my shadow whose favourite spot was perched on my hip as I did my work one handed.

At last that year came to an end and the girls and I, along with the other wives and children, lined the quay in Portsmouth Dockyard as HMS Loch Fada slid slowly alongside, all of us eagerly seeking out the face of our particular loved one. I spotted John but as I held the girls up and started to wave, he moved out of sight and I knew he didn't want any unseemly displays of public emotion. However, as we walked up the gangway and he looked at me properly I could see just what he was feeling – horror! For a friend had lent me a cream mink coat (yes, I know – but that was before any thought of animal rights had seeped into either my or the public's consciousness) and written all over my husband's face was "where the hell did she get *that*?"

After the euphoria of John's return, it was difficult to settle down. He seemed different in subtle ways which were difficult to identify. There was a shut-down, secret part of him which I didn't understand, a worldliness, a lack of interest in me and his daughters. Added to this, veiled rumours and clues I could not ignore hinted that, far from pining for me, he had found consolation elsewhere. I remembered my father's dire warnings about sailors with 'a wife in every port'. Was John Watson - as shipmates, after a drink too many, hinted with a wink and a nudge - a bit of a lad? And why, when this happened, did he shush them with an embarrassed laugh? But I loved him too much to open a Pandora's Box of accusations, so I locked the lid and kept these anxieties to myself.

One day in May, 1961, John came home with momentous news - he was to be seconded to the Malayan Navy as captain of one of their small fleet of fast patrol vessels. And we were to go with him! What is more we would travel first class on a P & O liner. To a girl who had never even crossed the English Channel, this all sounded so exotic I could hardly believe it was true. But there was a big problem. Could we take Lou-Lou to the tropics? Wouldn't the heat be too much for her let alone the strange bugs and diseases which must surely abound? But to our amazement the Great Ormond Street doctors said that, far from being too much, the heat and humidity would actually put much less strain on her heart than coping with British winters. In fact, they felt it would be positively good for her. We had a last holiday in Cornwall with John's mother and Sarah. Probably because she was upset about our departure, Grandmama, as the children called her, was absolutely impossible and, as always, John seemed in thrall to her and her moods. I couldn't wait for the holiday and its attendant tensions to end. And I couldn't wait for our great adventure to begin.

On a sunny morning in August, we found ourselves leaning over the crowded rails of the SS Stratheden, throwing streamers and waving goodbye to loved ones far below. Then, as a band played poignant songs of farewell, the ship – all 24,000 tons of her - inched slowly away, nudged by tugboats through Tilbury Docks and out into the Thames. We stayed up on deck awhile, John holding Mary-Louise in his arms, Victoria as always perched on my hip, as the ship slid past the bustling docks, now long gone, making her way towards the open sea. My heart filled with excitement - we were off and we would not return for two and a half years.

116

S E V E N

THE SS STRATHEDEN WAS LAUNCHED in 1937 and had plied the route between London and Australia until WWII, when she became a troopship. Now she had only two more years as part of P & O's fleet of passenger liners before being withdrawn from service. Unlike the floating funfairs which are the leviathan cruise-ships of the present day, the Stratheden's charm lay in her under-stated elegance and slightly faded grandeur. And for the next six weeks this beautiful ship was to be our home.

On our first night at sea we made our way to the dining room. I had tucked the girls into bed, knowing that the ship's experienced nannies would be baby-sitting. Now we were getting to know our affable host, the ship's doctor, and fellow diners. I studied the menu which read like a gourmet's dream. Should I have the prawns or the lobster bisque? Suddenly and unexpectedly a wave of panic hit me - I knew with absolute certainty that my babies had clambered out of bed, opened the porthole and were about to plunge into the sea. I jumped up and ran, hundreds of eyes following me as I sprinted out of the dining room. So great was my terror that I forgot which deck our cabin was on. Up and down endless stairs, along miles of corridors I raced. B deck, E, deck, where is it? Oh God, would I be in time? At last I found the cabin and, hands shaking, opened the door. Had they plunged to their doom? No.

Life soon settled into a wonderful routine. In the mornings the girls went to the ship's nursery whilst we strolled the decks and socialised. In the afternoons we swam and played with the children. In the evenings we danced and ate vast quantities of utterly delicious food. What bliss it was to be together. Once again we were best friends, making the most of every carefree moment, as happy as we had ever been. And the country girl from Gloucestershire, the 'lass' from the Lord Mayor's Office thought to herself: yes, I can do sophisticated.

As we entered the Bay of Biscay and passengers began to succumb to sea-sickness. John issued a stern warning to his three girls:

"We are a naval family - we will *not* be sick." So we weren't.

After visiting the Rock of Gibraltar the ship sailed onward across the Mediterranean to Port Said and the entrance to the Suez Canal. Here we joined the others vessels anchored in the Great Bitter Lakes awaiting the passage of the north-bound convoy. Finally, our long procession of ships set off on the slow, 16-hour, 103-mile journey south along the canal to Aden. This was an extraordinary, unforgettable experience which now and then became surreal when the line of ships ahead rounded a bend in the canal and appeared to glide through the desert sands – truly like ships of the desert.

Some of our fellow passengers were more congenial than others. One in particular, a colonel's wife travelling to India with her daughter, could not have been more obnoxious. A large woman with a red face and a braying voice, she had an infuriating air of superiority and had instilled this smug self-importance in her teenage daughter. However, the girl was not always as sophisticated as she thought she was. One evening, as she entered the bar, her mother boomed:

"Dahling – here you are at last! What will you have to drink?"

"Oh, a large John Thomas, please."

Tee hee, such fun to titter at her expense! Better still, the mother was about to meet her social come-uppance.

Traditional entertainers during the transit of the Canal were the Gully-Gully men, Arab magicians said to be from one family whose specialty was to produce chicks from thin air. Our Gully-Gully man had boarded the Stratheden at Port Said and, after a performance for the children, it was our turn. We took our seats for the show, Mrs. Colonel, clad in an unfortunate satin gown from which her vast bosom overflowed, sat in the middle of the front row, as of right. The Gully-Gully man in his long white djellabah and red fez moved about the audience, plucking chicks from an ear here, a nose there, a sleeve, a pocket, a shoe so that soon we were all laughing uncontrollably. But I swear the man was a psychologist because, as his grand finale, he honed in on Mrs. Colonel. No part of her was spared. He pulled chicks from her mouth, her ears, her nose, her hair. They hopped onto her lap, they scuttled up her skirts and finally an avalanche of chicks erupted from her massive breasts, more and more and more and more until, shrieking like a banshee, she gathered up her skirts

118

and fled, and was not seen in public for several days. As for the Gully-Gully man, he received a standing ovation and far more tips than perhaps he was expecting.

Once through the Canal our voyage continued: the Gulf of Suez, the Red Sea, through the narrow, pirate-ridden Strait of Hormuz into the Gulf of Aden, then across the romantically named Arabian Sea until one morning we awoke to see a great archway on the edge of a harbour where the ship had quietly docked as we slept. It was the Gateway to India and beyond it lay Bombay. With only 24 hours in this astonishing city, one was left with no more than a snapshot of memories. Years later, I met an Indian couple who asked me what I thought of Bombay, their home city. I waxed lyrical but felt bound to add:

"But it was terrible to see so much poverty - the beggars, the poor little children...."

"The beggars? Oh, they've all gone," he interrupted.

"How wonderful! What happened?" I asked, imagining a sort of Shangri La where the formerly destitute now lived in comfort.

"Oh", he said airily, "they've all been moved out."

Down the Indian coast we sailed, rounding the southernmost tip of Ceylon (now Sri Lanka) and out into the mighty Indian Ocean with its long, heavy swell. Day after day our voyage continued, sometimes accompanied by schools of dolphins and porpoises, sometimes by whales which rose from the deep, vast and majestic, to swim beside us for a while before returning to their mysterious world beneath the waves, leaving only flying fish and the lonely seabirds in their wake.

Now the horizon surrounded us in a great azure circle where sea met sky. At night the stars, wheeling in their blue-black heaven, seemed to beckon, guiding us on our oriental odyssey, whilst the sea, phosphorescent, hypnotic, as enticing as a Siren, tempted one to leap into the cool haven of its depths. So far from land, we forgot the outside world, the past, the future, as our shipboard life became our one reality.

Finally, we awoke on a day as hot and steamy as a sauna to find ourselves in the Strait of Malacca, the narrow stretch of sea which separates the emerald shores of western Malaya and the Indonesian island of Sumatra. We were nearing the end of this extraordinary journey and would soon reach our destination, Singapore.

Rotting vegetation and sewage were the perfumes of the East which greeted us as we disembarked into the steamy heat of Singapore.

But other senses quickly took over as we drove through the teeming city - rickshaws, carts and hooting cabs, discordant music, strident voices, mangy dogs, pigs in pokes, canaries in rattan cages, fat babies beaming from their mother's backs, old men puffing on long clay pipes, washing on poles, street markets, temples with lip-lilted roofs, dark alleys where opium dens still lurked - there was something strange and extraordinary to see on every side. In the more affluent areas we passed smart shops, old colonial hotels and houses set in shady gardens, but not a single high-rise building (although two years later we attended the opening of Singapore's first skyscraper, an hotel which rose to a dizzying ten storeys). Then we drove up the main Bukit Tima road until we reached the island's northern shores. Here a causeway linked Singapore with the Malayan mainland. As this was ostensibly a border crossing, there was a Customs post at one end where, we would soon discover, cute, blonde-haired children softened the hearts of the normally aggressive officers who, after cooing at them for a moment or two, always waved us through.

Whilst we waited to be allotted a married quarter, we stayed at a little Chinese-run hotel in Johore Bahru, a small town on the southern tip of the Malay Peninsula. As I looked out of the window on our first morning, I saw an old lady tottering on tiny bound feet, bearing testament to a barbaric custom thankfully now a thing of the past.

The Malayan Navy's headquarters was not, as one might suppose, in Malaya itself but situated within the vast British Naval Base on the northern shores of Singapore island and it was here that we expected to live. However, a shock awaited us when we learned that, despite this being an accompanied posting, John was not entitled to a married quarter until he was 25 in June the following year. This was a serious financial setback which meant that, as the days passed, we had to tighten our belts until all four of us were squashed into one hot, cramped hotel room and eating the cheapest dish on the menu – the surprisingly delicious and nourishing fried rice. After six weeks, by which time the Watson coffers were almost empty, John informed his superiors that he was bringing his family to the base the next day and we would camp there until we were given somewhere to live. His threat worked and within a week we were ensconced in a beautiful, roomy flat set on a hill overlooking the barracks.

Singapore is only 100 miles north of the equator and our new home was built to cater for its humid, tropical climate, with big airy rooms, glassless wall-to-wall windows, rattan furniture, cool stone floors and ceilings fans which circulated the hot, steamy air into a semblance of coolness. Hibiscus, bougainvillea and jasmine scrambled up from the gardens onto our wide balcony whilst flame trees and jacaranda perfumed the air and were home to exotic birds. We soon got used to the tiny green geckos which lived on the ceiling, especially when we learned that, without them, a building is said to be haunted.

Snakes, however, were another matter entirely. There were so many varieties that a long shelf in our doctor's surgery was devoted to jars holding snakes pickled in formaldehyde so that if one was bitten, the attacker could be identified and the antidote, if there was one, administered before death could claim another victim. One day a 24-foot python was found in the stretch of jungle below our apartment. It was fast asleep and along its coiled length were 12 chicken-shaped lumps. Unfortunately, my children developed a very hands-on approach to snakes. They were playing outside one day when I heard them come in and ask the amah for a knife. Perhaps the afternoon heat had stultified my senses because several moments passed before I thought: "a knife?" and raced downstairs in time to see them chopping off the head of a snake. I even came home one afternoon to find Victoria walking down the hill waving a small, highly-venomous – and luckily dead - pit viper by the tail, chanting, "snaky, snaky, snaky." I tried to steer clear of reptiles although one day I glanced up into a tree and saw a huge, dragon-like lizard at least five-foot long, which returned my gaze from fathomless, prehistoric eyes. I moved first.

John was delighted with his new job as captain of Sri Trengannu ('Sri' meaning 'Lord' and 'Trengannu' the name of a Malay State) one of the Malayan Navy's fleet of fast patrol boats on which, with his crew, he would spend two weeks of every month patrolling the waters of Malaya's east and west coasts. He took a crash course in Malay, a simple language with only one tense, which he had to learn so that he could communicate fully with his crew. With his help, the children and I also learned some useful Malay, such as the first few lines of The Three Bears.

I, meanwhile, become a lady of leisure, thanks to that ultimate luxury, an amah. In fact, help was a necessity because the torrid heat was so enervating for we thin-blooded Europeans. Our amah, Ah Lin, was a kind, gentle woman in her forties, always immaculately dressed in the traditional uniform of wide black trouser and starched, high-collared white tunic. She did everything, so no more cooking, housework, washing or ironing for me - whoopee! Having discussed the day's menus with Ah Lin, rung my food orders through to the various merchants who delivered to the door, I was free to spend the morning shopping, making clothes suitable for

121

the climate, visiting the hairdressers, learning to play Mah Jong or having coffee and lunch with new friends. It was amazing how quickly I took to my new role!

This was the first time I had been part of a group of naval wives and soon I was forging friendships which would last for years to come. All of us understood both the best and the worst of what life as a naval wife entailed. Joan, Wynn, Lulu, Robbie, Dorothy - together we enjoyed the fun of our new life, supported one another when our husbands were at sea and comforted each other when things went wrong.

We bought a car, the fashionable and affordable Mini, and then I learned to drive, firstly in the safety of our barracks with my neighbour Joan as my teacher, then out into the British naval base. Finally it was time for a proper instructor and a man was recommended who, by way reference, said he was the Sultan of Johore's cousin. I was duly impressed although, as time went by and every other person seemed to claim the same regal relationship, the awe wore off. However, teach me he did until the day he declared me ready for the driving test. I duly turned up at the test centre in Johore Bahru and sat with a nervous group waiting to be interrogated on the Highway Code by a truly fearsome Chinese man who must, one felt, have seen the inside of a torture chamber. If one passed this hurdle then it was time for part two of the ordeal, which was to reverse your car through a long 'L' of bollards set very close to ones vehicle. If you touched a bollard, that was that – failure. Joan, my ace teacher, had become so nervous that she failed this stage four times. However, perhaps because I was driving a tiny car, I succeeded. Then an examiner jumped in beside me and out we went into the narrow streets of Johore Bahru. He was so busy telling me about his nineteenth-cousin-once-removed, the Sultan of Johore, (yawn) that he didn't seem to care when, as we crawled through a crowded market, a coolie stepped out in front of us. He had a yoke across his shoulders from which hung a line of huge fish and, even though I braked hard, the last fish hit the windscreen, making the poor man stagger. We drove into a narrow lane and were held up behind a desultory buffalo cart. When I eventually edged past it, I could not help noticing that the creature had the end of a bamboo pole stuck in its bottom, which the driver, lolling in his seat, moved from left to right to indicate direction. H'm, I thought, no wonder you're walking so slowly, dear buffalo, I would too if I had a pole stuck up my bum. Finally, we stopped on the seafront where I enjoyed the view whilst my tester continued to prove his genealogical link to the sultanate. At last he looked at his watch:

"Oh, is that time? You pass, okay. Quick, back to base."

By the afternoon, the heat of the day was at its most intense and for this reason the navy operated 'tropical routine' with work starting at seven in the morning and ending early. Schools too finished at mid-day. In the afternoons we, like most families, went to the Officer's Club where we could swim and relax around the pool and, above all, keep cool. It was the epicentre of social life, the place where everyone gathered, gossiped, swam and swapped invitations. Life became a round of cocktails, supper-and-cinema evenings, pool parties, barbecues, lunches, dinners, dances and even grand balls. There were no more lonely evenings for girls when our husbands were at sea, for we were always taken by friends. It was even quite acceptable for a married woman to go to parties alone, especially as women were hugely outnumbered by men and we were therefore much in demand.

John didn't like dancing. I could drag him onto the floor where he would shuffle around for a while, but that was all. He much preferred to prop up the bar, talking shop with naval pals. On the other hand, I, like all my girlfriends, just wanted to dance, dance, dance the steamy nights away; quick steps, fox trots, languorous waltzes, the cha-cha, tango, rock and roll, the jive - it was all utterly exhilarating, but none more so than the Twist, the new dance craze which was sweeping the world. 'Let's twist again, like we did last summer, let's twist again, last we did last year'. The moment Chubby Checker started belting out his twelve-bar blues, even non-dancers like John were up on their feet, unable to resist the rhythm. One day someone put a new record on their turntable. It was a song called 'Love Me Do' and the artists were a group of Liverpudlians none of us had heard of – the Beatles. We were instantly hooked.

On Saturday nights groups of us would sometimes go to the Straits View Hotel in Johore Bahru where one could sit overlooking the ocean, eat, drink and dance. The hotel's cabaret was mediocre except for one very popular act; a squat, middle-aged Chinese woman, dressed in a 'You Tarzan, Me Jane' jungle-print bikini, whose specialty was to writhe and wrestle with a fifteen-foot python, both fascinating and horrible in equal measures.

At weekends the hotel was frequented by rubber planters from up-country, glad of the chance to relax now that the Malayan Emergency had ended and eager for a bit of life away from their isolated plantations. They seemed to me to have stepped from the pages of a Somerset Maugham novel, men of the British Empire, harrumphing as they downed their stengahs, shouting 'boy' at the waiters when they wanted a refill, their vocabulary littered with 'old chaps' and 'don't-ya-knows'. They favoured wide, knee-length khaki shorts, starched so stiffly that when they sat back in their rattan chairs, legs akimbo, a rather nasty view could not be avoided.

The girls also settled down quickly and happily, making new friends with other children in the barracks. Soon it was time for Mary-Louise to start school and 'Hilltops', a little school in Johore Bahru, was recommended. We went to investigate. The school was in a traditional Malay house perched on high stilts, under which chickens scratched and sleepy cats drowsed in the shade. Unusually for that era, it was multiracial, with Malay, Chinese, Tamil and European children. It was very small with only twenty or so pupils and I could sense at once that the children were happy and well taught. The headmistress showed us round and, as we went into the nursery class, Victoria pointed to a tiny Tamil boy and announced:

"I want dat choclick boy."

Dressed in her crisp apple-green uniform, Lou-Lou was soon going off to school each morning with four other little friends from the Malayan Barracks. Left behind, Torla, as we called her, was bitterly upset and day after day sobbed that she wanted the 'choclick boy'. She had also developed an obsession with clothes. No sooner had I dressed her than she would run to her bedroom, tear of what she was wearing and choose something else, try it on only to discard it, until a pile of clean but crumpled clothes lay on the floor. Even worse was her fixation with cosmetics, raiding my dressing table for lipsticks which she applied liberally to the lower part of her face, varnishing her tiny fingers up to the knuckle and, of course, ruining my cosmetics in the process. At last, surveying the damage from yet another foray, I lost patience:

"You're a *naughty girl*!" I scolded, "don't you *dare* touch my make-up again, do you understand?"

Several weeks later a friend said:

"Look, I've got the sweetest photo of Torla at Annabelle's birthday party." And there she was, sitting on a swing surrounded by a group of admiring little boys, surveying herself in *my* compact as she applied *my* lipstick. Could this, I asked myself, be a sign? I mean, snakes, clothes and lipstick were surely rather odd preoccupations for such a young child. Clearly what was needed were more cerebral pursuits. Within a week Victoria, aged three and a half, joined her sister at Hilltops School, insisting bossily on sitting next to the chocklick boy, whose name was Verjakma and who immediately became her friend.

Both girls loved the pool and quickly learned to swim, albeit underwater like little frogs, returning to the surface now and then for a gasp of air. Our neighbours, Joan and Philip Barker, were as yet childless and so made a great fuss of them. Philip's first encounter with Victoria was unusual to say the least. He had just brought his ship back from patrol and was enjoying an afternoon siesta on his sofa when a small voice woke him up:

"Look," said Torla, for it was she, "I dot no knickers on."

On opening his eyes, he saw a tiny girl holding up her skirt to reveal that indeed she had not! They showered her with presents including green goggles with matching nose clip and flippers, chosen to match her green and white polka-dot bikini.

The high diving board at the club was normally the domain of teenage boys and young men, who would strut to the end before plunging like cormorants into the water. Now and then, John – like other dads - would take the girls up to the top and, with one screaming child under each arm, jump. One day, we heard a bit of a commotion and looked up to see a long tail-back down the steps, all impatient for their turn. Then I saw the reason for the hold-up, for who should flop forward to the end of the diving board, flippers, goggles, nose-clip all in place, but Victoria. She posed at the end, waiting until sure she was the centre of attention, then jumped. There was a round of applause.

As well as snake charming, the children in the block developed their own bush telegraph, although one based on plumbing rather than drums. One evening, as I returned to the bathroom where the girls were splashing, I heard a small, disembodied voice. I paused to listen. Surely, that was little Simon from downstairs?

"Are you inna barf, Lou-Lou?"

"Yes," replied Lou-Lou, pressing her mouth to the circular overflow just below the taps, "I'm inna barf. Is Penelope inna barf?"

"Yes, she's inna barf. Is Torla inna barf?"

Victoria slid past her sister and took her place at the 'mike':

"I," she announced importantly, "is inna barf too."

One day Victoria received a party invitation and the following Saturday, with Torla wearing her prettiest dress, the three of us set off. The address on the card read 'Istana, Bukit Serene, Johore Bahru'. Unable to find it, I wound down the window and asked a passerby for directions. He got very excited, pointing and waving his arms in the air and shouting 'Istana!, Istana!'. We soon understood his excitement when we drove in through gilded gates, winding our way through lush gardens until we reached an exquisite building sparkling in the sun, beautiful as a wedding cake.

"Oh my goodness, girls," I said, "it's a *palace*! So *that's* what 'Istana' means."

As we entered a great marble hall we were presented to a tall, plumply handsome man attired in traditional Malay dress. He was none other than the Sultan of Johore, Tunku Ismail Al-Khalid. (Oh, how I wished I had not been wearing shorts!) He greeted us with great warmth, talking sweetly to the girls until there was a stir of activity and there, coming down a sweeping staircase, surrounded by a retinue of servants, was the birthday girl.

"My daughter," said the Sultan, his face wreathed in smiles, clearly a besotted father.

The tiny girl was wearing an emerald green dress, and a necklace of jade and filigreed gold hung from her neck to her waist. Victoria remembers thinking "oh, she looks just like a princess," which, of course, she was. She tells of how, after tea, the children ran wild around the palace. The Sultan, a great animal lover, even had a private zoo where a friendly elephant, clearly mistaking Lou-Lou's nose for a currant bun, reached out and took it gently in his trunk.

I had longed to ask the Sultan how many wives he had but did not dare. However, with the aid of Google, I can now see that he had only two 'official' wives, the first dying tragically after a car crash. He had seven sons, only three of whom survived to adulthood. However, there is no reference to a girl born in 1959, Victoria's school friend. Thus, the birthday girl's mother must have been a member of his harem - an 'unofficial' wife.

Tunku Ismail asked me if I had a son and, as we were to find with all Orientals, commiserated that I had not. However, when we later met his eldest son, the Tunku Mahkota (Crown Prince) Mahmud Iskander, I felt that it was *I* who should have commiserated with the Sultan. For, in contrast to his good, gentle father, beloved by all, Mahmud was a dissolute, deeply unpleasant man in his thirties whose vicious nature would lead to convictions on charges of brutal assaults and finally murder, all of which were overturned by his father. The Sultan disinherited him, although he revoked this on his deathbed – an event which caused controversy because, some people argued, the old man was comatose at the end of his life and would therefore probably have been unable to sign the necessary documents. Whatever the truth, Mahmud Iskander not only became the 24th Sultan of Johore but, at the time of writing, is now the Yang di-Pertuan Agong (King) of Malaya.

The Yang di-Pertuan Agong is elected from among the Sultans of the country's nine States and even though his duties are largely ceremonial he is still effectively the constitutional monarch. One day we heard that the then Yang di-Pertuan Agong, Tunku Syed Putra of the State of Perlis, was to visit and review his Navy, and that wives and children were expected to attend the march past. I, like all the other mothers, explained the importance of the occasion to the children and stressed that they should be on their best behaviour. On the appointed day, the families were marshalled round the edge of the parade ground and the band struck up. His Majesty – a tiny man with so much gold about his person he appeared to glitter - stepped onto the saluting dais. The troops began the march past, officers bearing drawn swords heading each detachment. It was all very impressive. Suddenly, Victoria spotted a familiar face at the head of his ship's company.

"Da-dee!" she cried joyfully and, with surprising accuracy for one so small, lobbed her teddy bear at him. Without losing step, he kicked it to one side where it lay, gracing this solemn occasion until the end. Da-dee, however, was not amused.

Not everything was wonderful about life in Singapore. Books (lifeblood to both John and I) were a rare commodity, circulated amongst friends like gold dust. Other than the odd Chinese opera, whose white-faced singers and strange instruments kept up a pentatonic screech like cats in traps for hour after endless hour, there was little or no culture. We once attended a performance by a troupe of visiting flamenco dancers, but as our seats were in the front row and the stage was very high, all we saw were their top halves which rather, one felt, defeated the object. The only newspaper was The Straits Times, which featured stories of haunted rambutan trees, attacks by water buffalo and mass hysteria at girls' schools. Once, when the temperature dropped to 75 degrees, its headlines screamed SINGAPORE SHIVERS.

Another drawback to living in this exotic place was the visitors. Never a month passed without someone ringing up to ask if they could come and stay. Indeed, one friend lived with us for months, giving birth and bringing her baby home to us. The long-suffering Ah Lin never complained although I always took over the cooking when we had visitors and made sure guests tipped her handsomely for her services.

And then there was the drinking culture which was so much part of the naval and ex-pat scene. Whether it was a glass or two of ice-cold Pimms or non-stop whiskies, there was always a constant flow of booze. We were young, life often felt like a non-stop party and drinking was just part of that. Most of us knew when to stop but plenty more, mostly men, had problems. Since he had become an officer, John's drinking had escalated. He was not an alcoholic but he was unpredictable. He would be fine for a while, drinking moderately so that our evenings out ended happily. But if he had his drinking boots on, then I knew we were in for a rough time. On these occasions he just could not stop, knocking back glass after glass until he was out of control, paying for everyone if a group of us were eating out, buying expensive bottles of wine, tipping waiters extravagantly, insisting we go on to a nightclub – all on a lowly Sub-Lieutenants pay. Even worse, he sometimes became indiscrete, boasting of his female conquests to whoever cared to listen. By the next morning, of course, he had completely forgotten what he had said or done. Now and then he would disappear, coming home next morning as though nothing had happened. Virtually every row we had was about a drink-related incident. He was not a bad-tempered man and certainly not a violent one. However, one morning when I had screamed and shrieked and protested after yet another debacle, and when he was no doubt nursing a sore head, he lost his cool and lashed out, aiming a boxer's right fist at my chin. I ducked and his knuckles went right through the wardrobe door. We both stopped and stared at it, a natural pause between rounds. Then - ding, ding, seconds out - he pulled his bleeding hand out of the wardrobe and this time didn't miss his target, his blow knocking me sideways onto the floor. I expect he thought that would be that but, enraged, I leapt up and grabbed him, shaking him backwards and forwards like a terrier with a rat, until his teeth rattled. Every button on his shirt flew off, the sleeve tore away from the shoulder and his watch flew to the ground, shattered. Finally, he managed to get free and shoved me aside before grabbing a clean shirt and stalking off. Later, when we made up, he remarked:

"You know, it's you should box for the Malayan Navy, not me."

He never did hit me again. But the wardrobe door took some explaining.

It is only fair to say that he was by no means the only man in the barracks to drink this heavily. And we were not the only couple to argue.

Because windows were glassless, every shouted word of a row was audible to the entire block. Neighbouring flats would fall silent as we all listened in, relishing every moment, smug in the knowledge that, on this occasion, we were not the couple at loggerheads. The most spectacular row peaked when a woman threw her entire dinner service, plate by plate, at her erring husband and the wall.

In this hedonistic environment, flirtations abounded, both innocent and less so. Sometimes these attentions came from the most unexpected quarters. New Year' Eve, 1962, found us onboard a ship in Singapore harbour. Like every other ship in the curving bay, its rigging was ablaze with lights. Guests in evening dress strolled the decks sipping champagne, music and laughter filled the balmy air, and at midnight a great arc of fireworks lit up the night sky. It was all unbelievably glamorous and I was glad to be wearing my gorgeous turquoise 'mermaid' dress.

Amongst our group of friends was an unfamiliar face; a Sikh dressed in the uniform of the Royal Naval Reserve. Brij Singh, an intelligent, charming man, was on the short side with a hint of a pot belly, his white turban soaring to a giddy point above his black-bearded face. He entertained us with a fund of fascinating tales. One, which was truly horrific, happened during the Partition of India and Pakistan in 1947, when he and his brother ran fifty miles to escape death at the hands of murderous mobs, leaving behind relatives, many of whom were slaughtered. The following year represented India in the first post-war Olympics, which were held in London. Not surprisingly, they competed in the marathon. At the moment, he told us, his wife and children were away for three months on their annual trip back to Calcutta. At some point I danced with him – just once.

The next evening as we sat in our apartment with friends, having a 'hair of the dog' and mulling over the previous night, the phone rang. John answered:

"Hello, this is Brij Singh. May I speak to your vife?"

John handed the phone to me, looking intrigued.

"Hello," I said cautiously.

"Hello, my darling," murmured a deep, syrupy voice, "did you sleep? I didn't. I just couldn't stop thinking about you and last night, the night vee met, the night vee fell in love."

What?

"Er, I don't know what you're talking about," I spluttered whilst behind me the room went silent.

"Oh, how silly of me - you can't speak because your husband is there. I' vill ring you ven he's out so vee can arrange to meet. Tomorrow morning?"

I could feel my jaw descending floor-wards.

"Look, I'm afraid you've made a mistake, I,..."

"Made a mistake? But you returned my signal ven vee danced."

"Signal? What on earth do you mean?"

"I squveezed your hand, you squveezed mine back, I could tell you felt the same."

"Well, you're wrong. I did *not* give you a signal and I *certainly* can't meet you. And, and... anyway, I must go, we've got guests."

I put the phone down and the muffled giggles exploded into laughter.

"What on earth was that all about?" asked John, and my dusky suitor became the stock joke for days to come. John did not seem at all concerned that someone had made this overt play for his wife and because Brij Singh now seemed to have attached himself to our circle of friends, we continued to bump into him socially. Never once did he mention the phone call and I therefore assumed he had recovered from his temporary infatuation.

But I was wrong. A couple of month's later he arrived one afternoon, unannounced.

"Oh, hello Brij," I said, "do come in. Would you like a cup of tea?"

Without a word he frog-marched me backwards across the room, shoved me against a wall and, putting a hand on each side of my shoulders, growled: "Unless you submit to me, I shall stab you. And I'm not joking - every Sikh carries a dagger."

Ohmygawd, what to do? Ah Lin was out and the apartments seemed quiet and deserted in the afternoon heat. But then I heard the welcome sound of children laughing in the garden. My girls! Now, if I could just get to the window... Like a pair of crabs performing some strange ritual dance, we shuffled along the wall, face-to-face.

"Darlings," I called brightly over my shoulder as we grappled, "come upstairs, someone's come to see you."

As we heard their footsteps pitter-pat up the stairs, he sprang away from me. "Don't you *dare* try that again," I hissed *soto voce* just before my little rescuers scampered in. He had the grace to look shame-faced.

The weather was exhausting, the relentless sun followed by monsoon downpours, which cooled us for an hour or two before making the atmosphere even more humid. To escape the heat one year, John and I took a short holiday in the Cameron Highlands, some 300 miles north of Singapore. We left home before sunrise, passing the endless rubber plantations where figures already flitted between the slender trees, their lanterns like fireflies in the early dawn. Then, after a long, long drive up the country's one (virtually empty) main road and a night spent in a government rest house, the next morning found us winding our way through the quaint old capital of Kuala Lumpur. At last, however, we began the final climb, zig-zagging up and up towards our destination. At 5000 feet we stopped to look back at the view. Dense jungle - the oldest primary forest in the world - covered the hillsides which were dotted here and there with tea plantations, silver waterfalls cascaded into lakes, whilst green and misty mountains stretched away to be lost in the clouds. As we stood there glorying in the view, the cool breeze like a blessing on our cheeks, the sounds of the jungle exotic in our ears, two things happened. Above the shriek and chatter of monkeys, the relentless frogs, the music of the birds, we heard a tiger's roar, primeval, awesome and very, very close. Then, like a mirage, a group of people stepped out of the forest, father, mother and three small children. They were *Orang Aslis* – 'people of the forest' - whose way of life had remained unchanged for thousands of years. Their tiny, brown bodies were naked although the man wore a cloak-like garment flung over one shoulder and carried a long (poisoned?) blowpipe in one hand. For a moment they stood there, a tableau from pre-history, before melting back into the forest as silently as they had come.

On the journey home, we wound our way back along the west coast, heading for the old Dutch town of Malacca. Coming to a bridgeless river, we drove nervously onto a ferry made of logs. As the ferryman heaved on the chains which hauled us across, he informed us cheerfully that a lorry had gone over the side the week before. Any crocodiles we asked? Plenty, he said.

Insects! How we hated them! Platoons of ants invaded the kitchen whilst enormous cockroaches, almost impossible to kill, emerged at night, scattering like a bronze army if one turned on a light. Our worst enemies, though, were the mosquitoes against which one waged a constant battle. Once evening fell, arms and legs were covered with insect repellent whilst mosquito nets swathed our beds and Tiger Balm coils burned on

131

bedside tables. For not only were their bites irritating, they could also be the bearers of dangerous diseases.

In a far corner of the barracks was a small open prison whose occupants worked as groundsmen and gardeners within the environs. The gardeners – or *kebuns* to use the Malay word - were great favourites with the children, who called them 'the likka-lakkaboons'. One of them was a handsome Tamil with shining black skin and lustrous eyes. Every morning my beautiful, blonde neighbour Joan and I leant over our balconies to say good morning whilst he cut us each a blossom and, Romeo-like, handed them up. One day we dared to ask why he was in prison and he told us a heartbreaking tale of love, jealousy and betrayal, culminating in his murder of the man who had impugned his wife's honour. A crime of passion, we thought sadly, oh, the poor, poor man. However, when we mentioned this tragedy to the guard who oversaw the kebuns' work, he said:

"Murder? No, he was an accountant's clerk and got three years for embezzlement."

But I digress. One of the kebuns' tasks was to spray the grounds with an anti-mosquito insecticide, but perhaps they had been too busy handing flowers to ladies or playing with children for they overlooked a rusty, water-filled tin behind the Wendy house, which became an unseen breeding ground for mosquitoes. One particular batch contained a deadly disease - viral meningitis.

Lou-Lou became ill. Listless and feverish, she complained of a terrible headache. I took her to Reg, the Malayan Navy's doctor, who had the unfortunate title of 'worst doctor in the world' because of his general laxity. Luckily, because others in the barracks had come forward with the same symptoms, he knew at once that she had meningitis and she was rushed to the British Military Hospital in Singapore. Here they performed an immediate lumbar puncture and, after days of desperate worry, she began to recover and at last came home. Then tragedy struck when, whilst the barracks was still being searched for the source of the disease, a baby died.

By then I, too, had begun to experience similar symptoms, which Dr Reg declared were not meningitis. As my headache became more and more excruciating, I went to him again but he dismissed me, privately telling John my symptoms were psychosomatic because I was worried about my daughter. Finally, I collapsed and the learned doctor was summonsed to our flat in the middle of the night. Yes, he admitted at last, it was meningitis but I was now too ill to be moved to hospital.

132

"Oh well, I'll just have to do a lumbar puncture myself," he said. He hurried away, returning later to announce cheerfully that he'd never done one before. "...but never mind," he added, "here goes."

Fortunately, I was too ill to be frightened as he jabbed away, causing my arms and legs to jerk in all directions until at last he got the needle into the right part of my spine. I was ill for quite a long time but, strange to say, the after effects were more disturbing than the illness, for I became deeply depressed and also developed what I can only call psychotic tendencies. I would sit in the midst of a group of chattering, laughing friends, and find myself thinking:

"If they don't shut up I'm going to get a knife and stab them." It was terrifying and I truly believed I was going mad. But fortunately for everyone, this phase passed and I had no recourse to the carving knife!

At some point in 1963 rumours reached me that John had a Malay mistress in Port Swettenham, a place his ship visited every month. I didn't want to believe it but something told me it was true. Equally, I knew I was too much of a coward to confront him and thus rock the boat of our marriage. What if I did tackle him and thus precipitated a crisis? I couldn't leave him as we were thousands of miles from home, I had no money of my own and - my main concern - I had two little girls to think of. So I did nothing and tried to carry on as though all was well.

In the summer of 1963 we were invited to a rather grand reception on board an aircraft carrier and, as John was away on patrol, I went with friends. The huge flight deck was crowded with people of so many nationalities that it looked like a United Nations melting-pot. Suddenly, two squads of Royal Marines, immaculate in white uniforms and ceremonial helmets, marched along the deck carrying long plush ropes with which they gently divided the guests, forming an avenue down the middle. At the same time music could be heard, faint at first but drawing ever nearer until, as the crowd finally separated like the parting of the Red Sea, a Royal Marine band appeared from the hangar below, raised – miraculously so it seemed to us – on an aircraft lift. They paused for a moment to heighten the drama before marching up and down between the crowd, now gasping and applauding in admiration both for the men and their music. It was totally spectacular and one of those moments when I felt proud to be British.

A group of VIP's stood near us, an Admiral and an Air Vice-Marshal with the usual sycophantic posse hovering around them.

"Look," whispered the girl I was standing with, "he's rather gorgeous, isn't he?"

The man she meant was the Air Vice-Marshal's aide-de-camp, and he was indeed gorgeous, immensely tall with a handsome, hawk-like face, his shoulders festooned in the gold epaulets of his rank. And was his aloof air arrogance or just boredom? It was hard to tell. For a moment he looked in our direction and, thinking our gawping had been spotted, we turned away, giggling.

I had forgotten all about him when, some time later, I heard a deep voice behind me:

"Do you always stare at strangers?"

I spun round and there stood the gorgeous one, no longer on duty and most definitely not aloof.

"I really do want an answer," he said, smiling down at me, "such bad manners, you know, staring, or so my grandmother taught me."

What could one do but laugh and then, for a timeless while, enjoy the delicious repartee of flirtation until, all too soon, it was time to leave. As I shook hands with the stranger, attraction sizzled between us like summer lightning. I turned as I left the flight deck and could see him, head and shoulders above everyone else, looking my way. He waved.

"We're meeting the Lancasters at the Straits View," said Philip as we drove out of the dockyard, "and they're bringing some friends."

Absorbed with thoughts of my brief encounter, I wasn't listening. Being so openly admired was a heady feeling and what is more it was a salve to my heart, still aching from the latest revelations about my husband.

We waited at the bar of the Straits View Hotel for the rest of our party to arrive until Joan exclaimed: "Oh, here they are," and, turning, who should I see in the group coming towards us but the object of my thoughts. He headed straight for me.

"What on earth are you doing here?" I whispered, as someone said: "oh Barbara, I see you've already met Jay."

"The Lancasters asked me," said Jay, "they're old friends. How about that? Now I really *do* believe in fate."

I felt myself reddening and looked away. A flirtation at a cocktail party was one thing, but now I could see I would have to be careful. We were seated round a large, circular table, about to order dinner, when Jay got up and asked the man beside me to change places.

"Well?" he said, seeing my embarrassment, "do you want me to sit next to you or not?"

Of course I did. For the rest of the evening we noticed no-one else. But I'm sure they noticed us. I learned a little about him. He was 27, an Old Harrovian, and his tour of duty in Singapore would end in a few month's time. He had one more year to serve in the RAF after which he planned to become a wild-life photographer, that being his passion. At the end of the evening he bent and kissed my cheek, black stubble grazing my skin, whispering in my ear:

"Would you like to have dinner with me one evening?"

"Yes," I said without a second's hesitation.

"Okay, I'll call you."

I spent a sleepless night, my mind in turmoil. Should I go out with this man if he asked me? My conscience told me it would be wrong but my ego answered: 'wrong or not, it doesn't seem to stop your husband. Here's your chance to get even.' Back and forth flew the debate but in the end, conscience won and I decided I would definitely say 'no' when – if - Jay called, which he did the very next day. He invited me out to dinner. And how did I respond?

"Oh, thank you, I'd love to."

For the two days before our date, the interior tussle went on:

'Thou - Shalt - Not - Commit - Adultery', intoned Conscience, with Old Testament sternness.

'Hey, you're jumping the gun, aren't you?' chuckled Ego, 'dinner's hardly adultery.'

Conscience: 'Cancel it *immediately.*'

Ego: 'Oh shut up, I'm going.'

We dined al fresco beside the sea, alone but for an old Chinese man in a tin shack who cooked us fish fresh from the ocean. Then we walked barefoot on the sands, the sea dark and mysterious, shallow waves swirling like cream about our ankles, tiny night creatures serenading us with their ceaseless music, the day's heat not yet spent. On that night began my romance with Jay, a passionate love affair which lasted just three months before he returned to England, which, for all that I knew it was wrong, healed me, reminding me that I was a desirable woman. Now, almost fifty years on, I remember it as a deeply romantic interlude, a transit of Venus set against the heady, exotic background of the tropics, reminding me of those days so long ago when I was young and, yes, beautiful.

In October 1963 we left Singapore. Our leaving was dramatic as a communist uprising had triggered a full-scale security alert and we were forced to travel from the barracks to the docks in an armoured convoy, driving through streets filled with sullen, threatening crowds.

Our voyage on the SS Chitral lacked the excitement and anticipation of the outward journey. We were desperately sad to leave Singapore, we would miss our countless friends, the easy way of life, the parties, the fun. Ahead lay the reality of a cold northern climate and a harder life. We had had our Swinging Sixties. Our Dolce Vita was over.

We were not looking forward to an English winter, not least because Lou-Lou's health was deteriorating. She had become pale and tired easily, squatting down and speaking in a breathless little voice. How would she fair without the tropical humidity and heat to ease the strain on her heart? I had consulted Dr Reg before we left who once again lived up to his title of 'worst doctor in the world' by giving me a huge jar containing 1000 penicillin tablets with instructions to give her one every day 'to ward off infection'. When I showed these to the ship's doctor, such was his disgust that he seized the jar, rushed to the nearest porthole and flung it into the sea.

A month later, we stood on Chitral's deck and saw the white cliffs of Dover, those gleaming sentinels which should stir the hearts of travellers returning to their native land. All I felt, though, was a sense of foreboding. What, I wondered, lay ahead? Fortunately, I did not know.

E I G H T

IT WAS TO GRANTCHESTER HOUSE that we returned on the 1st of November, 1963. The children were thrilled to be back. They adored their Grandmama and staying in a school where everything was child centred was paradise to them. As for Sarah, she was the best auntie in the world, never without a story, a game of make-believe, a picture to paint, a special place to explore. She was a constant source of fun, endlessly patient, endlessly loving. Sarah was a nurse, trained at St Thomas's Hospital, one of the elite 'Nightingales'. Now aged 25, she was a midwife and worked in a nearby suburb. One day she took the girls for a ride round the district.

"You know," she said, "I cycle all round here delivering babies."

There was silence from the back seat until a puzzled voice asked:

"But Auntie, how d'you get them all on the bike?"

The children might be happy but things weren't going so well for the adults. John had a long leave and I had anticipated we would stay with his mother for a couple of weeks before returning to our home on the south coast, which, now the tenants had left, stood empty. But it was not to be. The girls caught mumps but even after they recovered both John and his mother insisted we stay. This might have been alright if the school had not been in full swing, which meant that my mother-in-law worked all day yet, come the evening when she was clearly tired, would allow no-one to help her make the supper. The longer we stayed the more tetchy she became and, for some reason, I seemed to be the person who irritated her most. As we sat round the dining table she would suddenly make remarks about an anonymous somebody (clearly me) who had annoyed her in a variety of ways. How, for example, she despised liars:

"...the sort of person who says she was the Lord Mayor of Bristol's secretary when she was nothing but a filing clerk," whilst another unnamed person was vain and stupid as well as being so lazy that she expected her husband to keep her without lifting a finger. There was no answering back as she would gather up the dishes with a great clatter and we'd all hurry after her to the kitchen to help wash up in an atmosphere fraught with animosity.

The longer this continued the more nervous I became. In the back of my mind I knew she reminded me of someone, but who? Suddenly I got it; she was like Daphne, my hated stepmother – they were both unpredictable and it was this I could not bear.

As the days went by, I could feel the happy, confident, popular women who had returned from Singapore reverting to the nervous girl I had been during the Daphne years. What could I have done to make her dislike me so? Had we returned from the Far East older, worldlier, less in need of her motherly advice? Did she feel her hold on us loosen? Did she envy us our rather glamorous life in Singapore? Who knows.

There was a shocking cessation to this domestic tension when, on the 22nd November, 1963, John ran in from the pub to tell us that President John F Kennedy had been shot dead in Dallas, Texas. We sat glued to the television as the hideous scene was shown over and over again; the President waving from the back of his open-topped car, the fatal shot, Jackie Kennedy holding his dying body in her blood-splattered arms - not just us, but the whole world reeled from the horror of his assassination.

Soon, though, hostilities resumed between my mother-in-law and I, coming to a head when she leapt from her bedroom one morning, grabbing me by the shoulders, shaking me and screaming abuse in my face. Just as a moment came all those years ago when I had turned the tables on my hated stepmother, I now knew that enough was enough. I demanded of John that we return to our own home at once, but he refused. Finally, I rang my sister and asked if the girls and I could stay with her, and of course, she agreed. This caused uproar. John swore he would divorce me if I left and I rather wished he would. But I had made up my mind - I was going. My resolve lasted until our taxi arrived and I opened the door on a freezing, foggy world whilst behind me John, his mother and Sarah begged me not to take the children, particularly the delicate Lou-Lou, out into this terrible weather. I knew immediately that they were right and that I could not jeopardise my delicate daughter's health. So I stayed and a fragile armistice prevailed until we finally left. However, Lou-Lou remained with her grandmother, where she could go to school without having to leave the warmth of the house, and did not come home until the following spring.

Within a very short time we had sold our bungalow and bought a house in the pretty little coast town of Emsworh. Nothing could have been more different from the featureless estate in Waterlooville. The houses were ultra-modern in design and built round a central green where all the old trees remained. At the end of our little garden ran a stream and beyond it a marshy area where willow trees flourished. Best of all, we were just yards from the beautiful waters of Langstone Harbour. Oh, I told myself, we're going to be so happy here.

N I N E

I STOOD IN OUR GARDEN one April evening in 1964. The sky to the east was still faintly tinged with pink, the birds in the willows murmured and rustled as they settled down to sleep and I could hear the girls, my darlings, chattering happily in their bedroom. Soon I would go up and kiss them goodnight. But for a few more moments I wanted to savour the quiet sense of peace and happiness which filled my heart on this, my 27th birthday.

My parents had been down for the weekend, the adored Granddad working his little granddaughters into a frenzy, as he always did. Tiggy, as ever that kind, down-to-earth soul whose company I so enjoyed. I had even had a card from John and remembering birthdays was not his strongest suite.

He was now navigator of HMS Carysfort, which had sailed in March for naval manoeuvres in the Mediterranean. He had seemed genuinely sad at this latest parting as, since escaping from his mother's tyranny and moving to this delightful spot, we had been blissfully happy.

Before he left we had had a wonderful reunion with my brother Richard, who had now left the army and was working with his father. He had driven down from Gloucestershire to introduce his fiancée, a sulky girl we did not much care for. However, they were clearly deeply in love and that was what really mattered.

As we stood waving goodbye at the end of their visit, a terrible fear suddenly and inexplicably engulfed me.

"Oh," I said, "there's going to be an accident, I know it - Richard's going to die."

"Don't be silly," said John, putting his arm round me as we walked back into the house, "they'll be fine. But if you're worried, why don't you phone tonight and put your mind at rest?"

Oh, the relief, when I rang and learned that they were safely home. The spectre of Lou-Lou's failing health still hung over me like a pall but on this birthday evening, in my mood of happiness and optimism, I simply thanked God for all the good things in my life and prayed that one day soon she would be better.

Two days later the telephone rang:

"Hello, it's Dad."

"Oh Daddy," I cried, "what a lovely weekend we had, I..."

He interrupted me, his voice juddering with shock:

"Oh, Barbie, the most dreadful thing's happened – Richard's been in a terrible accident. They're operating on him now but they don't know if they can save him."

Oh God, oh God, my darling brother.

Somehow my poor father, stuttering and gasping, managed to tell me what had happened. Richard had been driving Dad's lorry back from Gloucester and was spotted by a police car crossing a double white line. The policeman pulled him over and they were standing between the car and the lorry when a huge articulated lorry - one of the new breed of juggernauts - careered round the corner on the wrong side of the road and smashed into them, throwing the two men high into the air. The policeman was killed instantly. My brother's life now hung in the balance. Richard survived the operation but the next morning my father called to say that he had died in the night.

"Daddy darling, I'll be down as soon as I can."

I rang off and leaned against the wall, my body shaking with the horror of it, my mind in freefall. No, no, it couldn't be true, not Richard, not our Dicky Doughnut, he couldn't be dead. But he was. His pure soul had departed leaving behind a beautiful young body smashed beyond recognition. The boy born on his mother's birthday 24 years ago, had now gone to join her.

Now my one coherent thought was 'John, I need John.' I sent him a cable: 'Richard killed in accident. Please come home.' I knew the Navy would fly him back on compassionate grounds and that, with him at my side, I would find the strength to support my poor dear father and Tiggy. However, there was silence from Gibraltar.

Before I left, I rang my mother-in-law who had not spoken to me since our falling out. I told her what had happened and there was a shocked pause. Then, in a strong, calm voice she said:

141

"Barbara, I am so, so sorry. I want you to know that whatever has come between us is over. I am here for you. Do you understand?"

My eyes filled with tears as I felt her strength and kindness pouring down the phone. I took the girls to stay with a friend and by the following day was on my way to Gloucestershire.

The next week passed in a haze of misery. My father stiff, unbending in his grief, afraid that if once he cried he would never stop; Tiggy grimly coping; Granny desolate at the loss of her beloved grandson; the poor little fiancée inconsolable, all her dreams dashed; the rest of the family grieving for the boy we all loved; the countless friends who jammed the church, the tears, the flowers, the tributes to this young man's generous heart, his loving spirit, his *joie de vivre*, all that he had been.

Then it was over and we who loved Richard had to try and pick up the threads of life. For my father this was well nigh impossible, for his son had lived at home, they had worked together and, of course, he had now lost not only his first wife but also his youngest child. He sank into depression and never fully recovered from the tragedy.

There was a trial. The lorry driver was fined one pound and banned from driving for life. My father was outraged by the apparent lenience of this sentence, the callous value placed on a human life and was consumed with hatred for the man who had killed his son. But there was a tragic codicil to this when, ten years later, a small paragraph in the paper reported the suicide of the lorry driver who had never forgiven himself for the deaths his carelessness had caused.

John rang me when I got home. He was sympathetic but there was something stilted about our conversation which worried me.

"Did you get my cable?" I asked.

"Yes", he said, "but I couldn't come home because we're on this NATO exercise."

"But surely they'd have given you compassionate leave?"

There was a slight pause and I guessed he had not even asked. I rang off, consoling myself with the thought that the ship would be back in Portsmouth in a month's time and then all would be well.

It wasn't. He was morose, snappy with the children, escaping to the pub even more often than usual, unwilling to talk about Richard's death for more than a few moments. Then one evening he sat in the kitchen, slumped, silent, grim, as I prepared supper. I couldn't bear it any more, I had to know what was wrong.

"What *is* the matter?" I asked, "you've been so odd since you got back. Just tell me what it is."

He stared at me for a moment then buried his head in his hands. Suddenly, as if he'd told me himself, I knew.

"You've met someone else, haven't you?"

He nodded. This was truly shocking. I knew there had been other women in his life, but liked to think they had all been passing fancies. I had found out about them by accident, by names and telephone numbers carelessly left about, by hints from other people, by abruptly finished phone calls, by his indiscrete and usually drunken boasting. He had always denied everything. Now he was telling the truth and I knew that this time it was different.

"Tell me about her."

He began to speak, his face suddenly animated, words tumbling out like a waterfall:

"Well, her name's Gillian and I'm, well, we've fallen in love. She's an army officer's wife and she's got four children. The youngest is only six months. Honestly, the sweetest little thing you've ever seen..."

Four children? A six month old baby? For God's sake, he was a bad enough father to his own kids, let alone someone else's.

"I know, I know, it all sounds terrible but the thing is, she's such *fun.*"

Such fun? Suddenly I was angry.

"Oh, such fun is she? So what do you want to do about it? Leave me? Go back to her for a bit more *fun*?"

"Yes," he said, his voice breaking.

"Well, if you're going, you can bloody well go right now."

He ran out of the kitchen and up the stairs, returning minutes later with his holdall. We stood in the hall, frozen in the moment, staring at each other.

"I'm sorry," he said.

Now we were both crying, our arms tight around each other for a brief moment before he broke away and walked out of our lives. We had been married for seven years.

As the door closed behind him I slid to the floor, howling, wailing, as the combined anguish of my brother's death and now my husband's desertion overwhelmed me. Sadness already weighed me down like a sack of stones and now this. What had happened to that boy and girl who'd fallen so deeply, achingly in love? What was it W. H. Auden wrote, albeit in another context? 'I thought that love would last forever: I was wrong.'

143

For the first time I acknowledged that, whereas getting married so young had worked for me, it was very different for him. To his credit he had never once shown resentment at our hurried wedding but now I could see that he was not ready to be tied down, could not, did not want, to handle the responsibility of a family. What is more, being a naval officer gave him the perfect out. Instead of being stifled by married life, he could sail away, forget us for a while and enjoy the freedom of a bachelor life. He had once been so deeply spiritual and yet this too seemed to have gone.

All my insecurities flooded to the surface. What was wrong with me? Dowdy? Clingy? Didn't much like pubs? Too tied up with my daughters? Was I as lazy as his mother insisted? Should I have got a job and not bothered about my fragile daughter? Was I boring? Dull instead of fun? Oh how that hurt, for the one thing I knew I could do, indeed wanted to do, was make people laugh, make them happy. And over and above these thoughts, the spectre of my own affair with Jay stabbed at my conscience and hissed: 'it serves you right.'

Suddenly I smelt cooking – I'd forgotten that dish in the oven. Hoping they would not notice my red eyes, I called the girls in for supper.

"Where's Daddy gone?" they asked.

"Oh he's been called back to his ship."

"But he didn't even say goodbye."

In the days that followed, during the sleepless nights, the pale dawns when sorrow renewed itself for the coming day, I tried to put my emotional turmoil to one side and turn my mind to practical considerations - like money. We had separate bank accounts and John had always paid the school fees. I sent him the latest bill which was promptly returned without a note. It was then I realised I was truly on my own. What's more I was broke. My father had given me Richard's prized Borgward car, so I sold the glamorous but useless Austin Atlantic we had foolishly bought (pale metallic blue with squashy red leather seats and terminal engine trouble) and got a temporary secretarial job at the local sailing school. And, although I told my mother-in-law and friends that John had gone, I did not tell my father what had happened because I didn't want 'I told you so' ringing in my ears.

Emotionally I was a mess, either shouting at the dear children or crying in front of them, spoiling them or burdening their little minds with my worries, alternately hating John, cursing the day we'd met, or willing to forgive anything if only he'd come back.

One evening a couple of months later he rang.

"What do you want?" I asked coldly.

"Can I come home?" he asked and immediately I succumbed,

But at soon as he was back I found I could not contain my rage and resentment. He, on the other hand, was furious that I had sold his car. For three days we shouted and argued until once again he walked out, no doubt glad to get away from this harridan and back to the mother of four, who, he had charmingly confided, was "like a sack of potatoes in bed".

But I had to put all this behind me and deal with an even graver crisis. Mary-Louise's health was deteriorating. Now she was always tired, squatting breathless and blue-lipped. It was hard to watch, heartbreaking when she gasped:

"When I …grow up I…want to be a…ballet-dancer."

I had begged Great Ormond Street to operate, but although there was now a procedure to correct Fallot's Tetralogy, it was still in its infancy and they wanted to wait for the optimum moment which would give her the best chance. There was some progress when, in July, she was admitted to hospital so that they could carry out a cardiac catheterisation which would determine the exact nature of the abnormalities in her heart. A fine catheter would be inserted into an artery in her groin and guided into the vessels of her heart. This procedure, I was told, was not without risk but the hospital had performed it countless times and had never had a problem.

But, in Lou-Lou's case, something went dreadfully wrong, precipitating her to the verge of heart-failure. She was put in an oxygen tent and connected to a ventilator. For hour after hour, through an endless night, I sat beside her, watching the ventilator's movements, holding my own breath when the pump seemed to hesitate, certain that her heart had stopped.

"You had better get her father here," said the ward sister next morning. I knew what that meant and felt sick with fear. HMS Carysfort was in Portsmouth but when I rang, the officer of the watch sounded cagey and, clearly knowing we had separated, told me that Lieutenant Watson was unavailable.

"But this is urgent," I said, "his daughter is very ill."

"I'll see he gets your message," was all he said.

But although I rang the ship again and again John did not call back Then I contacted the Admiralty but was passed from one department to another until at last I gave up. Next I called SAAFA (the Soldiers, Sailors and Airmen's Association). Surely this charity would help me?

"What rank's your husband, dear?" asked a woman in a voice so bored I could imagine her with the receiver tucked under her chin whilst she filed her nails.

"He's a lieutenant."

"Oh, we don't deal with *officers*," she said as though talking about a contagious disease, "only ratings. Sorry love."

Oh, thanks very much.

Finally, I did what I should have done in the first place and called my mother-in-law.

"Can't get hold of him?" she said grimly, "just you leave it to me."

The next day he walked into the ward, handsome and debonair. I glared at him over the oxygen tent:

"You bastard," I hissed, "to think you had to be dragged back to your own daughter's sickbed. I don't just hate you, I *despise* you."

He had no reply but several days later, when Lou-Lou's life was out of danger, her father and I left the hospital, John to catch a train back to Portsmouth and me to Esher, where my mother-in-law and Sarah waited, bastions of kindness, strength and comfort, caring for Victoria in my absence. Before John left, we agreed that this was no time for enmity. He told me the Gibraltar romance was over and all he wanted was to come home. Hard though it seemed, hard though it would be, we were once again struggling towards reconciliation. This, we both knew, was not for our sakes but for our children.

After this brush with death Mary-Louise's condition worsened and the hospital decided they must bring forward her operation, which they scheduled for the beginning of October. Now more than ever aware that she might not survive, I did not want little Victoria to suffer any of the stress and sadness that lay ahead. I asked Joan and Philip Barker, our Singapore neighbours who now lived near us, if she could stay with them for a month and, dear souls that they were, they immediately agreed. Then Lou-Lou and I went to Grantchester House to await the day I both longed for and dreaded.

More tests were carried out and then Mr Waterson, the surgeon who would be heading the team, spelled out the risks. His message was stark and uncompromising – they had only recently started carrying out full repairs of Fallots Tetralogy and there was a high risk of mortality. So far they had operated on seven children and four of them had died. I immediately lost my nerve and said I didn't want him to proceed.

"In that case she will not live much longer."

Now there was no turning back although, to add to the tension, the operation was twice delayed. Her seventh birthday came and went but at last, at the beginning of November, she was admitted and a day set for the operation.

"It will take all day," the ward sister told me, "so you and your husband must be here by 7a.m."

HMS Carysfort was now on exercise in the Atlantic, somewhere off the Irish coast. I sent John a cable asking him to come home for the operation and received a reply which said:

"Explain reason why my presence needed, soonest."

Why was he needed? Sickened, I didn't bother to answer. That evening he rang on a ship-to-shore radio. He couldn't come back, he explained patiently, because: "...a ship can't sail without a navigator." Oh, *now* I understood; we couldn't possibly let his daughter's life-or-death operation impede the efficiency of the Royal Navy.

The day before the operation, the ward sister once again reminded me that we should arrive early.

"Well, I'll be here but my husband can't come."

"But he's *got* to come," she insisted, "we can't go ahead unless you're both here."

And I knew why. If Lou-Lou should die, both parents needed to be there to support each other. I stared at her, my nerves a-jangle, then burst into tears.

"What's the matter," she said, "what's going on?"

"It's not that he *can't* come – he *won't*."

This wonderful, calm, angel of a woman's face darkened with anger.

"Won't come, eh? We'll see about that. *I'll* bloody well make him come."

She rang the Admiralty and this time they sprang into action. John was winched off Carysfort by helicopter and flown to Shannon airport where a plane was standing by to take him to London. A waiting car then sped him to the hospital. He strode in like a hero.

Lou-Lou's favourite toy was a boy-doll called Timothy, soft bodied and cuddly. The night before her operation, she 'operated' on Timothy, cutting his chest open and 'making him better' with a sticking plaster. Seeing this, I realised that her little mind had quite a keen understanding of what lay ahead.

Leaving her that night was the worst moment of my life. As we left the ward, we looked back at her one last time, sitting up in bed with

Timothy in her arms, countless wires attached to her head (and some for boy-doll) which would monitor her brain function the following day. As we walked out into the night, I was certain I would never see her alive again. I felt faint, near to collapse, my legs buckling. John and my mother-in-law half-carried me into the nearest pub where we ordered brandies. We all needed them. My mother-in-law and John were ashen and, when I caught my reflection in a mirror, I saw an old woman.

We arrived the next morning in time to kiss her as she lay sleepily on the trolley, clutching Timothy in her arms, then watched as she was wheeled away to the operating theatre. And then the long wait began. Now that he was here and could see - had been forced to face - the gravity of the situation, John stepped up to the mark and was the tower of strength I had longed for. Hours passed. We sat there in silence, pretending to read, jumping every time the door opened, trying not to visualise her sternum being sawn open, her rib cage levered apart...

After what seemed an age Mr Waterson appeared:

"Well," he said, "we've got her on the by-pass machine so she's safe for the moment. If you want to go out for a while, do it now."

We knew this meant that our daughter's heart had been stopped and her blood was now being circulated through the machine. The minutes, the endless hours, ticked on and on as we waited, hardly daring to breath, to hope, I prayed an endless mantra:

"Please God don't let her die, please God don't let her die, please God..."

Not until six o'clock did the surgeon re-appear. He looked exhausted.

"It's over," he said, "we've re-started her heart and..."

We leapt joyfully to our feet, but he held up a restraining hand.

"No, don't get too excited, we've still a long way to go. During the operation the by-pass machine was doing all the work, but now she's on her own and we have to wait and see whether her heart can cope. She'll be back in intensive care soon and you'll be able to see her."

"Oh, thank you so, so much," I gasped, even though the words seemed utterly inadequate.

We waited on a balcony where children's beds had been pushed to watch a firework display and all of a sudden we realised it was Bonfire Night. The children squealed happily at every bang and flash, but to us it only added a surreal element to this nightmare day.

Later, we were shown into the room where our little girl lay, a tiny figure linked to banks of monitors, her naked body festooned with needles, catheters and drainage tubes, a blood transfusion dripping slowly into her arm, an oxygen mask over her face, a broad dressing down the centre of her chest. The bed was surrounded by medical staff and the window was open to the cold night air to keep her body cool – it was an utterly shocking sight. But as we stood there her eyes opened and suddenly the fingers of one hand moved slightly – she'd seen us, she was waving!

This pioneering operation, undertaken by two surgeons with a twenty-two-strong team, had taken eleven hours. During that time, twenty-four pints of blood had been used. In the days and weeks that followed, she moved slowly, often painfully, towards recovery until at last I heard those longed-for words "you can take her home". It was an indescribable joy to walk out of the hospital with her, knowing that this terrible ordeal was over. Although she was thin, frail and pale, she was no longer blue. She had made it! Her heart was no longer 'broken' - and nor was mine.

A few weeks later, something happened which emphasised the tragically thin line dividing life from death, joy from sorrow. During my daily train journey to the hospital I had met a woman who not only lived in Hinchley Wood but who, by an extraordinary coincidence, had a little girl, Heather, who was also awaiting a heart operation in Great Ormond Street, although for a less serious abnormality. Indeed, the two children's beds were next to each other and they became friends.

A few weeks after Lou-Lou's discharge, en route for her first check-up, I drove past the local church and saw a small white coffin being lifted out of a hearse and carried into the church. It was Heather's funeral, for she had died of complications following her operation.

"Mummy," asked my little girl, "what's in that box?"

We returned to Emsworth in December. Instead of leaving Victoria for a month, we had been away for nearly three. I had written, called, sent little presents, and Joan had constantly assured me that all was well. Now I was walking up the path for the longed-for reunion, a waif-like Lou-Lou at my side. The front door opened and Victoria flew out and into my arms. But the bonnie little girl I'd left had disappeared, replaced by a white, stick-thin child, her eyes shadowed and anxious. I looked over her head at Joan, both our faces taut with pain.

"I'm *so, so* sorry," said this dear and wonderful friend, "you had enough on your plate I just couldn't bring myself to tell you."

For Victoria had lost her appetite, woken screaming from

nightmares, crying for her Mummy, even sleep walking. Now she looked even frailer than her sister. I was consumed with guilt.

Early one morning, just before Christmas, I lay in bed, my two pale, skinny girls tucked in my arms. The question *du jour* was whether I thought Santa would come.

"Yes, of *course* he'll come," I said, "and what's more, I bet you'll get extra special presents this year because he'll have heard what brave girls you've both been."

Three weeks had passed since the three of us had returned home and now I tightened my arms about them, thanking God that 1964 - this year from hell - had come to an end, a year when my emotions had ricocheted from one extreme to the other, from happiness to happiness, pausing on the way for grief and jealousy, sorrow and despair, apprehension and fear, to take their turn. So immersed was I in the dramas of family life that the rest of the world had passed me by. I scarcely noticed when Nelson Mandela was sentenced to life imprisonment or the escalation and pointless savagery of the Vietnam War. The Pope condemned oral contraceptives, mini-skirts appeared for the first time, Beatles mania reached a crescendo, the death sentence was abolished - all this went over my head. Now, as 1965 approached, I could once again give thanks not only for the miraculous operation which had saved my daughter's life, but that my marriage appeared to have survived and we were once again a united family.

"I love you Mummy," said Victoria, snuggling in.

"Oh do you darling, why's that?"

"Because you're warm."

T E N

IT WAS FEBRUARY, 1965. Both girls were happily settled in school, Mary-Louise now stronger than she had ever been, and I realised that I could safely look for a full-time job. I saw an advertisement for a school secretary at a primary school and, having reached the short list, was called for interview.

Afterwards, I sat with the other applicants nervously awaiting the outcome. At last a lady emerged to announce that Mrs X had been successful, adding "but will Mrs Watson stay behind." Stay behind? I was instantly swept back to my school days. Was I about to be accused of forging my references and given a hundred lines? I was ushered in to confront the Board once again.

"Mrs Watson," said the Chairman, "We feel you would make a very good teacher. Have you ever considered teaching as a career?"

Then, whilst I was still catching my breath, she told me that a member of staff had fallen ill, they couldn't find a replacement and consequently had a vacancy. If I was interested, I could start the following week on a month's trial.

"But I'm not trained," I stuttered, "I wouldn't know what to do."

"Oh, don't worry you'll get all the help you need."

Yes, I know it sounds unbelievable, but it happened, and the following Monday morning found me in a classroom on a tough housing estate with forty six-year-old dervishes whirling and shrieking around me. After the first day as I staggered into bed exhausted, I was prepared to give up. After the first week, I realised I loved it, even though chaos still reigned. After the trial month - with the constant help of the headmistress and other teachers who popped in and out of the classroom to guide and encourage me, and help me prepare lessons - order and calm were restored. More to the point I could see that the children were happily learning. By the end of my second term I had been give a one-year contract as an unqualified teacher at a big primary school on nearby Hayling Island and then was accepted for teacher-training at Bishop Otter College in Chichester.

How different teacher training was in the 1960's. At Bishop Otter we studied child psychology and child development, we learned about history's great educators, we had endless opportunities to improve ourselves through academic subjects and every possible creative art. What we never found out, though, was *how* and *what* we should be teaching. No, we were told, this would stifle our own creativity as teachers as well as placing limitations on the children. Our task was to create a rich and varied environment in which children would want to learn. French education with its rigid curriculum was held up as a stern reminder. It might be a good way to instil rote learning, or 'chalk and talk' as they called it, but was in every other way stifling. We were encouraged to cast aside such parameters and think for ourselves. One particular maths lecturer extolled the virtues of allowing children the freedom to calculate using, say, eight as a base number.

"Er, excuse me," I said, rising hesitantly from my seat in the big lecture hall, "how does this help children if they then have to conform to society's norm, like buying a bus ticket? Wouldn't it confuse them?"

He stared at me in utter disdain for a moment before snapping: "Sit down, woman, I really don't know why people like you are at this college."

Thus, when we were out on teaching practise in local primary schools, my fellow students and I, like drowning souls, grabbed at every idea, every teaching method we saw. I realised then how fortunate I was to have had actual teaching experience. What I already knew and what my fellow students now saw in schools was that, however casual things might seem, a teacher's principle task was to ensure that children became literate and numerate, for without these basic building blocks of learning, no child can flourish. There appeared to be no guidelines, no supervision of what and how teachers taught and although, as I saw for myself, most teachers were doing a wonderful job, the system allowed the lazy and apathetic to slip through the net. It seems to me that somewhere between the easy-going 1960's and the strict curriculum still in operation as I write, lies a happy medium where guidelines and assessments exist but where teachers have the freedom to use their own creativity, imagination and knowledge of individual children's needs to create a perfect learning and teaching environment.

I left Bishop Otter as one of the few students to gain a Distinction and, even better, with a job at Emsworth Primary School, only a mile from our home.

"D'you know what, Mummy, now you're a teacher you're not half as grumpy as you used to be," said Lou-Lou one evening.

"Oh, thank you very much, darling," said the former grump.

I found teaching very, very hard work. Other than reading schemes, we had no printed material on which to draw and were expected to make an ever-changing collection of work cards and teaching materials for other subjects. I never had less than forty children in my class and there was no such thing as a teaching assistant. One had to be highly organised, setting tasks for groups of children according to their ability whilst at the same time tackling the constant battle of hearing each child read.

My classroom in Emsworth was a prefabricated hut set away from the main school and about 50 yards from a railway line. One playtime, a little boy came sobbing to tell me that so-and-so had thrown his Action Man onto the roof. I borrowed a ladder from the caretaker, set it against the classroom wall and clambered up. As I balanced precariously on the top, trying to retrieve the wretched toy just out of reach on the filthy roof, a train rumbled past. I saw faces staring at me from the windows and for a moment reflected on the unglamorous nature of my job. It was but a passing thought, however, for to me teaching was the most wonderful, the most fulfilling job in the world. When a struggling child learns to read, or writes a few lines, or suddenly grasps the basics of number. When a clever child exceeds one's expectations. When a silent child opens up, a sad child confides. When a class laughs together, sings and dances together, creates together. That is learning. That is the joy.

TALES FROM THE CLASSROOM

Whilst at college I took a group of children from the East End of London to the seaside. As we watched the seagulls wheeling above the waves, I explained that birds have very light, strong, hollow bones which make it easier for them to fly. There was silence for a moment then one little boy said: 'Cor, 'e's bloody marvellous in 'e, old God?'

153

Luke was the local Methodist minister's son. He was a quiet little chap who rarely wanted to share his news with the class. So when he whispered one day that he had something important to say, I asked the children to stop what they were doing and listen. Luke turned his chair round and clambered onto the seat. Gripping the back of it, he bent his head in apparent prayer before leaning over and surveying his congregation from left to right. Then he began his sermon:

'Good morning evwybody. Many of you will have heard of my dog, Topsy. Well, you will be vewy sowwy to hear that she's got twouble wiv her waterworks.'

Then he climbed down and got on with his writing.

****

As any primary school teacher will tell you, Christmas sees a frenzy of activity in school: making cards and presents, decorating classrooms, the carol service, parties and so on. The highlight, of course, is the annual nativity play. One year I decided it would be fun to put on a nativity with a difference, using puppets made by the children. On the appointed afternoon, the mothers trooped in and the show began. However, all was not well in Bethlehem for a squabble quickly broke out between Mary and Joseph, the latter solving the problem by beating ten bells out of the Virgin and Child. Two of the Wise Men, perhaps remembering Punch & Judy shows they had seen, joined in and soon papier mache heads were rolling into the audience. Chaos ensued, the Virgin Mary burst into tears and the curtain was rung down. Never again, I thought.

****

Another Christmas I decided to ask Brian, a quiet, withdrawn boy, if he would like to be Joseph as I felt it would boost his confidence Yes, he said, he would. However, by the time the third rehearsal had taken place, it was clear I had made a big mistake, for just standing up in front of his classmates almost paralysed him with nerves and I could see that it would be agonising for him to perform in front of an audience.

"Would you rather be a shepherd?" I asked.

"Oh yes please!" he gasped with palpable relief.

The next day his mother arrived in the classroom, a red-faced *virago dragging Brian by the wrist. How dare I do this to her boy? He was so disappointed he'd cried himself to sleep. I was a right cow, I shouldn't be let anywhere near kids because I didn't know bugger-all about them. And anyway what about her, eh? Had I stopped to think how she felt? She'd told everyone Brian was going to be Joseph and now all he was was a bloody shepherd with a bloody tea-towel on his head. Whilst she ranted on in this vein, Brian stood beside her, mortified by the fuss, near to tears. I suggested we go and see the headmaster to sort this out but she swept off, following up the next day with a five-page letter to the Head. I was guilt-ridden. Had the poor little fellow really cried himself to sleep?*

"I'm very, very sorry, Brian, you know I didn't mean to upset you. How would you like to be one of the Wise Men's pages?"

"Oh no," he said, "I want to be a shepherd."

****

The Christmas story obviously intrigued Peter.

"Was Jesus the son of God?" he asked.

"Yes, that's what the Bible tells us."

"So God was his Dad?"

"Um...," I said, feeling unequal to the task of explaining the Holy Trinity.

"And Mary was his mother?"

"Er, yes," I said cautiously, guessing where this was going.

"But wasn't she married to Joseph?"

"Well, yes she was."

"Well then," he said and, giving me a nudge-nudge-wink-wink sort of look, he went back to his desk.

****

It was the last day of term and my class was noisy and excitable at the thought of the holidays ahead. With an hour 'til home-time, I decided to settle them down with a story and soon they were engrossed in the tale, although, as usual, Robert - constantly naughty, always adorable - was causing a disturbance and, also as usual, the ghost of Joyce Grenfell hovered above me:

"...so later that day – Robert - the Knight decided to search for Princess Crystal. Perhaps she was lost deep in the forest – wasn't she Robert? - but as he rode into a clearing what should he see but – Robert,

155

will you please stop that – *but a fearsome dragon with huge* - Robert, will you be quiet - *now where was I, oh yes, with flames pouring from his nostrils. So the Knight drew his trusty sword and galloped forward, for he knew the princess's life was in danger and* – oh, for goodness sake, Robert, now what?"

"*Miss,*" *said the boy sitting next to him,* "*Robert's crying.*"

"*Crying? Robert, what's the matter?*"

"*He's got a bead stuck up his nose, Miss,*" *said the spokesman. Robert's muffled sobs now became a roar.*

"*A bead stuck up his nose? Robert come here and let me look.*"

I peered cautiously up his small, runny nostrils and sure enough, there was a red bead lodged at the top. Immediate action was clearly required so I took a hairgrip out of my hair and carefully pushed it up the tiny orifice. The rest of the class leaned forward, for this real live drama was better than any story.

"*Now children* – *stop crying Robert, it'll be alright* – *now children, I'm sure you all know it is VERY SILLY INDEED to put a bead up your nose, don't you?.*"

"*Yes...Mrs...Wat...son,*" *they chanted.*

"*...and of course if you should accidentally put a bead up your nose, you should never, never try to get it out yourself as that could be very dangerous. No, no, don't worry Robert, hold still, I've nearly got it.*"

But then, disaster, for just as I was about to retrieve the errant bead it disappeared into unknown territory. En route for the brain? Oh help! I ran into the next room, gabbled an explanation to the teacher with a request to look after my class, grabbed Robert's hand and raced to my car. Within minutes we were at the nearby Cottage Hospital where a doctor, wielding what looked like a long-handled crochet hook, swiftly retrieved the bead. I congratulated him, adding that I had had no luck trying to get it out with my hairpin.

"*I hope you realise that that was VERY SILLY INDEED?*" *said the doctor severely.   Robert gave me an accusing look.*

****

John had written to say that whilst on patrol in the Persian Gulf, his ship had captured an Arab dhow loaded with munitions – gunrunners.   He had headed a boarding party which overcame the armed crew and then sailed the dhow back into harbour where the hapless men were handed over to

156

the authorities. In school next morning I said:

"Well children I've got something exciting to tell you. My husband is a sailor and he and some other sailors caught ten pirates who had lots of guns in their boat."

'What happened to the pirates?" someone asked.

"Oh, I expect they had to go to prison," I said vaguely.

"Yeah," piped up a knowledgeable voice, "they caught my Dad an' give 'im five years."

****

It was often when children were recounting their 'news' that one got the clearest insight into what their home lives were like. None was more dramatic than Ann, a waif of a child who, skinny and shabbily dressed, looked like an advertisement for a children's charity. Yet she was a happy, confident little girl, and I somehow felt her home was a happy one, if a bit on the wild side. Her mum, like many women on the estate, worked at a factory producing women's sanitary items or, as the kids called it, 'up the Tampax'.

Whenever Ann announced that she had news to tell, a frisson of excitement ran round the classroom and an expectant silence fell until, taking a deep breath, our little drama queen was off at breakneck speed:

"Well, Saterdee our Dad gets drunk. Our Mum starts shoutin' you're nuffin' but a boozer, our Dad frows 'is beer at our Mum, our Mum 'its our Dad, our Dad 'its our Mum, our Mum starts screamin', our nipper runs upstairs and gets inna bed wiv our baby, I runs next door'n gets our Nan, our Nan comes runnin' in, our Nan 'its our Dad wiv 'er 'andbag, our Dad 'its our Nan, our Nan says keep yer 'ands off me mate, our Mum shouts quick run downa pub 'n get our Billy, I runs downa pub 'n gets our Billy, our Billy runs back, 'e 'its our Dad, our Dad falls over 'n 'its 'is 'ead onna telly, our Dad starts bleedin', our Mum shouts now lookit me carpet, our Nan shouts quick calla amblance, our Mum shouts no calla cops…"

When at last the saga ends, we all sink back and a hush falls over the classroom

"Cor," says a little voice, "I wish I lived up your 'ouse."

I met Ann's parents when they came to an Open Evening and it was clear they were devoted to their daughter. As they left, her Dad paid me an enormous compliment: "Our Ann loves it in your class. You can 'it 'er all you like."

157

I had just started teaching at Emsworth Primary School when John received that most sought-after of postings - two and a half years at HMS Mercury, the navy's communications school which was based in the beautiful Hampshire village of East Meon, an easy drive from Emsworth. So began a period which was the nearest we ever got to normal family life. Oh, how wonderful to be ordinary, just like millions of other families, both of us working, bringing up our children, enjoying a simple social life, visiting our families, going on holiday, arguing, loving, laughing. There were no desperate dramas, no partings, no infidelities, no resentments. And it was in this outwardly mundane life that we found happiness. The boy I had married seemed to re-emerge and I found myself hoping that he need never go to sea again.

The girls too loved life in Emsworth, where they not only made lots of friends but also had both countryside and the seashore as their playgrounds. It was now that Lou-Lou, who had been in perfect health since her heart operation, developed a special rapport with elderly people and had several old folk she used to visit regularly. The strangest of these was an ancient lady who had once been a Baptist missionary in India and who lent her religious tracts and books about saintly children who converted the heathen masses. The old soul was obsessed with the thought that she had fleas and so cut her hair into a jagged, half bald helmet and gave her head a daily dowsing with disinfectant. She was an odd friend for a child of eight or nine, but a sweet and harmless one. We did not then know that one day Lou-Lou's affinity with old people, the compassion for others she showed so early on, would play a key part in her professional life.

Because of her heart problem and the drama of her operation, Lou-Lou seemed to have been the centre of attention in the family. Added to this, she was also proving to be a very bright child, often top of her class, receiving countless prizes on Speech Day and made a prefect at the first opportunity.

Victoria, on the other hand, although just as bright, was a bit of a maverick who had her own ideas on what she liked, the subjects she was prepared to work hard at and those which did not interest her. This did not sit well with the staff at her old-fashioned girls' school who could not fault her intelligence but preferred conformity. (One of her teachers wrote on her report: 'Victoria appears to think she is entitled to short rests'!) We decided that something was needed which would allow her to develop her greatest talent – music. For, from the moment she could talk she could sing, humming in a sweet, high voice and in perfect tune. Both her granddad and grandmother had pianos from which, when visiting them, she could not be torn and on which her tiny fingers wandered, untrained yet in total harmony. What she wanted more than anything in the world was a 'nanno' and on her eighth birthday, her generous grandmother made this dream come true.

The day after the piano was delivered she had a cold and could not go to school. I, on the other hand, had a class of forty waiting for me and so – with the guilt and divided loyalty which every working mother will recognise – asked my neighbour to keep an eye on her and went to work. I rushed home at lunch time to find her engrossed at the piano and when I came back at the end of the afternoon, she was waiting at the door.

"Quick, Mummy, come and listen", she cried, rushing to the piano, "I've written a song."

I stood beside her, loyally ready to applaud whatever she'd done, but to my astonishment she sang a poignant song about a soldier saying farewell to his sweetheart, knowing he will never return. The accompaniment, played with both hands, was different to the melody she sang. It was at that moment I knew she had inherited the music gene from both sides of the family and had a true gift from God. Piano classes were quickly arranged and from then on she blossomed, both as a musician and a singer, developing a voice with an extraordinary range most unusual in such a young child. Her cousin, Lydia, was equally musically gifted and one day my sister took the two girls to a Promenade Concert at the Royal Albert Hall, where they heard Yehudi Menuhin perform. Afterwards, they went to the stage door in the hope of getting his autograph and as he signed her programme, Victoria graciously told him that she thought he had played 'quite well'.

"How kind of you to say so," said one of the world's greatest violinists

She had also inherited her father's wit and, another unexpected accomplishment, she was a mimic. Whilst her teachers might have been pleased to see her concentrating on what they were saying, they would not have known that she was studying their speech patterns and body language. Then, come the evening, she would put on a show, appearing from behind the sitting room curtains to deliver a wickedly accurate impression of her latest victim.

One Christmas term the school announced a talent competition which the girls decided to enter. After much discussion we hit upon an idea which we were sure would be a winner – their act would be called Last Night of the Proms. Every year we loved watching this on television, particularly the bit at the end when a lady with big hair and bigger bosoms sang 'Rule Britannia' in a ringing contralto voice. Our preparations began. I made Victoria, who was now nine, a royal blue satin dress, which, with a wig, loads of jewellery and some judicious stuffing down her vest, looked suitably over the top. To make her as tall as possible, she balanced on her sister's shoulders, with the dress's floor-length skirt covering them both. She perfected the anthem in her deepest, fruitiest voice and every time she sang, we laughed until we cried. Oh, this would bring the house down!

And so to the concert. On went the Watson girls and Victoria gave of her best, but as they were about to exit left, Mrs Luxford, the headmistress, leapt to her feet and in her deep Margaret Thatcher voice cried:

"Encore! Encore! All together girls, join in!"

Victoria, realising she had a hit on her hands, threw herself into the role, flinging her arms wide, swaying from side to side whilst beneath her skirt, the hapless Lou-Lou staggered under her load. On and on went the performance until at last, to thunderous applause, the audience let them go. No-one laughed at all - they thought it was serious.

That evening Mrs Luxford rang me:

"Mrs Watson," she said, "your daughter's performance was one of the most inspiring things I've seen in my life. I was moved to tears."

"That's strange," I said, "so was I."

Another naval couple lived next door to us and their two daughters, Sally and Gillian, went to school with our girls and became good friends. Equally, their mother Irene and I became very close. One day Mary-Louise and Sally rushed into the house.

"There's a donkey derby on next week and we're going to go in for it!" they cried.

Lou-Lou was so excited in the days before the event that she could hardly sleep. But at last the great day dawned and immaculately attired in new cream trousers, a borrowed velvet riding hat pulled well down over her curls, we set forth. This may just have been a donkey derby in a nearby field but she was taking the event as seriously as the Horse of the Year Show and there was a look of steely determination on her little face as she selected her mount. He was knocked of knee and withered of shank, and had a nasty gleam in his eye. I think his name was Lucky. But to Lou-Lou, he was an Arab stallion. Soon they were under starter's orders and then they were off - and, oh dear, so was my girl, landing with a bump whilst the rest of the field galloped on. But up she leapt, raced after him, hurled herself aboard and clung on grimly until, seconds later, Lucky did his bucking bronco act again and off she fell. And so it continued as the other seven children and their steeds disappeared towards the winning post - she fell off, she raced to catch up, she clambered back onboard, he flung her off again, she hurled herself across the saddle, she slide off the other side... But finally, heroically, sobbing, bruised, velvet cap over one eye, our girl crossed the finishing line. Yes, she was last, but she'd made it. To me it was still incredible that she no longer gasped for breath and was as active as any other child. I rushed to gather up my wounded heroine, not knowing whether to laugh or cry.

Whilst we were engrossed in this drama, Irene and I had not noticed that Gillian and Victoria had disappeared, off down at the end of the field where a small fun fair had been set up. Once we had found them, we all hurried home so that I could pop poor, bruised Lou-Lou into the bath.

A week or so later the four girls came to find me.

"Torla and Gilly have got something to tell you," said Sally mysteriously. And out came a tale which made my blood run cold. One of the men at the funfair had befriended the two little girls and given them sweets and free rides. Then he had shown them his car parked behind the fair and asked if they would like to go for a drive with him. Oh my God.

"Well, thank goodness you didn't," I said calmly.

"Well, I wanted to go 'cos he was really nice, but Gilly wouldn't let me," piped up Victoria.

Irene and I rang the police, and two women officers arrived at the house. The older, a sergeant, gently encouraged the girls to tell their tale and, feeling very important, they vied with each other to give the best description of the man, the colour of his car and so on. She nodded at each new twist to the tale until they came to a halt.

"Is that all?" she asked, "you can't remember anything else?"
No, they said. And then she let them have it. In a very quiet, calm voice she told them just how silly, how stupid they were. Liked him had they? Did they expect bad men to have horns and flashing lights on their heads? Did they realise they could have been taken away and never seen again? Never see their homes again, their mummies and daddies, their family, their friends. Bad things could have been done to them. Soon they were both sobbing until at last she told them to cheer up but never to forget what she had said. A week later she rang to say they had arrested a man at a fun fair further down the coast, the same outfit which had been at the donkey

derby. The girls' description had been very helpful in linking him to actual assaults on children.

John had been at HMS Mercury for eighteen months when he came home with bad news - he was going to sea again, this time in HMS Hampshire. The man originally appointed had been withdrawn from the posting on compassionate grounds and John was to take his place. This meant we would lose a whole year of our time together and we were both terribly upset. We knew the officer he was replacing and so I rang him, hoping that nothing too awful had happened.

"Oh, it's just that I couldn't face leaving my family," he said when I asked him why he had pulled out. I was outraged.

"You couldn't bear to leave your family? Well, guess what, now John has to leave his. Do you think *he* can bear it?" Do you think *we* can?"

I had never known John so reluctant to leave us and, after eighteen months of domestic happiness, I was heartbroken. But go he did and I found myself one sad morning driving away from Portsmouth Dockyard, half-blinded by tears and, as I had so many times before, preparing to face life without him. Oh please God, I prayed, please don't let anything go wrong this time.

E L E V E N

TIME PASSES, OF COURSE, and after a long period without him, the girls and I joined the other families on the quayside for yet another happy homecoming. The following weekend whilst John was at the pub, I decided to tidy our box room which was jammed with the possessions he had brought back from the ship. As I worked my way through - hanging up clothes, sorting out books, filling the laundry basket – I came across a cardboard carton full of letters and recognised my writing.

"Oh, how sweet," I thought, "he's kept all my letters."

I sat down on the floor to read a few but quickly realised that most of the envelopes were addressed in unknown hands. I opened one. 'My darling John,' it started and, to my horror, I found myself reading a love letter. I read another and another, each from a different woman and from a different place, enabling me to trace John's conquests round the world: Gibraltar of course, Malta, Singapore, Hong Kong, Japan, New Zealand, Australia, Brazil, Chile... The Hong Kong correspondent was particularly effusive. Written on thick cream notepaper bearing a Hilton Hotel crest, she addressed him as her 'Dearest Mr Owl Eyes' and apparently it was his luxuriant eye lashes which turned her on. It was also clear that they had known each other for some years.

Each new letter just added to my pain but although I knew I should stop reading them, I couldn't. When I got to the bottom of the box I carried it downstairs and arranged the letters into piles, one for each member of his fan club. There were thirteen. Unlucky for me but clearly not for him. My own letters I threw into the dustbin.

My discovery was a hideous shock. So he had had umpteen affairs? No surprise there. In fact there was part of me which understood that, for men away from their wives for months, even years at a time, other women were perhaps a natural response to human desires. Indeed, I had seen this for myself in Singapore. No, what added to my pain was the fact that, as in the past, he did not seem to care whether I found out or not Did these women mean so much to him that he not only kept all their letters but had also carried on lengthy correspondences? No wonder he only had time to write to me rarely – and to his children precisely once. And as he carried the box into our home didn't he stop to think that not only were its contents highly incriminating but that when I found it, as I was bound to do, I would be deeply hurt? This total lack of respect or consideration for my feelings felt like the ultimate humiliation.

As I wait for him to come home, a black cloud of misery descends upon me. I know I have to confront him yet dread plunging us back into turmoil. We'd found peace and happiness during his time at Mercury but now what? More scenes, more accusations? Can I bear to go through it all again? Equally, I know the letters are grounds for divorce. Isn't it time I ended this farce of a marriage? So says one side of my brain whilst the other cries, "No, no, I still love him." And what about the children, what is best for them? Would they be happier without him in their life or was a pretty useless father better than nothing?

I hear his car arrive and hurry to open the door. Glimpsing his face, grinning and flushed with drink, I am filled with a bitter rage.

"You bastard," I think, and, as he approaches, I slam the glass panelled door with all my might. It breaks, sending fragments of glass tumbling to the ground where they lie between us like the shattered shards of our marriage. The shock freezes us and for a second we stand looking at each other through the doorframe's jagged edges. John speaks first:

"Why on *earth* did you do that?" he asks - mildly in the circumstances. He steps gingerly over the pile of glass closely followed by a small, bespectacled man who, I can't help noticing, has a comb sticking out of his unkempt hair.

"Hey, why on earth did you do that? What a bloody mess, this is going to cost us a bob or two," John is saying, "mind the glass Gordon - oh, by the way, darling, this is Gordon, he's a psychiatrist. Come on in and have a drink."

"How d'you do," says the strange little man brightly.

"Hello," I reply curtly, thinking: oh for God's sake, I can't be bothered to make small talk at a time like this. He trots behind us into the sitting room.

"Now, Barbara, it is Barbara isn't it? I can't *tell* you how much I admire your gesture..."

Across the room, John has seen the pile of letters and is immediately sober.

"Talk your way out of *that,*" I hiss as he hurriedly sweeps them up and deposits them in the box under the table.

Man-with-comb-in-hair, apparently oblivious to the rising tension, prattles on: "... I'd go so far as to call it a wonderful gesture, slamming that door! Your husband's late for lunch, he's had a drop too much, you're angry and you're not afraid to show it. My word how brave! Yes, a very strong personality, no repressed emotions there and if everyone..."

John and I stare at each other, speechless in the face of this farce, whilst between us, like an unexploded bomb, lie the letters.

"...went for the grand gesture, why, I wouldn't have many patients left, would I, ha, ha, ha, and..."

Oh for heaven's sake, *shut up.*

"You've got a comb stuck in your hair," I snap over my shoulder.

"A comb?" he cries, reaching into his birds nest to retrieve it, "oh, my *comb,* oh *thank you,* I've been looking for it all *day,* I couldn't *be* more grateful! You know, there are combs and combs and this one is..."

At last, John steps in to stem the flow:

"Look, Gordon, would you mind going, we're..."

"Oh, of course, how thoughtless of me, you must be dying to have lunch. See you tomorrow in the pub?" And he leaves, his feet crackling over the broken glass, his stream of consciousness gradually fading away into the distance.

Then silence. Suddenly I feel drained, no fight left. I slump into an armchair. John sits down too and stares at the floor. In the past he has always flatly denied the accusations I have periodically flung at him but now, with the evidence heaped on our dining table, there is no way out. The room is completely still, the air charged with a dark energy. I find myself wishing desperately that I could rewind the clock. I do not have the strength, cannot bear, more trouble. But it is too late.

"Well?" I say at last.

He shakes his head

"Thirteen different women," I say, "*thirteen. "*

His answer is seared on my memory:

"Well, they were all nice girls."

Nice girls? Oh, thank goodness for that, *such* a relief. He looks up at me, his eyes blank, opaque, telling me nothing. In fact, what else is there to say? At last, I pierce the silence:

"I'm sorry, I've had enough. I want a divorce."

"Well, I don't."

I consulted a solicitor, reluctantly trotting out the unsavoury details which were threatening to torpedo my marriage. He listened impassively until I had finished, then said:

"Where are these letters?"

"They've disappeared. I think my husband has destroyed them."

"Pity, they would have provided concrete evidence of adultery. But I suppose we would have his behaviour when your daughter was ill, we could certainly cite mental cruelty on that..."

"Oh, I know how dreadful it all sounds," I interrupted, "but he's not all bad. He's a lovely man most of the time, he hardly ever loses his temper and we usually get on really well, especially when he's at home."

"H'm," he said peering over his half-moon spectacles, "it sounds to me as though you are not ready for a divorce."

He also warned me that such scandalous evidence was likely to find itself splashed across the News of the World – 'Naval Officer Had Thirteen Mistresses' - and I should therefore make no hasty decisions.

I'd gone into the solicitor's office feeling militant and left feeling relieved, for even after this latest body blow I knew I did not want to end our marriage until we had tried to rebuild it. I resolved to go home and persuade John to do what he hated doing; talk things through. I also decided to be as honest with him as I hoped he would be with me - I was going to tell him about my affair with Jay. This was weighing particularly heavily on my conscience because I had met Jay again the previous year when he had been in the area. We had had dinner together a couple of times but the Singapore magic had gone. So, although I would never see him again, it seemed wrong not to tell John. I did not relish the prospect.

That evening, I told him I had seen a solicitor, that I had plenty of grounds for a divorce but would much rather try to make our marriage work. Yes, he said, that was what he wanted too.

"First of all, though," I said, "I've got something to tell you. I don't want to but I'd be a hypocrite if I didn't. I have had an affair too."

He stared at me, horror contorting his face.

"You've had an *affair?* Who with?"

"Jay N....."

"Jay N....?"

He glared at me, speechless for a moment before leaping up,

taking the stairs two at a time and rushing into the bathroom from whence I heard the sound of vomiting. After a while he came back, his face ashen, and stood with his back to me looking out of the window.

"The bastard," he snapped, "I'm going to break his bloody legs."

"You couldn't," I shot back spitefully, "he's much bigger than you."

Now his anger spilled over, he ranted and raved in an endless stream until he ran out of insults, ending with:

"...and do you know what? You disgust me."

"Disgust you? How *dare* you say that after what you've done. Now perhaps you know how I feel every time I hear about yet another bloody woman, let alone *thirteen* all at once."

He didn't reply. This is going nowhere, I thought, perhaps it really is the end. But I pressed on:

"Look, you must try and see things from my point of view. It's bad enough knowing what goes on when you're away, but why can't you be discreet about it? Don't you respect me enough to make sure I never find out? Can't you see how humiliated I feel? Look at the state you're in because of what I've just told you. Just imagine how I felt finding all those letters."

Tension, taut as wire, stretched out the silence. But at last he nodded, as though acknowledging the logic of what I had said. Then he put his head in his hands and in a low voice said:

"I don't know how to explain this to you, but when I go to sea and have to leave you and the girls behind, it hurts so much that the only way I can get through it is to put you out of my mind so I can sort of forget you. And the other thing you must believe is that you're the only woman I have ever loved. These others meant nothing."

Out of sight, out of mind. I didn't know whether this made me feel better or worse but I knew it was the truth. I jumped up and ran to him. He put his arms round me and at last I cried, hard, painful tears that washed away grievance and turned it into grief. When at last I stopped, he asked:

"Try again?"

"Yes," I said, "try again."

'Hope Springs eternal in the human breast', wrote Alexander Pope, and I continued to hope that we could repair our marriage, put an end to this latest conflict and maintain a loving home for our children. But irreparable harm had been done. On top of this was the fact that, although we had made our marriage work for those eighteen precious months when

167

he was shore-based at HMS Mercury, sea-going life and family life were largely incompatible. John's life in the Navy was male-dominated, highly regimented and disciplined, with set routines, rules and regulations. The comradeship of the officers and men created a tight-knit ship's company where every man knew his place and his own responsibilities. Their central *raison d'etre* was related to war and the prevention of war. Their day-to-day life was to ensure that they and their ship were in a constant state of readiness. When the ship went into a foreign port, their duty was to 'Show the Flag' and open the ship to visitors. 'Showing the Flag', in the case of the officers, meant a round of official visits to local dignitaries and cocktail parties on the ship, to which everyone was expected to contribute in accordance with their rank. This added to the expense of effectively running two households, one at home and one at sea. But being in port was also the opportunity to relax and enjoy themselves. And, my goodness, John did.

Coming home from this male bastion was difficult for him. He found himself, as he once put it, trying to force his way into a 'little female clique', and he didn't find that easy. But then, nor did we. He was right, my girls and I *were* a 'little female clique', we even called ourselves Three Girls Together. When he returned, the routines we had established all came to a grinding halt. The car was handed back to him, our weekends were once again dominated by pub opening hours and the girls could no longer be the centre of my life. I resented his constant criticism of the children, the piles of extra washing, the different food he liked, in fact the complete turnaround in our lives. So it was not an easy transition for any of us.

Somehow, though, we stumbled on until, navigating the shoals and whirlpools in our relationship, we found ourselves back in tranquil waters. For John was a Jekyll & Hyde. Removed from the temptations of a sailor's life, he was a different person, easy to live with and far from the ogre I may have made him sound. He was even-tempered and home loving, never happier than when he was discussing the next meal or when he could settle down with his beloved books. He was charismatic, witty and often funny beyond words, an intellectual who studied naval and military history, but not above watching silly television programmes. And despite everything, we still loved each other, even though I sometimes wondered how that love had survived. So we settled down, allowing our problems to sink away like sludge in a stream.

One thing the girls and I noticed was that John was far better off than we were.   Whereas I always seemed to be struggling to balance the household budget, he was never short of money for trips to the pub, clothes for himself and other little luxuries. One evening I drove him to a Mess dinner, the girls in their pyjamas and dressing gowns in the back of the car. We watched as he walked up the steps, resplendent in naval Mess undress, part of his extensive uniform made-to-measure by the Savile Row tailors, Gieves & Hawkes. As we drove away a perplexed voice asked:

"Mummy, why is Daddy so rich when we're so poor?"

No answer to that one, darling.

At the end of 1968 I fell prey to a strange 'flu-like illness. For two weeks, my sweet daughters looked after me, Lou-Lou, with her armful of Brownie badges, even cooking supper every night (newly launched products like Vesta beef curries, Smash instant mashed potato and Instant Whip puddings were, I'm afraid to say, the current favourites). Afterwards, I found it hard to recover and over the coming months peculiar symptoms began to occur: if I had so much as a sip of alcohol, I collapsed, writhing in pain; I felt as though there was a painful grapefruit-sized 'something' in my chest; I suffered night sweats and I was constantly exhausted. After a while, I went to see my doctor who was unsympathetic and unhelpful.

"You get a pain when you drink? Simple solution – don't drink."

Every few weeks I would return, hoping that this time he would take my symptoms seriously. But he never did.

"Pains in your chest? Oh, it's probably rheumatism, take these pills. Night sweats? Well, there is a bug going round. You're always tired? Well, we'll take a blood test." Slight anaemia showed up so he told me to take iron pills and eat raw liver. I tried going to other doctors in the practice, craftily waiting until my own GP was off-duty. But they, reading my notes, were equally unhelpful. When I became so exhausted I was finding it hard to function, I decided to try one more time. My doctor looked at me kindly:

"Mrs Watson," he said, "even though I know these symptoms are very real to you, I want you to understand that there's nothing at all the matter with you. In other words, this is all in your mind. So really, you should see this as good news, try to forget your preoccupation with your health and just get on with life."

So I was a hypochondriac, was I? This felt like such an insult that I gave up going to the surgery. But I did not recover. I was losing weight and looked ghastly. I bought one of the newly fashionable wigs hoping that this would improve my appearance. But all I saw in the mirror was the same gaunt face.

169

"Oh dear," I said one day, "I look terrible."

"I know," said Lou-Lou earnestly, "you look just like Cruella de Vil." Trouble was she was right.

The time was fast approaching when Mary-Louise would be moving on to a secondary school. The Ministry of Defence gave grants towards boarding schools to ensure continuity of secondary education, especially when service families were posted abroad. I did not like the idea of an elitist school for my children and was very happy when we found King Edwards School, Witley, in Surrey. It was founded in the 16th century by King Edward VI at the behest of the saintly Nicholas Ridley, Bishop of London, who drew the young king's attention to the plight of London's destitute children and suggested that Bridewell Hospital down by the Thames - 'a wide, large house that would wonderfully serve to lodge Christ himself' - could be used as both home and school for some of these unfortunate boys. The gentle, philanthropic King agreed and signed a charter in 1553, the very year in which he died aged just 15. Within two years, Bishop Ridley was also dead, burned at the stake by Edward's successor, the terrible 'Bloody Mary'. In 1867 the school moved to Surrey and, by the time Mary-Louise joined, had become co-educational. I particularly liked the school's egalitarian philosophy whereby, even though it was a public school, pupils came from all walks of life.

Now I had read all the Angela Brazil school stories when I was a girl and Lou-Lou had read Enid Blyton's 'Mallory Towers' and 'The Chalet School' books, so we knew all about the jolly life at boarding school, the midnight feasts, the rivalry, the lacrosse matches, the fun and escapades enjoyed by all. So it was with rising excitement that we packed the trunk emblazoned with her initials and prepared for the big day.

Suddenly, she was gone, the house seemed empty and, oh, how much we missed her. However, I consoled myself that she would be happy as a lark and looked forward to hearing from her. Then came the first of a stream of phone calls, my child's heartbroken sobs echoing down the line, her little voice begging me to come and bring her home. She was desperately homesick. As she told me recently, she felt that the moment she arrived was the moment her childhood ended. Suddenly, there was no room for make-believe and dressing up, for putting on little shows or running wild on the seashore. Suddenly she was expected to conform to rules and regulations, keep to a strict timetable, sleep on hard beds in a cold dormitory with girls she did not know, eat food she hated, wash in antediluvian bathrooms. Suddenly her sister had gone, her friends had gone, and there was no Mummy to kiss her and tuck her in at night. She sobbed all through her first weekend home but, even though every maternal instinct told me not to, I gritted my teeth and took her back on Sunday night. The school had said this homesickness was common with new children and would soon pass, but as I was leaving she ran after me, crying piteously and clinging to me. I have never felt a worse parent in my life than having to leave her there, out of my care, out of my control. What had I done? Gradually, however, she recovered and by the second term had begun to settle down, make new friends and enjoy all the boundless opportunities the school had to offer.

At the beginning of 1970 John received a new posting. He was to be captain of a minesweeper based in Hong Kong. Unbelievably, it was an accompanied posting, which meant that, seven years after our return from Singapore, we were off to the Far East again. It seemed heaven sent. He would leave in February and Victoria and I would follow at the end of the Easter term. In the few weeks before he left he was particularly tender and loving, and we were longing for two and a half years together in Hong Kong. He also realised that I was far from well. A row of pea-sized lumps had appeared in my neck and he insisted I go back to the doctor. This time I was sent to hospital for tests but came back with the good news that they were harmless sebaceous cysts. Perhaps, after all, I was just tired? With newfound gentleness, John reassured me that once we got to Hong Kong, I could stop working, rest and get better.

We were having lunch on his last day in Emsworth when the telephone rang.

"Hello", said a tearful voice, "could I *please, please* speak to John Watson. My husband's been killed in a plane crash and John was one of his best friends and… and if I could just, if he would just…oh, oh," and she burst into the most heartrending sobs.

"Oh my God," I gasped, "how absolutely terrible, I'll get him at once."

I ran back into the sitting room and gave John the gist of the call. Grim faced he stalked into the hall and grabbed the phone.

"How *dare* you call me at home," he snarled, "you know damn well what I've always said…"

Then he shut the door. But I had heard enough and a familiar grey mist of anguish began to well up inside me. Oh no, it was all about to

171

start again, the bitter rows, the recriminations, the sheer misery. Something like panic swept through me. I could not, I just could *not* go through all that again, not now when he was being so loving, not now when I felt so ill. What is more, our lives were in transition, our home let and John was leaving for the Far East the next day. Was I now to light the blue touch paper which would blow all this apart? He walked back into the room, saw my stricken face and dropped to his knees, holding my hands in his:

"I'm sorry," he said, "I'm so terribly sorry."

But in that moment I made up my mind; I couldn't stand this so I would slam the shutters.

"Don't tell me anything," I said, standing up and pushing him away, "because I don't want to know. I'm going upstairs to have a rest."

Half way across the room I turned: "Just tell me this - has her husband really been killed in a plane crash?"

"No, of course not."

It was my final day at Emsworth Primary School. In a couple of week's time Victoria and I would be setting off for Hong Kong. I was bone weary, the last few weeks had passed in a blur of preparations for the move. And despite the fact that the medical profession said my symptoms were imaginary, I felt weaker with every day that passed. If this was psychosomatic, I dreaded to think what a real illness would be like. Finally, that long, last day ended. I had said goodbye to my friends on the staff, goodbye to the dear children who had meant so much to me. Now, as I walked wearily out of the school gates, longing for home and a cup of tea, a woman I knew stopped me. She was also a naval wife and had recently developed unbearable delusions of grandeur following her husband's posting to the Royal Yacht Britannia or, as she coyly put it, 'the Royal Ya-chet'.

"Oh Barbara, just the person I wanted to see. Could you tell me how you got into teaching? Now that Peter's on royal duty - Her Majesty is *charming* by the way, Peter and she get on *frightfully* well - I've decided to get a little part-time job, something easy like teaching."

Easy? Oh, shut up you stupid woman.

T W E L V E

WE HELD OUR BREATH as the RAF VC10 came in to land at Kai Tak airport, swooping so low over towering apartment blocks that we could see little figures and rows of washing on the roofs. Then, after one last stomach-churning turn, the plane landed on a runway which was no more than a narrow causeway jutting out into Hong Kong harbour. This was said to be one of the most difficult landings in the world which only the most experienced pilots were allowed to make.

For Victoria and I, the long flight was over. John was there to meet us and soon we were driving up the precipitous, switch-backed road to The Peak, almost at the top of Mount Austen, where our married quarter was located. I breathed a sigh of relief. We'd made it!

That evening, as Victoria was happy to spend the evening with a new friend, John suggested we go down to the Hilton Hotel for a drink to celebrate my arrival. I tried to disguise my gaunt face with make-up but it was no good, Cruella De Vil stared back defiantly from the mirror. I found my wig and pulled it on which, if anything, made matters worse. But as we walked out to the car and I saw what has to be one of the most magical sights on earth - Hong Kong by night - I forgot my fatigue in the exhilaration of the moment.

"Actually," said John, as we walked into the hotel, "I've brought you here to meet a very good friend of mine."

"Oh, who is he?" I asked, but he was on his way to the bar and didn't hear. I looked round the room at the sophisticated, cosmopolitan crowd and felt I ought to hide. Compared with these beautiful, exquisitely dressed women, I was a wreck, haggard and travel worn, with the ghastly wig hiding my lank hair. Somehow, though, it didn't seem to matter because, even though Lou-Lou was now far away, John, Victoria and I were

173

together. He had been so loving before he left for Hong Kong and so, with the 'air crash widow' conveniently hidden in the 'amnesia' section of my brain, I allowed myself to feel optimistic. Everything was going to be fine. In fact I couldn't believe how lucky we were. Our new home was a beautiful apartment overlooking the sea, we would have an amah to look after us again and an exciting social life to look forward to. I even began to feel hopeful about my health. Perhaps I was just worn out and now that I could really rest, would soon get better. After all, my GP had said I was a hypochondriac so maybe he was right.

John was talking to a man at the bar whom I guessed must be the friend we'd come to meet. I hoped they'd come over soon. Meanwhile, I went on people watching: the tiny Chinese girls, their hair glistening blue-black, their faces like perfect flowers; the Indian women so elegant in their dazzling saris, the brash American tourists... I spotted a woman on the far side of the room and guessed, as she moved confidently amongst the tables, greeting people, conjuring up waiters with a snap of her fingers, that she must work here. She was plainish and quite a bit older than me but I looked at her admiringly, taking in the expensive clothes, her poise and effortless social ease. She reached the bar and tapped John on the shoulder. He turned and, with a smile, bent to kiss her on both cheeks. Then they came over.

"Darling," he said, "I want you to meet my good friend Sally."

She was, he told me, manager of the Hilton coffee shop and could not have been more charming, welcoming me to Hong Kong, asking about the flight, the apartment, our girls. Within minutes, she was offering to introduce me to her hairdresser, her tailor, take me shopping, introduce me to her friends.

"I know they'll all *adore* you," she gushed, "oh, and I'm having a party next weekend, you and John simply *must* come."

"Her parties are legendary," John adds, as though he's been to lots.

I notice her beautifully manicured nails and the way she curls her fingers round his hand as he lights her cigarette. And I notice that although he's smiling he seems a little tense. Somewhere at the back of my mind a tiny warning light clicks on. Images begin to form. I see Hong Kong Hilton envelopes, lots of them. I see a box stuffed with letters. Letters! That's it, she's one of the Gang of Thirteen. And, oh my God, she's the one whose letters all began 'Dearest Mr Owl Eyes'. Their voices seem to fade away. I vaguely hear John telling me she has the most wonderful penthouse apartment at the top of the hotel and her babbling on about what *fun* we're all going to have.

Outrage fights with exhaustion, clarity with confusion. What should I do? What's the etiquette for such a situation? Do I burst into tears and run out? Or hiss "I know who you are lady" and throw my drink in her face? Or do I behave like a woman of the world, as sophisticated as she is, and accept the situation? Then what, share him? After all, I've apparently shared him with her for years. But a wave of nausea sweeps over me and I suddenly feel too ill and miserable to do anything at all. I can see Sally has noticed the change in me and her voice falters. I hold her gaze and in that moment am certain she knows I've guessed their secret. I realise too that that is enough. I have no need to sweep out or make a scene. I need not be smilingly grateful for all her offers of help. From now on, I decide, however often we meet, I will never speak to her again. But for the moment I simply become icily monosyllabic.

John has picked up the tension between us and after a few more minutes of stilted conversation between them I stand up and ask him to take me home. On the drive up to the Peak his rage erupts. He is furious that I could be so rude to Sally.

"How *dare* you," he shouts, "especially as she was so kind."

He is utterly ashamed of me, he says. Is this how I plan to treat all his friends? What on earth possessed me to put on a performance like that? And in the Hilton of all places. But I cut him short.

"What possessed me? I'll tell you what possessed me. I suddenly realised who she is. 'Dearest Mr bloody Owl Eyes', that's who, one of your Gang of Thirteen. Remember them? How *dare* you introduce me to your girlfriend."

As we drove back to our new home, I felt all my hopes of love and happiness shatter, piercing my heart like splintered ice. He'd not changed, I'd not changed, nothing had changed. How could I be so stupid as to pretend otherwise when trust had gone from our marriage long ago? And yet I knew that by the morning I would have forgiven him, I would bury another pain somewhere deep inside me and allow things to go on exactly the same as before. So ended my first day in Hong Kong.

There was no time to carry on our animosity, however, because the next morning I received a call from the Medical Centre down in the naval base. Steve, the junior doctor there, wanted to see me. He was a young South African who had had to leave his country because, as a 'Cape Coloured' – which was what people of mixed race were called during

Apartheid - he could not train as a doctor, let alone practice as one. He and John had become friends and he was interested when he heard about my mysterious symptoms. He had done some research and now had a few ideas. All the same, I was astonished to learn that he'd made arrangements for me to be admitted to the British Military Hospital in Kowloon the following morning.

And so, almost 18 months after my strange symptoms had begun and just three days after we'd arrived in Hong Kong, I found myself in hospital undergoing a whole battery of tests. It was a huge relief to be taken seriously at last, no longer labelled a hypochondriac. Now, when doctors asked me whether I had a pain if I drank alcohol, or if I had night sweats, I could say 'yes'. They no longer called the line of lumps in my neck 'sebaceous cysts' but knew they were lymph glands which were suspiciously swollen. Clearly, they were on track and, like medical detectives, were about to crack this case. Now I felt certain I would soon get some treatment for whatever was wrong and, oh, how wonderful it would be to feel well again!

On Sunday, John arrived at the hospital with Dr Steve and the senior medical officer from the naval base. Moments later, the consultant physician and two other hospital doctors walked in with a nurse, who came and stood beside me. The little room was packed. What on earth was going on?

"We believe we know what's wrong with you," says the consultant bluntly, "we think you have a rare form of cancer called Hodgkins Disease which attack the lymphatic system. We can't treat you here. You'll have to go back to the UK."

My head begins to spin. Everyone seems to be talking at once but I feel detached, far away, and their voices are loud, so loud. John sounds angry. He doesn't want me to go home, he is shouting, why can't I be treated here? Someone answers him:

"We haven't got the specialists or the facilities to treat her. This is a serious illness and it's remained undiagnosed for far too long. If she doesn't go back now and get the proper treatment, she'll be dead in six months."

The nurse takes my hand. I feel nothing, no emotion, no fear, just a bleak emptiness. I look at Dr Steve and he gives me his lovely, gentle smile. I will be flown home on Tuesday, he tells me quietly, and taken to Queen Alexandra's Military Hospital in London.

My gaze drifts past him, through the window to the harbour, wide, exotic, pulsating with life: fishing junks with huge crimson sails, cruise liners, shabby freighters, tug boats, the green Star Ferries bustling busily from shore to shore, tiny sampans bobbing in the swell, the sombre grey of naval vessels. Out there a myriad hearts beat, countless destinies unfurl; so many souls, so many emotions, yet all a mystery to me. I was to have been part of this wonderfully alien place but now everything has changed and I am leaving before my new life has had a chance to begin.

As we make our way home, my weary brain begins to absorb the fact that, like my mother, I am going to die young. This thought is swiftly replaced by another which, with the gathering menace of a storm, starts to whirl through my mind, over and over and over again - my daughters, my darlings, my precious girls, what will they do without me? And for the first time, I am truly afraid.

The shadows lengthen as our car climbs the Peak. The sun sets. Night is upon us.

Next day, the practicalities of the situation have to be faced. I know that Mary-Louise, however devastated she might be by the news, has her grandmother and beloved Auntie Sarah to look after her. Anyway, however ill, I will soon be in England myself. My biggest worry now is for Victoria. I remember the forlorn five-year-old waif who greeted me when, after a three-month absence, I returned to collect her following Lou-Lou's heart operation. It is enough that she now has to come to terms with her mother's life-threatening illness, let alone be left behind in this unfamiliar place. What is more, John's record as a father is not good and I fear he might not look after her. Should she stay and if so who with? Or should she come back with us, even though she is too young to go to boarding school with her sister? It is at this point that an unexpected angel steps into the frame.

Pat, another naval wife, is a fat, motherly, practical woman and a stranger to me until a few days ago. She suggests that Victoria moves in with her family, goes to the same school as her daughter, Victoria's new friend Clucky, and spends weekends with John in our nearby flat. We put the idea to her and she agrees. She also faces the bad news of my illness with a courage that astounds me.

As the days progress, Pat becomes my comforter, my driving force, the one who lifts me from despair. She listens and nods as I tell her about Victoria, just ten years old, my musical, clever, sensitive child who does not fit willingly into the mould and who has once before found herself separated from her mother in equally serious circumstances. I also, as tactfully as possible, mention that John may not be as attentive a father as one would wish. She assures me that she will care for my daughter as though she were her own, and I believe her. Then she helps me pack for the sad return journey, firmly putting aside my best clothes because, she says: "You'll need them for all the parties when you get back."

Finally, before John and I leave for the airport, she gives me an exquisite green jade horse.

"This is your talisman," she says, "whenever you look at it, just *believe* you will get better. And remember, it's only a loan. I want it back when you return."

Pat's optimism seemed to renew my inner strength and as the plane took off from Kai Tak next morning, exactly one week after our arrival, I swore that, no matter what lay ahead, I would survive for the sake of my children.

The return flight could not have been more different from our joyous trip the week before. In RAF terms I was now a casualty evacuation, or CasiVac. At every refuelling stop I was whisked away to be examined by a medical team before the next leg of the flight. This was both reassuring and confusing. On the one hand, I felt grateful that my condition was being taken so seriously, glad too that now I could give in, stop trying to cope. I was also experiencing something close to relief, for fear of the unknown was, I now realised, worse than facing the truth. At the same time, this level of attention was frightening as it re-enforced the fact that I was indeed very ill. It also made me feel strangely out of control, a passive part in the way my immediate destiny seemed to have been taken out of my hands.

My darling father and Tiggy were there to meet us when we returned to Brizenorton, and waved us goodbye as the ambulance headed for London. My father later told me that when he saw me I looked like my mother in her dying days and feared he would soon lose yet another of his loved ones.

I came home to an English Spring, the countryside bright with daffodils, leaves burgeoning on the trees in that green so beautiful it almost hurts the eyes. By the time we reached London the sun was setting, turning the grey waters of the Thames to fire and promising a bright tomorrow. But I felt far from bright when the ambulance pulled up outside Queen Alexandra's Military Hospital on the Thames Embankment and I was taken up the stairs to Barry Ward.

178

The Millbank, as it was known, was a red brick building next door to the original Tate Gallery, built in 1905 as a flagship hospital for Queen Alexandra's Royal Nursing Corp. Barry Ward was named in honour of General James Barry, a renowned military surgeon to whom a strange tale is attached - when he died, the woman who laid out his body saw that 'he' was, in fact, a woman. He – or rather she - is thought to have been born Margaret-Ann Bulkley, a greengrocer's daughter from County Cork in Eire who, disguised as a young man, managed to enroll in medical school in Edinburgh. Despite being just over five foot tall, with a tiny frame and what an ambassador's daughter described as 'a most peculiar squeaky voice and mincing manner', her secret was never discovered, not least one suspects because of a terrifying temper which made people fear her. Florence Nightingale even described her as 'a brute, the most hardened creature I ever met throughout the army'.

But as I settled into the hospital I had other things to think about than the history of this extraordinary character. A round of often painful tests began, culminating in the removal of the lymph nodes in my neck, which were found to be malignant. This final diagnosis came on my 33rd birthday and when a doctor came to tell me that the results were positive, I asked him plaintively:

"Aren't I a bit young for this?"

"No," he said, "in fact you're a bit old because it's usually much younger people who get Hodgkins. In fact, it's quite rare in women as it's a disease normally associated with young men."

The ward was run by a Sister of the old school, a tough, uncompromising woman who ruled us, nurses and patients alike, with a steely determination and yet cared for the sick with the greatest skill and compassion. That there were no hospital super-bugs in those days was no doubt due in no small measure to women like her who, like a truffle hound, honed in on the slightest speck of dirt. Whilst everyone well enough was expected to be up and dressed each day - "come on, girl, stir your stumps, don't just lie there looking sorry for yourself" - she could tell at a glance if a patient was feeling ill and would immediately pop her back in, propped up with extra pillows, whilst a nurse was dispatched for medication or a cup of tea. With her at the helm we felt secure.

The day after I arrived, Sister told me they had only had one other female patient with Hodgkins Disease throughout the time she had worked at the hospital and that, by coincidence, she was on the ward now. I was introduced to Lilian, a plump little lady from Yorkshire, and was eager to

179

hear what her treatment involved and how near she was to recovery.

"Oh no, loove," she said, "you don't recoover from Hodgkins. I've had it for four years. I just come in when it gets bad and they somehow keep me going. They think I might last another year, if I'm lucky."

A six-week course of radiation began in the nearby Westminster Hospital. Because the disease involved most of my chest, neck and under-arm area I had to have 'mantle radiotherapy' to cover this wide area. The effect of being bombarded with such a large amount of radiation was overwhelming. I became ever more nauseous and so weak it was hard to make the short walk between the two hospitals.

I was in the Millbank for nearly three months – unthinkable these days – and quickly got used not only to the routines of the ward but also to being ill. In some strange way, having this rare cancer became just part of my day-to-day life and as such not so frightening. I had complete faith in the doctors treating me and, of course, I was in the company of women who all had serious illnesses, so mine seemed no big deal. One day three or four of us stood round the bed of a woman with breast cancer. She was very ill indeed. She was an opera singer and had just been singing for us in a frail but heartbreakingly beautiful voice. Now she gave us some advice which I have never forgotten:

"We owe it to our families to keep going no matter how ill we are," she said, "we must never, ever give up because tomorrow there could be a medical breakthrough which could change everything."

A week later she died.

Far from being hard done by, I felt surrounded by love. I had countless visitors, cards by the score, bouquets from people I had never even met and at weekends, when we were allowed home – which for me was now at Grantchester House, where my mother-in-law and Sarah looked after me with the greatest tenderness and care. I was also comforted by the thought that Mary-Louise was not unduly upset by my illness. My sudden return from Hong Kong had delighted her because it meant Mummy was home again and, reassured by the family, she knew I would soon be better.

Then, in June 1970, came the happy interlude of my sister-in-law Sarah's wedding to an army chaplain, a shy and utterly delightful man named Peter White. They had known each other for a number of years and were the most perfect couple. Having waited so long to get married, they applied themselves to the task of making babies and had three children – two boys and a girl – in quick succession. And Sarah, to the manner born, became not just a busy mother but the wife of a Church of England priest.

The day finally came when my blood tests were clear of the disease and I was discharged. I could hardly believe that my skirmish with death was over, that I would not after all be leaving my children motherless. In the past months, I had met and become close to other women who had not been so fortunate and whose lives were now over. My own good luck therefore took on an even greater significance. I felt changed, blessed, lifted above the petty and the everyday. From now on, I resolved, I would make the most of every minute, every hour, every day of this sweet, sweet life.

TH I R T E E N

AT THE END OF JULY, Lou-Lou and I flew back to Hong Kong. We had prepared carefully for the trip, folding tissue paper round the clothes we planned to arrive in, as I did not wish to look like a bag lady this time. We had even invested in something new on the market - paper knickers especially designed for travel, a pack of three each, which we donned, stiff and crackly, for the first leg of the journey. We were en route to Bahrein when two of the crew pulled up a section of the floor in the aisle beside us, lowered a ladder and disappeared into whatever lay beneath. After a while they emerged, smiling pleasantly, and disappeared back into the cockpit. We thought no more about it until we landed in Bahrein, when the captain announced that a piece of the aircraft had fallen off during the flight - oh great - and we would therefore have to spend the night at the RAF base whilst a new part was flown out. We were getting impatient by the time the plane took off twenty-four hours later and headed for Gan in the middle of the Indian Ocean. We waited for many hours in the balmy heat of this tiny tropical island until the aircraft once again took off. This was to be the last leg of our journey so on went the last pair of crinkly knicks. But suddenly, more bad news, a typhoon had hit Hong Kong and the plane would be unable to land there. Instead, we were diverted to Singapore where we waited and waited, marooned in a grotty hotel and unable to leave Changi airport. By the time we reached Hong Kong we had been wearing the third pair of pants for such a long time that they had almost disintegrated. Even so, when we arrived four days later than expected, we looked immaculate and no-one would have guessed that under our clothes our knickers hung in shreds like economy grass skirts. John and Victoria were there to meet us and soon we were winding our way up to our lofty home.

    I was as overjoyed to see Victoria as she was to see me. She said little about her time without me and I assumed that all had been well. In fact she had been very unhappy, not really fitting in with her temporary family despite the kind and motherly Pat.   Added to this, she not only worried about her mother and missed me but saw hardly anything of her father. She attended the Island School and it was here that a beacon of light entered her life in the form of an extraordinary woman called Jackie Pullinger, her piano teacher. Jackie was an Evangelical Christian missionary who believed it was her vocation to work with prostitutes and drug addicts, but when no missionary society would accept her, she sought the advice of a minister in Shoreditch who told her to: "Buy a one way ticket on a boat going as far away as you can afford, and pray to know when to get off." Hong Kong proved to be her destination and, when Victoria met her, she was already working with heroin addicts in Kowloon's Walled City, which was controlled by the criminal Triad gangs and was such a dangerous place that not even the police dared to patrol it, thus allowing the area the freedom to become a major centre for the opium trade. Jackie was the only Westerner and the only woman ever to have been allowed into this dark and desperate place, and her destined work continues to this day.

Even though our family was reunited, there were only six weeks of the school holidays to spend together before the girls returned to England and we determined to make the most of every precious moment.

Our apartment was perched almost at the top of Mount Austin which, at just under 2000 feet, just missed mountain status but was still the highest point on Hong Kong Island. It was often shrouded in mist yet this only added to its charm. From our windows we looked out over the South China Sea, deep, beautiful, stretching away to strange and distant shores. Chinese fishing junks, with their great, square-rigged sails, followed its currents, wending their way between the myriad islands which dotted the ocean. Buzzards and eagles circled lazily on the thermals whilst below us dense woodlands tumbled down the rocks and crags of the mountain's side. Small fishing villages dotted the coast along this sparsely populated side of the island, whilst on every hand lay nature in all its lavish glory: rainbow-hued butterflies, brilliantly plumaged birds, gold-tinged lizards, exotic plants and tiny insects darting iridescent in the sun. Behind us lay the other side of the island and a different yet equally magnificent view of the city, the harbour and, beyond it, Kowloon and the mainland, all of which erupted into a neon kaleidoscope of colour once darkness fell.

Zig-zagging round umpteen hairpin bends meant that driving to town was slow and slightly hair-raising. In fact, the quickest way was to take the Peak Tram, the funicular railway which chugged almost vertically down the hillside, so that in half an hour we were in Central district and every girl's shopping paradise.

Lane Crawfords was the nearest thing to a Western department store at that time, its beauty department staffed by intimidatingly beautiful Chinese girls. Once I went there with a friend whose penchant was for vivid eye shadows. She decided to buy some and asked one of these lovely creatures for advice:

"Wha' colour you wearin'?" asked the girl.

"Oh, it's Lancôme's 'Peacock Jewel'," said my friend, smiling modestly.

"Well," replied the girl, "it look ab-so-loo-lee *awfoo*."

I bought a jar of moisturiser and was rather taken with the description printed on the side, which boldly declared that 'this cream is the enemy of little winkles.'

The girls and I were much more interested in things oriental. A huge 'Chinese Emporium', stocking goods from mainland China, became a favourite destination. This monument to consumerism was a real paradox, for even as it lured the public - including countless tourists from the United States - into its depths, anti-American slogans denouncing the 'American Running Dogs' blared forth from loudspeakers in ear-splitting Cantonese. Inside lay an Aladdin's cave selling everything from smelly slabs of dried fish, cheap plastic sandals, coolie hats and painted parasols to jade ornaments, oriental rugs and the finest Thai silks.

For my daughters, the jam-packed stalls in 'the alleys' were the biggest draw. In these narrow lanes threaded between de Voeux Road and Queens Road one could find a thousand things a girl could not live without: shoes and sandals, tee shirts and toys, sun hats, bikinis, tiny cloth dolls, fans, pin cushions, junk jewellery, handbags and every possible thing you could clip, tie or pin to your hair, all at pocket-money prices. Wherever one shopped, one bargained and it was even said that to get the lowest price of all you should arrive just as the stalls were opening in the morning, as the Chinese considered it bad luck to turn down an offer, however low, from the first customer of the day.

We explored the street markets, taking in the strange foods and stranger odours. We hurried past certain windows, blanching at the sight of huge glass flagons of snake and rat wine, tightly and repulsively packed with their entwined bodies. We chanced upon little green-roofed temples from which aromatic incense drifted upwards in pale wisps, carrying incantations to unknown gods. Sometimes we would enter a narrow lane where the usual cacophony of voices had fallen silent and the loudest sound was the staccato click and clatter of mah jong tiles. Here and there, old ladies sat gossiping in the shade, needles flashing in arthritic fingers as they stitched intricate patterns on linens and silks. We saw logs fashioned into coffins. We saw shops filled with the accoutrements of death where mourners could buy the necessities for the afterlife – from cars and televisions to chopsticks and noodles - all made of paper to be burnt at the grave of the dear departed.

The juxtaposition of wealth and poverty was evident on every side: squatters' shacks perched on the top of luxury hotels, skeletal rickshaw men, their stick-thin legs corded like wire, weaving in and out of the traffic with their well-fed passengers, homeless beggars jostling millionaire matrons in designer clothes, even the wretched souls living in sewers with the rats, all packed into the same small island.

One day we took a ferry out to Lantau, once the haunt of pirates and smugglers, and the largest of Hong Kong's many islands. It lay at the mouth of the Pearl River and at that time was still all but deserted save for a scattering of fishing villages around its shores and, on its highest peak, the Buddhist monastery of Po Lin. We caught a ramshackle bus which took us up the precipitous mountain passes, the single-track road so close to the edge that the vertigo-inducing view made one doubt ones sanity in ever boarding this rickety vehicle. But it was worth the nail-biting ride because the temple at Po Lin, floating above the clouds like a heavenly mirage, was a sacred place, a place of tranquility, where red-robed monks chanted before a gilded Buddha and a great brass gong reverberated, sending waves of peace and holiness into ones very heart.

Every day and on every side, there was something new and extraordinary to see in this incredible, noisy, smelly, swarming city, which seemed both the most alien and the most electrifying place in the world.

The amahs' quarters were at the back of the apartments, interlinked with stairs and doorways. Amongst the women who looked after our community of sixteen naval families, our amah – another Ah Lin - was the undoubted leader. A tough lady in her fifties, she had a raucous voice and a laugh which threatened the eardrums. The intense radiotherapy had taken its toll and I tired very easily, so I was relieved to have an amah to help me around the home. However, on my return from England I quickly realised that she was not very keen on me. It was clear she had much preferred looking after John, who hadn't told her what to do and in any case was often absent. So relations between us were a little frosty for a while until, little by little, we reached a tacit understanding; whilst I might appear to be mistress of the household, Ah Lin was actually the boss. That suited both of us even though it required more diplomacy on my part than on hers.

This woman whom I grew to know so well had endured unimaginable hardship and tragedy. She was one of thirteen children, born and raised in Canton where her parents were farmers. They were poor but never hungry until, as a result of Chairman Mao's Great Leap Forward and his countless disastrous changes to the cultivation of the land, crops failed and catastrophe struck – starvation. During The Great Famine, which lasted from 1958 to 1961, fifteen million people starved to death including seven of Ah Lin's siblings. Even when thousands of starving people besieged the huge warehouses packed with grain from former harvests, officials, fearing to disobey central government's orders, refused to open the doors, leaving them to fall, dying where they fell outside the gates. Ah Lin never forgot this. She never wasted anything. Once I found five dried-out peas on a saucer in the fridge and threw them away. On discovering they had gone, she berated me for such needless waste. How she escaped from mainland China to Hong Kong I do not know but she had since invested so cleverly on the stock exchange that she was rumoured to be the richest amah in the colony. Yet, despite her capitalist tendencies, a well-thumbed copy of Chairman Mao's Little Red Book still lay on her bedside table.

Her most endearing quality was her wild eccentricity. We hadn't quite grasped this side of her character when, before the girls' summer holiday ended, we decided to have a dinner party to thank Dr Steve, whose brilliant diagnosis had saved my life. My neighbour showed me a brass bell set into the floor beneath the dining table. By pressing this with my foot, she said, I could unobtrusively summon the amah as the meal progressed. The very thought of this, I have to admit, made me feel awfully grand and just the tiniest bit 'Upstairs, Downstairs'. Goodness me, it would be like summoning ones own butler! A few days before the dinner I showed Ah Lin the bell and explained that when it rang in the kitchen she should come in and I would tell her what was wanted.

"Okay, missy," she said, "you plessy bell, me come, yeah?"

There were eight of us round the table and all went well as we ate the first course. Then I pressed the hidden bell whilst continuing to talk graciously to my guests. Ah Lin came hurrying out of the kitchen.

186

"Someone at flont door, me go!" she shrieked as she rushed past us.

"No, no Ah Lin, it's me, I'm..." I called after her, feeling my face turning red. But she was already in the hall, opening the front door. She came back, shaking her head.

"Hey, tha' funny - bell ling, no-one there."

"*No* Ah Lin, it was *me.*"

"But why *you* ling flont door bell, I no unnerstan'?"

"It was *this* bell," I mutter, pressing it again to demonstrate, "the one I showed you." But she'd heard it ring and was off again.

"No-one there!" she shouts from the hall, "someone play tlick on us, maybe small boy. I go find."

I run after her.

"Ah Lin, come back," I call as she clatters down the stairs, "come and look, the *bell's* under the *table*."

"Bell unner tayboo? Why bell unner tayboo?" suddenly it dawns on her, "oh, I remem'er, you show me!"

"Look," I say, abandoning my attempt at being the lady of the manor, "just help me clear the plates and we'll bring in the next course."

And so the dinner continues, Ah Lin trotting in and out, chatting happily with everyone as she plonks the dishes down on the table. We get to the cheese.

"Ah Lin," I call, "could we have some biscuits please."

She trots in with a large packet of crackers and - choog, choog, choog - empties the lot onto a plate, crumbs and all. But, hey, who cares? With Ah Lin at the helm there could be no delusions of grandeur and, thanks to her, any future parties would be the better for informality. I also saw her more clearly as a woman whose role was to serve but who was not servile, who was funny but not a figure of fun, who kowtowed to no one.

The evening ended on a high when Victoria, doing her best to join in the conversation, leaned towards Dr Steve:

"I hear you're an African," she said earnestly.

The summer holidays were drawing to an end and the day came when the girls, along with all the other children returning to boarding school, had to fly back to England. For Victoria, the ordeal of starting a new school was also about to begin and I prayed she would not be as homesick as her sister and would soon settle down. It was heart wrenching to part with them, knowing they would not be back until Christmas, knowing too that in those days before computers, emails and cheap phone calls, our only contact would be by letter. As the parents trailed miserably out of the airport, most of the mothers in tears, the childless days ahead seemed bleak.

Victoria, perhaps predictably, did not settle down at school. Her first eagerly awaited letter was short:

Dear Mummy and Daddy, Will you please tell *them* I don't eat fish or toad-in-the-hole, Love, Victoria.

Although we laughed, the underlying message was that she hated King Edwards School – and always would. However, there were compensations, of which the purpose-built music school was one, where sixteen music teachers were available to teach every possible instrument. Her piano lessons continued, and she soon started oboe and singing lessons. When she and her sister returned for their first Christmas in Hong Kong we gave her a guitar. We were invited onto an Australian ship and she was asked to perform. In her pure voice she sang one song after another, each more yearningly beautiful than the last, until these tough men were almost in tears, homesick for their own families.

With the children away at school, John and I were alone. He had been delighted and relieved to have me back after my illness and I, in what still felt like a state of grace following my recovery, wanted nothing more than for us to be happy. Not long after my return I came down to earth when he told me that people had been spreading gossip about him, suggesting that he had been seen with other women during my absence. He was very upset about it, he said, how could anyone think this of him when he was sick with worry about me?

"…so if you hear anything, ignore it."

For once, I believed him. How indeed could he have thought of straying when his wife was so ill?

"Who's been spreading these rumours?" I asked.

He named a woman whom I had never met although she had been one of the squadron wives who had sent flowers to me whilst I was in hospital. Ignoring this kindness, I rang and confronted her, saying how cruel I thought it was to spread such gossip about a man who thought his wife was dying. She um'd and ah'd uncomfortably but had nothing more to add. She could at least have apologised, I thought, as I rang off.

How naïve can you get? As time went on and I got to know people, enough hints were dropped to make me realise that the rumours were almost certainly true. What else had I expected, I asked myself? Had I already forgotten about the Hilton woman? Wasn't it time I accepted the fact that I was married to a philanderer, a man I could not trust? As if this was not enough, he was also drinking heavily. I hated having such sordid matters forced upon me, nullifying the resolves I had made in hospital, forcing me to face a reality I did not like. But what could I do about it? Nothing. I knew how to live with my Jekyll & Hyde husband, so I just got on with it. In any case, our new life was very pleasant.

Domestic life in the married quarters had a set pattern. Each morning the greengrocer, fishmonger and grocer arrived in their vans. The latter, Mr Cheung, was a tall and slightly threatening man who not only supplied groceries but virtually anything else from reels of cotton to fuse wire, no doubt adding his cut to the bill. Once a week a tiny man brought us orchids, selling them so cheaply that one could afford huge bunches of these glorious flowers. Now and then the Linen Man called, always by appointment so that one could invite friends to his 'show'. As we gathered round, he spread his wares on the carpet, each piece more beautiful than the last: tablecloths, napkins, nightgowns, guest towels and bed linens, building up to his grand finale of satin kimonos and cheongsams dazzlingly embellished with dragons, chrysanthemums and exotic birds. The conclusion was always the same, one was beguiled into buying these exquisite things, most of which were put in a drawer and never used.

As my strength began to return I started giving private English lessons. My students included a 17-year-old Japanese boy called Ryo Kakimoto. Ryo was extremely clever and sometimes, when we touched on a finer point of syntax, I would find myself stuck.

"Ah," I would say when he asked me to explain, "now that's something I want you to find out for yourself before our next lesson."

The moment he left, I would rush for my 'Fowler's Modern English Usage' to look it up. Strangely for such a clever person, he was a Jehovah's Witness and if we ever touched upon this, the rational part of his brain deserted him.

I had several Japanese students, the youngest a minute boy aged five who, left with me by his bowing parents, stared up in absolute terror at this alien woman, tall as a giant, with strange blue eyes and a sticky-out nose. But we soon made friends and began drawing houses – the corners of his roofs curved up whilst mine were straight.

One day I received a call from a Mr Liu who wanted me to teach his daughter. He owned a night club, he said, and asked me to meet him there. The club was a seedy building in the seediest area of Wanchai. There were several girls at reception all wearing white tops on which their names were emblazoned – Miss Jane, Miss Suzy, Miss Marigold… One of them, whose name I noticed from her tee-shirt was Miss Carry, took me through to Mr Liu. He was short, fat and menacing, like a Buddha without benevolence. He was sitting at a bar and as my eyes became accustomed to the gloom, I noticed that a dozen or so girls were lounging on sofas around the room. I also noticed that, apart from skimpy underwear, they seemed to have forgotten to get dressed. I left.

My favourite student was a Chinese film star who had appeared in many of Bruce Lee's martial art movies, including Enter the Dragon. She was exquisite, a porcelain doll in designer clothes who, for all her fame, was completely without affectation. Our weekly 'lessons' were held in any one of her boyfriend's string of restaurants and it soon became clear that she had no interest in improving her English in any way other than chatting. It was both fun and filling. Who said there was no such thing as a free lunch?

I was asked to stand in for a teacher at an army primary school but before starting, I had to sign a form under the Official Secrets Act, swearing not to divulge anything that happened whilst working there. Understandable, of course, as my activities with those six-year-olds were all very hush-hush. However, I am now about to risk prosecution by breaking nearly forty years of silence to reveal that the class hamster escaped from his cage and we had a helluva job catching it.

One day I was approached by the Red Cross Blood Donor unit and asked whether I would like to become part of their small team. Friends told me I should be flattered because as well as being considered suitable for the task, only women who looked good in the uniform – a very short American-style nurse's dress - were ever enrolled. Superficial? Our task was to tour the harbour in a sleek white motor boat, persuading sailors to give generously of their blood. The outfits helped.

"Well," I said to Mary, the gorgeous, green-eyed nursing sister who headed the team, "I can't bear needles or the sight of blood but I'll give it a go."

Although it did indeed make me squeamish, it was also great fun. I soon noticed an odd fact; that the less intelligent the donor, the less likely he was to faint. A jolly jack tar who had spent the previous evening downing pints of beer was only too happy to have a nice lie down and could not have cared less how much of his blood we siphoned off.

"Oh look," we'd joke as his precious donation began to fill the bag, "it's not blood, it's Guinness!"

More senior men, on the other hand, often turned white and sometimes passed out, and had to be revived with cups of hot, sweet tea.

John, now a Lieutenant Commander, relished his new job as captain of HMS Sheraton, one of a squadron of mine hunters. This was his second command, in a bigger ship and with a larger crew than he had had in Singapore. Although we had now been together for thirteen years, I had never before seen him in this, his natural habitat. The sea was in his blood, passed down from his grandfather, Frederick Prosser. It was in his stars too, for he was a Cancerian, a water sign. He had even been born in a cawl which, superstition has it, meant that he would never drown at sea. In Singapore, wives and children rarely went onboard the ships, perhaps in deference to the Muslim crew. Now I had a chance to see him doing the job he loved. He was a natural leader and it soon became clear that the ship's company thought highly of him. He seemed able to be both their commander and their friend, to alternate giving orders with man-to-man talks when someone needed help or advice, to socialise one night but go to sea the next, with every man taking on his particular duties whatever his rank. We spent many an evening with the ship's company and their wives in the beer-and-skittles atmosphere of the China Fleet Club. This was the chance for men, having had a couple of pints, to corner me and air the grievances they did not dare mention directly to John. These conversations usually started with, "you can tell the skipper from me...," and, having promised to do my best for the petitioner, I would then pass on a watered down version to my husband.

Many of the wives, especially the younger ones, found it hard to settle down when they first came to Hong Kong and I was frequently called upon to help them with problems of accommodation, schools, health and so on. Sometimes I would be asked to sort out spats between the girls.

"I hate that Jenny," one would say.

"Why?" I'd ask, trying to get to the bottom of the dispute.

"She thinks she's it."

When Margaret Miller arrived as the bride of Ordinary Seaman 'Dusty' Miller, she was just seventeen years old. She was a Scottish lighthouse-keeper's daughter and had never been far from the little fishing village where she was born, let alone abroad. Now she found herself on the other side of the world, thousands of miles from her family and everything she knew and understood, living in a teeming Asian city where every aspect of life seemed a mystery. She was sweet, naïve, and very, very dim. Dusty was a skinny lad of nineteen who was always in trouble on the ship. He and Margaret had been allotted a flat in a noisy high-rise block. Neither of them had a clue how to cope with married life in Hong Kong. Margaret found everything difficult from managing money and shopping to getting around the city. She rang me constantly to help her sort out one crisis after another. Then one day she told me she was pregnant. Poor mite, I thought, looking at her strained little face, how on earth is she going to cope with a baby? She really ought to be at home with her mum.

A tradition in the squadron was Families Day when wives and children were welcomed on board and the ship sailed out to one of the many beautiful islands for a day of swimming, picnicking and fun. The only exception was HMS Sheraton because John was adamant that he would not have women and kids trampling all over *his* ship. But the sailors and their wives nagged me and I nagged him until eventually he gave in.

It was a beautiful morning as the ship left the dockyard, turned right - or should I say to starboard? - and sailed slowly through Hong Kong harbour towards the open sea. I stood on the fo'c'sle chatting to the other women, all of us happy and excited. But I began to feel uneasy when, looking round, I seemed to see nothing but pregnant women. In fact, I knew that five of the wives were expecting babies but in planning the Families' Day had failed to take into account that being bounced about on the sea was not perhaps the wisest move when a baby is on the way. Margaret Miller was one of them and, at 5'2" with a baby in her tummy, she looked like a small, greasy-haired dumpling. Now these women were on a Royal Naval ship heading out into the South China Sea. Well, it was too late to turn back and I just prayed that all would be well. At the same time, I really hoped John hadn't noticed.

After about an hour, the ship dropped anchor off a little island and the families were all ferried ashore in Gemini dinghies, inflatable boats with powerful outboard engines which sped across the sea, slamming into the waves and bouncing their passengers uncomfortably hard in the process. Once ashore our special day began, paddling and swimming, building sandcastles, fishing in little rock pools, sharing picnics, sunbathing and gossiping, wandering off to explore the island - it was heaven.

But by mid-afternoon the sky began to darken and, knowing the unpredictable weather in these seas, John decided to get everyone back onboard as quickly as possible. When the Geminis had been hauled onto the deck, with engines running and anchors aweigh, we were ready to go when someone noticed that Dusty and Margaret were missing. Where on earth were they? Yet again a Gemini sped back to shore and a couple of sailors set off round the island to find them. We all waited anxiously. I glanced up at the bridge where John, grim faced, was pacing up and down. Twenty minutes, thirty minutes passed. By now the sky was darkening and a heavy swell beginning to run. But at last the boat returned bearing the missing pair. Margaret was shoved up the narrow vertical ladder at the side of the ship and deposited on the deck, closely followed by Dusty. They were both soaked to the skin.

"Come on Margaret,' I said, 'we'd better get you out of those wet clothes."

I was helping her down to John's cabin when, whoosh, her waters broke.

"Oh, Barbara," she gasped, "I think I've done a wee in ma..."

"No you haven't," I said, "I think your baby's on the way."

She was surprisingly calm as I got her clothes off, dried her, and tucked a blanket round her on John's bunk. She may have been calm, but I wasn't! With no doctor on board I knew that, if push literally came to shove, it would be down to me. When in doubt panic - so I did. Oh God, what d'you do? Push, push, when do I tell her to push? Boil a kettle, string, cut the cord! Scissors, I'd need a pair of scissors! And the placenta, what about the placenta? Oh no, I can't *possibly* do it! Please, please don't let this happen to me. Oh, pull yourself together woman, I told myself irritably, first babies always take hours to come. I took a deep breath.

"Have you had any pains yet?" I asked hopefully, handing her the cup of tea Dusty had just brought in.

"Aye," she said, "I've had them for a coupla hours but I didna take nay notice. I thought it were just the violent sexual intercourse did it."

Violent what? I glanced at Dusty who was looking sheepish. I knew he had been under five days' stoppage of shore leave for his latest misdemeanor so they must have been making up for lost time on the island.

"If we hadna fell off the rocks into the sea while we were doin' it," continued Margaret, 'it wouldna have been say bad, would it Barbara?"

No, I agreed, it wouldna. Dusty sidled round the door and, weasel-like, slunk away. I sent a message up to the bridge and John signalled ahead for an ambulance to meet us. For the next hour or so I timed her pains as they grew more frequent, praying that the ship would arrive in harbour before the baby arrived in the world. Meanwhile, one by one, three of the other mothers-to-be also showed signs of going into labour and the signals between ship and shore were red hot.

As Sheraton turned to enter the naval dockyard I looked out of the porthole and saw a line of ambulances lining the jetty. Suddenly I realised that Margaret had nothing dry to wear. I found a pair of John's underpants in a drawer and she struggled into them. Then I helped her into his naval issue raincoat. The buttons didn't quite fasten round her stomach and the hem trailed on the ground but at least she was covered up. When at last we were alongside, all four women were helped into ambulances and rushed away to hospital.

"That's the last time I have women on *my* ship," announced John as we drove home.

Oh, here we go, I thought, I'm never going to hear the last of this.

"Although," he added, "I *did* enjoy signalling 'request birthing', instead of berthing party'! Good God, all those ambulances - looked as if there'd been a disaster at sea!'

"There nearly was," I said, "and wait 'til I tell you about the 'violent sexual intercourse'."

We both began to laugh.

That night, Margaret had a little boy and, over the next 48 hours, three other Sheraton babies were also born.

How good it felt to be part of the Sheraton family and how lucky I was to have had that experience. On our last Christmas, I was asked to tour the ship and choose the best decorated mess deck. As I walked into the Petty Officer's mess, I glanced around at the tinsel and mock-scathingly said:

"Well, if you lot think I'm choosing *this* you've got another think coming. I mean, you could have made an effort boys."

But they were standing around looking rather solemn and for a moment I wondered if I had offended them. Then the Chief Petty Officer stepped forward and thanked me for all I had done in looking after the families. He whisked a cloth back from a strange shape on the table and presented me with a beautiful silver tray and matching candlesticks.

Our social life was busy although more sedate than the wild days in Singapore. Hong Kong was a melting pot of nations and so there was always someone new and interesting to talk to. In those days when Mao Tse Tung was still in power, it seemed to me that spies abounded. Were they or weren't they? I devised an easy test. You simply asked what someone did and if they replied: "lovely evening, isn't it?" or something equally vague, you would think, yawn, yawn, not another spy. However, I did once meet a man who, folk whispered, really was a secret agent. James Bond he wasn't. The poor man walked with the aid of sticks, his legs bound in calipers, his gaunt face telling a tale of constant pain. He had been the only survivor of a plane crash, his life saved because, when he realised they were going down, he wedged himself across the narrow walls in the lavatory. How he operated as a spy, I do not know.

A party of Fleet Street journalists visited the colony in July 1970 and I was asked to help entertain them. We met at the Press Club where, hanging in the hall, I saw the original of the horrifying Pulitzer Prize-winning photograph that would come to epitomise the tragedy of the Vietnam War; a little girl, Kim Phuc, running naked down a road, screaming in agony as napalm burnt through her skin.

Whilst talking to the journalists I mentioned my long family connection with journalism and that my grandmother, Florence Radford, had been a newspaper reporter in the early 20th century.

"Oh, I've heard of her," said one of them.

How thrilled Granny will be when she hears this, I thought, I'll write to her tonight. But when I got home I found a letter from my father bearing the sad news that Florence, my extraordinary grandmother, had died.

Some invitations were less welcome than others. One day, for reasons we were unable to understand, we received an invitation to dine with a Major General and his wife, whom John had met briefly some weeks before. However, I didn't know them and wasn't particularly looking forward to what I felt sure would be a stuffy evening. I was relieved when we were shown into a lavishly-furnished drawing room to find several people we knew amongst the twenty or so guests. We all sipped champagne for a while and then were called through to the dining room. Under dimmed chandeliers, the long candle-lit table shimmered with silver and crystal. Deep bowls of flowers scented the air. Exquisite porcelain and starched napery marked every place. It looked simply beautiful. But when we checked the seating plan I discovered that I had been placed at the top of the table on the Major General's right whilst John and our friends were all together at the other end. Next to me was a Rear Admiral and opposite an equally exalted officer and his wife, a haughty woman whose booming voice resembled a gibbon's, as, sadly, did her face. I glanced longingly down the table to where John sat, relaxed and enjoying himself. Why me, I thought, why am I stuck up here at the boring end? And what on earth am I supposed to *say* to all this top brass?   But I soon discovered that, in such company, all goes swimmingly if one simply exclaims 'but how *fascinating*' or 'how *amazing*' as they recount their exploits.

The first course came and went.   Then a line of white-gloved stewards entered, the first bearing aloft a silver salver on which reposed a huge roast turkey, the breast of which had been sliced and put back in place.   In my position at the top of the table, I was the first to be served and the steward zoomed in, lowering the platter to shoulder level.   My host was holding forth importantly and I was still trying my best to look fascinated and indeed amazed, so I was distracted as I glanced up briefly and, with a tablespoon and sharp-pronged fork, helped myself to turkey.   The steward moved on and I glanced down at my plate, and, to my horror saw that with one stab I had somehow managed to spear about ten slices of turkey, which now lay in a succulent, steaming heap on my plate.   Oh, oh, what to do?   Put some back?   Shovel the evidence into my handbag?   Share it out amongst my lofty companions?   All impossible, for even as they continued to babble, they were aiming laser-like and disapproving glances at my gross plateful.   The vegetables arrived and I tried unsuccessfully to camouflage my greed with *petit pois*, *haricots verts* and *pommes dauphinois*.   But worse was to come when, halfway round the table, there was an awkward pause because – thanks to my public gluttony - they ran out of turkey breast and the steward had to retire to cut more meat from the wretched bird.

Dear Lord, I pleaded urgently, please strike me down in a dead faint, or at least allow me to slide under the table and crawl quietly away. But there was no help forthcoming from the Almighty and I had to stagger through the rest of the evening thinking wistfully of our own parties with the inimitable Ah Lin as the mistress of ceremonies.

Far more to my taste were the Chinese Festivals which punctuated the year.   The first, and by far the most important, was Chinese New Year.   This took place in February and was the time when all the amahs received an extra month's wages and made the long train journey back to Canton to visit relatives.   For months Ah Lin stockpiled gifts and spent her spare time knitting sweaters.   On the day of the journey, she put on as many of them as could be squeezed under her coat (her Customs avoidance tactic) before waddling away down the hill like Humpty Dumpty.

In April the Qingming Festival found the Chinese population spring-cleaning their ancestor's graves, even taking out their bones to give them a good scrub.   The Dragon Boat Festival followed the next month, a thrilling affair when immensely long canoe-style boats with dragon heads and tails, crewed by 20 or 30 men, raced against each other, the 'stroke' standing amidships and beating out the rhythm on a huge drum. To me, however, the most magical of these events was the Moon Festival when processions wound their way up the Peak, their lanterns flickering in the dark like a host of tiny fireflies.

Hurricanes, or typhoons as they were known in the Far East, were part of Hong Kong's weather pattern. A well-established routine had been established in the colony giving warning of an approaching storm. When it seemed likely that it would hit us, schools and businesses shut, the airport closed, ocean going ships put out to sea, well away from the typhoon's path, whilst smaller vessels sped back to the safest harbours they could find. At home we all knew what to do: windows were roped shut and their glass criss-crossed with tape, plants and furniture were removed from balconies and breakable objects packed away. We filled baths and basins with water in case supplies were disrupted, whilst emergency food supplies, torches, candles and portable radios were all checked.

There had already been three minor typhoons in 1971 but on the 16th of August, the big one struck. Mary-Louise and Victoria were out for the summer holidays and we busied ourselves around the flat, getting ready for whatever lay in store. We were told that winds might reach 100 mph and so had pulled mattresses and bedding into the large, windowless hall located in the centre of the flat.

One by one husbands and fathers returned to the flats. HMS Sheraton was not big enough to warrant putting to sea and so we expected John back at any moment, but the afternoon ticked past and there was no sign of him. Perhaps he had decided to stay in the dockyard with his ship, we thought. But at last, when the wind had already reached storm force and trees were leaning sideways, he returned, staggering in, grinning, slurring, almost insensibly drunk. I pushed him ahead of me into the spare room and shoved him onto the bed where he fell, spread-eagled on his back, asleep almost as he hit the pillow. I looked at him with contempt. I hope the wind sucks the window out and you with it, I thought, as I shut the door and left him.

That night, as we bedded down in the hall, the full force of Typhoon Rose hit the colony, and our block of flats, perched on the top of Mount Austen, caught the full force of it, buffeting the building so that we could literally feel it sway. Outside, the wind reached 140 mph, screeching like a banshee, battering, smashing, destroying, sinking ships, drowning

197

sailors, as it whirled through the night. We kept our radio on and could hear SOS signals from ships in distress. Strangely, we were not frightened, the adrenaline of the moment keeping fear at bay. Then came the eye of the storm, that eerie zone when the winds drop and all is still, bringing with it a false sense of relief until the storm blows in again, this time from the opposite direction. But at last it whirled on its way and by morning all was calm.

John was up early, having slept right through the typhoon and, with no sign of a hangover, rushed off, anxious to get back to the dockyard to inspect his ship for damage.

Typhoon Rose left a trail of devastation in its wake. From our windows we could see uprooted trees, great chunks of road bitten away to roll down the mountainous slopes, overturned cars, fallen lampposts and telephone poles, whilst the coastline far below was littered with vessels which had run aground. Five thousand people were made homeless that night, 286 were injured and 130 souls lost their lives. It was the worst storm since Typhoon Wanda in 1962.

John had had a perilous encounter the previous year when, en route to Japan, Sheraton was hit by the edge of a typhoon. Giant waves struck the ship with such force that its massive fridge broke free and slide to one side, causing the ship to list dangerously. Every bit of manpower was needed to push the fridge back into place and so save the ship from capsizing. In 1909, John's grandfather Frederick Prosser's ship, HMS Kent, had also been hit by a typhoon and two sailors had died during the storm. Back in Plymouth, a fearful rumour swept through the naval base that the Kent has been sunk with all hands and, communications being slow back then, it was not for a week that the anxious families – including Frederick's wife, Lily - learnt the truth. These two incidents, separated by sixty-two years, took place in exactly the same stretch of water whilst sailing to exactly the same port - Nagasaki.

On the 31st December, 1971, we were invited to a New Year's Eve party at the exclusive Hong Kong Club. It proved to be a dull, low-key affair and I found myself, as on various other occasions, trying to avoid Sally, the woman from the Hilton. Now, as the midnight chimes faded, John turned to me and said:

"I don't know about you, but I'm ready to go home."

We had both had heavy colds and I still didn't feel too well, so I agreed at once. Soon we were winding our way up the Peak in the back of a taxi, talking amicably about the evening. We arrived home and I climbed out of the cab, waiting as John leaned forward, presumably to pay the driver - except that he wasn't paying, he was telling him to drive off.

As the cab's lights disappeared round the first bend and I stood alone outside the darkened building, unable to believe he had left me in such a cruel way on this, the first day of a new year, I had a sort of Ides of March moment. I suddenly saw things with total clarity and knew that, both physically and emotionally, he would always put himself first. He never had and never would be there for his daughters and me. We would never stand together in unity, whether in good times or adversity. My constant wish to put things right made me complicit, weak, giving out the signal that he could do whatever he liked and I would always want him back. Now I knew with an inner certainty that in the not too distant future our marriage would come to an end. He did not return for two days.

That was our last New Year in the Colony. We were returning to a new home and a new life. A few months previously, we had received a letter from John's mother telling us that the house next door to hers was for sale. It had been the property of an irascible old couple who never stopped squabbling even though they were clearly devoted to each other. They had been wonderful friends to Audrey Watson especially during the time when her marriage was disintegrating. Now, because old Colonel Cousins had died and his wife was in a nursing home, Cranmere, as the house was called, was on the market. As friends of the family, the executors were offering it to us at a very advantageous price. It was a lovely house, spacious, beautifully proportioned and with a big garden. Initially, it seemed out of the question but the more we pondered the idea the more we could see its benefits. John already knew that his next appointment was at the NATO headquarters in Northwood, to which he could drive quite easily. It had even been suggested that I teach at Grantchester House.

And so, with Audrey funding the deposit and mortgage repayments until we could sell our Emsworth house, the sale went ahead. Her kindness and fortitude during Lou-Lou's operation and my illness were something I would never forget. She had also spent Christmas with us in She had also spent Christmas with us in Hong Kong and had been the perfect guest; considerate, generous, fun, self-effacing when necessary and great company. I therefore had no qualms about living next door to her. Any misgivings I now had were reserved for my deteriorating relationship with my husband.

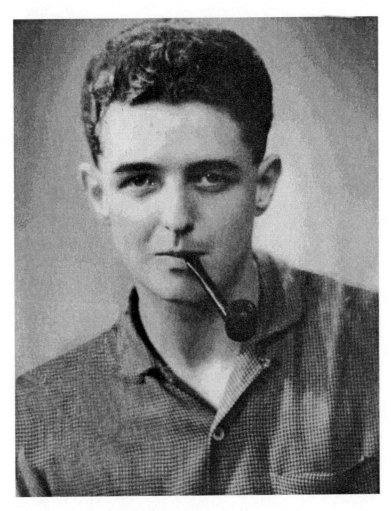

My darling brother, Richard Godfrey Davis.

'Three Girls Together' outside our new house
in Emsworth, Hampshire. 1964.

Victoria and Lou-Lou, September 1964.

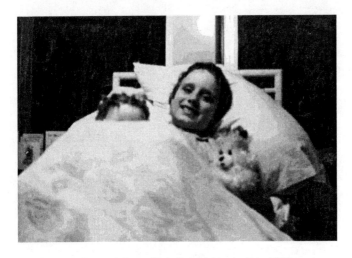

Great Ormond Street Hospital, 9th November, 1964.

John, Barbara and the girls
with Great Granny Lily Prosser.
Grantchester House, 1965.

The Perpetual Prize Winner, 1967.

A small Geisha girl, 1967.

Sarah and Peter White on their wedding day, June 1970.

Victoria as 'Miss Poppy' with her 2nd cousin Emma in attendance.

Mary–Louise and Dick on their wedding day
Amsterdam, August 1979.

With Dick's father, Diederik Hoebee, at the wedding, 1979.

Great Grandmother Audrey with Victoria and baby Michael,
The Hague, Holland. 1982

'I love oo so much, f.o.b'. Bebe and Michael, 1985

F O U R T E E N

'ABSENCE MAKES THE HEART GROW FONDER' goes the old proverb. It was certainly true for me when I came back to England in May, 1972. John was bringing HMS Sheraton back by sea, a voyage which would take three months and this breathing space was a blessing, allowing me to settle into a new life without having to worry about marital problems.

Despite my growing disillusionment with my husband, other areas of life were once again looking good. The new house was everything I had hoped for. My mother-in-law was warmly welcoming and had confirmed that she wanted me to join her staff. I was reunited with my sister, my parents, relatives and friends. Above all, my daughters' school was only an hour's drive away. Now we could look forward to their days out, weekends and holidays at home. I, in turn, could go to all the school events. After our long separation, how joyful it was to be together again.

Then came the bombshell. I had gone to the Westminster Hospital for a routine check-up and, after the usual tests, I was called into the consultant's office.

"Bad news," he said without preamble, "I'm afraid the Hodgkin's Disease is back. All your lymph nodes are swollen and your blood test is abnormal. However, until we do some more tests, it's hard to pinpoint exactly what parts of the body are affected. So we'd better get you in as soon as possible. We'll contact the Millbank and go from there."

I walked out into the summer sunshine in a daze. Even though I had been growing more and more tired during our final months in Hong Kong and the house moves in England, even though I had an excruciating pain in my back, even though the slightest sip of alcohol had me once again writhing in agony, I never for a moment thought the cancer had returned.

Now, as I made my way back to Waterloo Station, I wondered how I could have been so blind, or how my subconscious could have blanked out such obvious symptoms.

Back in Hinchley Wood I broke the news to my mother-in-law and reluctantly called my father and other members of the family. The following weekend we drove down to King Edward's School for the terrible task of telling my daughters I was ill again, down-playing it and assuring them that I would soon be better. How brave they were, how hard to hear this news and, at the ages of 13 and nearly 15, how difficult to bear the weight of it in a community where there were precious few people to comfort them.

Then there was John. His ship was somewhere in the Indian Ocean. His mother and I felt that he had quite enough responsibility in bringing Sheraton safely back to Portsmouth without burdening him with this bad news, so we decided not to tell him until we absolutely had to.

The following week found me back on Barry Ward and straight into another round of radiotherapy, this time covering the lower part of my body. Even though my chest was again involved, more radiation in that area was impossible and could kill me. For the next six weeks I walked round to the Westminster Hospital each weekday morning, lay on the couch to be 'zapped', only to find myself almost too weak and sick to dress myself and stagger back to the Millbank. Hand in hand with this went tests, tests and more tests. In those days before ultra-sound, CAT and MRI scans, other ways had to be found to view the inner workings of the body. One of the most excruciating was an injection of blue dye into my feet, which was then pumped up my legs into my body, thus making soft tissue visible when x-rayed. I was even injected with a radioactive isotope. Week after frustrating week passed until finally I learned that the disease had entered my spine as well as the more usually affected areas.

"What we are going to do," said the consultant, "is put you on an eighteen month programme of chemotherapy."

Chemotherapy? And for eighteen months? The only people I had ever known to have chemo were in advanced and irreversible stages of cancer. Here we go, I thought, order the wreaths.

"Oh dear," I said, "I suppose this means I'm seriously ill."

"Well, your illness *is* serious but giving patients these drugs at an earlier stage is the latest approach to treatment. In combination with radiotherapy, we feel it gives a far better chance of eradicating the disease. We'll be using a cocktail of drugs which have only just become available. So if you're up for it, we'll start as soon as possible."

212

Up for it? Of course I was. I knew I had another fight on my hands and my driving force was the same as last time: to survive for the sake of my children.

A few days later I received a cable from my husband: 'Arriving Simonstown 7th July. Suggest you fly out and join me.'

This was a double blow. Not only was such a trip impossible but I could hide the truth no longer. The next day I sent him a carefully worded reply: 'Hodgkin's returned. Now in spine. Do not worry as treatable.'

Although it seemed a stark message I knew from Sheraton's schedule that they would reach Durban on the 1st July and hoped he would ring me from there. Then I could reassure him. But Durban came and went, likewise Simonstown, Walvis Bay and Monrovia, but he neither called nor wrote.

How painfully familiar this all seemed, bringing back memories of Lou-Lou's operation. I asked myself why I had even expected him to care. I remembered my foreboding when he'd left me on the doorstep last New Year's Eve.   Now, true to my prophesy, another chunk of love had just crumbled away as he let me down yet again. Why, I asked myself, did I stick with this man, year after year? Why didn't I just go? The answer was one I simply hated - because I was too ill to be able to make a new life for my children and myself.

He did call eventually and, over a stilted conversation, I told him the unvarnished truth. Bad luck, I thought cynically, you'll be back soon and then you'll have to face it with me whether you like it or not.

HMS Sheraton and her sister ship, HMS Kirkliston, reached Portsmouth on the 24th August. Although he did not know it, this was to be John's last sea-going job in the Royal Navy. A few month's later he joined the NATO staff at Northwood in Middlesex.

An officer's promotion within the Royal Navy is automatic up to the rank of Lieutenant Commander. However, after a few years at this rank, promotion is by selection and lists are published twice a year showing who has moved up the promotional ladder. John's dedication to the Royal Navy was total. His regular reports had all been so good that he – we – almost took for granted that he would soon become a full Commander. Despite the problems in our private life I had always been immensely proud of his career as a naval officer. However, when year followed year and nothing happened he began to nurse the fear that he would become the thing he most dreaded - a 'passed over' Lt-Commander. So he threw himself into his new job with enormous energy, hoping that this time he would be noticed and his zeal would bring the reward he yearned for. He was also living at home and so had no alternative but to witness the progress of my treatment.

Before my chemotherapy could begin, a sample of bone marrow had to be obtained, an unpleasant but relatively straightforward procedure whereby a long needle is screwed down into the hip or sternum and a sample of bone marrow drawn out. However, it was my misfortune to have bones so dense that the procedure was carried out three times without success. It was a process that, even under light sedation, I found absolutely horrifying as well as painful. Equally, I knew that I would have to endure it a fourth time because without it my red and white blood cells and platelets could not be measured and, without this information, my treatment could not start.

"Well," said Sister after the third unsuccessful attempt, "you've apparently got bones like cast iron and they simply can't drill into them so we're sending you over to the Westminster to have it done there."

I was admitted to a ward full of cancer sufferers and, as day turned to night, I watched the doctors and nurses at their unceasing work. Finally, a young doctor came and slumped on the edge of my bed, eyes bloodshot with fatigue.

"Well," he said, "you're first on the list in the morning. It's a short procedure so you'll only have a light anaesthetic."

"Anaesthetic? Did you say anaesthetic?"

"Yes, but you'll only be out for twenty minutes at the most, so no need to worry."

"No, no," I babbled, "I'm not worried, I'm just so, so relieved!"

I don't think many people smile broadly on their way to the operating theatre, but I did.

With this ordeal behind me, my chemotherapy could start. I was to go into hospital every third week and stay for two days. Dosage, I learned, was calculated according to the height and weight of the patient. Even so I was unprepared for the two Smartie-sized hypodermics holding my first 'cocktail', which included elements from mustard gas (used by the Germans to gas troops during WWI) as well as from the periwinkle plant. In it all went, however, and very soon the inevitable side-effects started, so overwhelming that one wondered whether ones body could really withstand the onslaught. My reaction was so violent that it was two weeks before I recovered and was strong enough to go home, by which time my doctors had decided that the dose would have to be halved. What they had failed

214

to take into account was the density of my bones which gave a misleading weight when calculating the right amount.

And so the regime began and for the next eighteen months my life was divided into distinct segments – one week ill, one week recovering, one week almost normal, then back to hospital to start all over again.

Throughout this, my mother-in-law was there for me, rock solid, kind, strong. I had already started work in her school and even though my illness was proving far worse than anticipated, we decided that I should still go in whenever I could, whether for a couple of hours or a day, for to be with children was to forget ones troubles.

When we first discussed my employment, she had announced bluntly: "I don't know about these qualifications you *say* you've got, but they mean absolutely *nothing* to me. If you're going to teach here, you must understand that, at Grantchester House, everything is done *my* way."

'Her way' was a watered down version of the Montessori system combined with the teaching methods she had developed over many years. Even though her scathing dismissal of my credentials was infuriating and demeaning, I had to admit that the free-and-easy way I had run my huge primary school classes would never work in an environment where the main aim was to get children into top preparatory schools. In fact it was a hot-house, where rote learning, times tables and spelling were the order of the day, where English grammar was formally taught, where bad handwriting was not tolerated, where lessons were conducted quietly with children sitting in neat rows of desks, where they moved about the school in silent 'age order lines'. Everything about it went against the grain with me, but I quickly discovered that not only was the formality interspersed with fun but that none of the children seemed to mind. Indeed, they thrived in the quiet atmosphere and firm but gentle discipline. At the end of each day, Mrs Watson stood on the school steps and shook hands with each child as they filed up the path to their waiting parents. The school motto was 'Manners are the Happy Way of Doing Things' and, twee though this may now sound, is it not a good philosophy to instill in a child?

I, with my suspect qualifications, was never allowed to do more than assist in the teaching of academic subjects although I was entrusted with whole classes for art and crafts lessons.

Now that we worked together, my mother-in-law and I had a lot in common. Each afternoon at four we would mull over the day's events over a cup of tea: Danny the temperamental Irish gardener's latest tantrum; the late arrival of sausage rolls for lunch (a weekly treat handmade by Mr

Missing the local baker); gossip about parents and staff, problem children, sick children, funny children... Grantchester House was a world within a world and it was all endlessly fascinating.

Audrey Watson had a seemingly infinite supply of energy. None of the parents knew, for instance, that their children's esteemed headmistress played a major part in the preparation of school lunches. Each evening she stood in her kitchen, chopping vegetables, stirring vast vats of stew and mince, or cooking apples from the orchard at the end of her garden. The next day her general factotum, Mrs Long, would bustle about in her green overall, transforming everything into homely dishes which the children loved.

My mother-in-law was clearly very intelligent woman and yet her view of life sometimes verged on the bizarre. When I went in for our after-school chat one day she led me into the dining room, her holy of holies, and shut the door. Goodness, I thought, she obviously has something serious to tell me.

"Barbara," she said, lowering her voice, "have you noticed that the youths of today have arrows on their trousers pointing to their genital regions?"

Arrows pointing where? Had she flipped at last?

"Em, no, I can't say I have."

"Well, you look. It's on these ghastly blue-jean trousers they wear and I must say I think it's *most* unseemly. The worst thing is that the arrows are *red*."

What on earth did she mean? In the following weeks I found myself sneaking furtive glances at 'youths' but could see no evidence of this blatant signposting. Then at last, when looking at jeans in a shop one day, I noticed that the stitching at the end of the fly tapered off into an arrow-like shape. Voila! She was right! But as the stitching was miniscule, how had she spotted it?

Not all her rigidly held views were amusing or harmless. Because she was held in such high regard, parents – usually mothers - frequently turned to her for advice on all manner of problems. In the case of divorce, she was of the unswerving opinion that mothers should always have custody and that, after the split, children should have no further contact with their father. "No," she'd tell the weeping mother, "a clean break is best, otherwise it just confuses the child."

This stance was based on her own divorce after which her children were forbidden to have any contact with their father. John adhered to this ruling into middle age, although his sister, who adored her father and was heartbroken to lose him, managed to keep up an intermittent correspondence, saddening her still further because it had to be surreptitious.

Living in Hinchley Wood was a new experience for me. After exotic, sophisticated Hong Kong, after our seaside home in Emsworth, it was, well, suburban. I found it hard to settle down. By contrast, John was immediately at home in an area where he had known since boyhood. He found a pub he liked and joined Esher Cricket Club. He was as unpredictable as ever, for weeks on end the home-loving man who, although he drank heavily at weekends, appeared to like nothing better than a peaceful, normal domestic life. He was even-tempered and easy-going. Then, like a dam bursting its banks, he would suddenly break out, drinking himself into a state of collapse.

Neither had his womanising stopped. He now chose the days when I was in hospital for this, but as always never bothered to cover his tracks. Several times I came home, weak and nauseous after my chemotherapy, to find a woman's name and number left by the telephone and John nowhere to be seen. I became paranoid, telling myself never to look in his pockets or his wallet in case I found something that would upset me. Then, unable to resist, I would delve and there, every time, was the hurtful evidence I had known I would find.

His NATO job took him to Brussels from time to time and whenever I could, I drove to the airport to meet him. One such trip coincided with my chemotherapy so he said he would make his own way home. But when I woke up on day three, I didn't feel as sick and ill as usual and decided I would give him a surprise by meeting him.

That evening I waited behind the barrier for the Brussels flight to come through and soon saw his familiar figure. But surprise, surprise, he wasn't alone. Oh dear me no. John Watson, looking smugly pleased with himself, was arm-in-arm with a blonde who trotted along beside him on teetering heels. I was so astonished that they had passed me before I could move. Pulling myself together, I hurried after them and tapped him on the shoulder. He turned, blonde still clinging limpet-like to his arm.

"Welcome home," I said, between clenched teeth.

"Oh..." he spluttered, momentarily losing his cool. Then, quick as a flash, he turned to Blondie:

"May I introduce you to my fiancée," he said.

217

His fiancée?

"I'm *not* his fiancée," I snapped, "I'm his *wife*." Then I turned and rushed away, hoping I could get to the car and drive off without him, but after a few moments he caught up. He was furious.

"How *dare* you make a fool of me like that," he snarled, gripping my arm so tightly it hurt as he frog-marched me out to the car park.

"Oh, I'm *so* sorry to have embarrassed you. How *unfeeling* of me to hurry back from the hospital so I could come and meet you."

We drove home in a sullen silence but as we pulled up, I said:

"One of these days I'm going to leave you."

"Oh yes?" he sneered, "How many times have I heard that in the last few years? You'll *never* leave me and d'you know why? Because I'm your bloody meal ticket."

You arrogant, cheating pig, I thought, just you wait. If I ever recover from this illness, I *will* go. But for the moment I felt humiliated, powerless, trapped with a man I no longer loved.

I had been warned that if I had a cough, sore throat or a cold, my chemotherapy would have to be delayed, as it was too dangerous to proceed if the body was already coping with an infection, however slight. Some months into my treatment, I felt the first hint of a cold and rang the hospital for advice.

"Come in anyway, and we'll take a look at you," said Sister.

The doctor who came to my bedside was a pompous little man I had never seen before as he had only just been posted to the Millbank.

"I've got a sore throat," I said at once, "so I suppose my chemo will have to be cancelled."

"Cancelled?" he asked, "what for? Let me have a look."

He peered down my throat.

"Oh, that's nothing," he said, "we'll go ahead." He went away and returned with an enamel dish containing two huge hypodermics instead of one.

"No," I said, "I don't have that much, it made me really ill last year. It's because of my bones..."

"Your *bones*?" he said, "what *are* you talking about?"

"She's right," said the nurse assisting him, "they've halved her dose."

"Are you telling me how to do my job?" he snapped, making the poor girl cringe, and with that he found a vein, fixed up the drip and in went the lot.

I don't know how I managed to get home next day, but I did. By the evening my face, lips and even my tongue had swollen up and by the following morning I was so desperately ill that, not bothering to call an ambulance, John bundled me into the car and sped back to the Millbank.

This medical blunder proved almost fatal. Twice I felt myself slipping away, moving at great speed through a vortex-like tunnel towards a brilliant light, only, I presume, to be rejected at the Pearly Gates. One afternoon, John brought Lou-Lou to the hospital to see me. Suddenly I found myself floating high above them, disembodied, dispassionate, looking down at my own white body on the hospital bed, arms outstretched, cruciform, the two figures on either side holding my hands. I do not know how long this lasted before my spirit slipped back into its frail human form.

Almost twenty years later, I met an old friend from Esher who told me a strange tale. Without knowing that I was in hospital and critically ill, she awoke to see a ghostly me standing at the foot of her bed. Fortunately, my spectral visit was brief but it was enough to unnerve her and as soon as I disappeared, she shook her husband.

"Wake up," she said, "I've just seen Barbara's ghost. I think she's dead."

But of course, as she discovered next morning, I was not.

A pragmatic, down-to-earth woman, she was the last person to have imagined such a thing. However, this episode had always puzzled her:

"I've never been able to understand why you appeared to me and not to one of your family. After all, we were never that close."

My sentiments precisely; rather a pointless haunt!

It took me a long time to recover from this crisis but when I went back to the hospital a couple of months later, I discovered two things: the doctor concerned had been moved to another hospital and my notes had mysteriously vanished.

"I suppose I won't be able to go on with the chemo after this," I said hopefully, because I didn't feel I could bear it any longer.

"Oh no," I was told, "we'll give you a couple more weeks to get over this set-back and then we'll start again."

Amidst this suffering, my daughters remained the shining centre of my life. They were now moving into their teens. Mary-Louise acquired her first boyfriend, Jimmy, a fellow-student at King Edward's School. After a few months, she brought him home to lunch. But whilst he was friendly and self-assured, poor Lou-Lou nearly fainted with the embarrassment of it all, giggling insanely, toying with her lunch and swinging her shining curtain of hair over her face to hide her blushes. Like many a teenager, she became secretive, confiding in her best friend, Imogen, rather than her mother. I bought her a diary which had its own little lock and key. One day I found it on her bed, unlocked, and to my shame could not resist temptation. I picked it up and opened it at random. 'I hate Mummy,' is all I read before slamming it shut!

Victoria, on the other hand, told me everything. One day she rang from school:

"Wonderful news Mummy – I've been saved! Send me a Bible at once."

What? I thought perhaps her conversion was part of the school's Anglican tradition but I was wrong, for what had happened had distinctly sinister overtones. She had been 'converted' to the Children of God, a secretive quasi-religious cult which removed converts from their families, brainwashed them and introduced them to bizarre sexual practices. A strong-minded girl at King Edwards School had become obsessed with the cult and such was her force of character that she had managed to 'convert' dozens of other children. I was particularly worried because friends of my parents had lost their son to the sect, had no idea where he was and did not hear from him for over nine years. Thankfully, the craze at KES slowly died out.

Seeing the devastating effects of my chemotherapy was terribly hard for my daughters, made worse because there was no-one to comfort them. They could not turn to a child's usual source of reassurance – their mother. Their grandmother, even though she loved them dearly, adopted a stiff-upper-lip approach which did not allow for cuddles or tears. At school there was no-one who would listen or could truly understand. And as for their father, he simply ignored their distress. On leaving the hospital after my overdose crisis, Lou-Lou had turned and clung to him, distraught that I was so ill, shocked by what she had seen, only for him to push her away and put her in a taxi to Waterloo Station where, all on her own, she caught the train back to school. He also did something else, which to this day, she has never forgotten. In December, 1973, he told her that I was dying and that this would be my last Christmas, adding that she was not to tell a soul. He would not discuss it with her, leaving her to bear this unendurable sadness alone, my white face convincing her that what he said was true.

One day, John asked me if there was anything I would like to discuss.

"Like what?" I asked.

"Like your death," he said.

"But I'm not going to die."

"Yes you are."

"I'm not."

"You are."

"I'm not."

We batted the taboo subject back and forth like a poisoned ping-pong ball until at last I said:

"Where you got that idea from I don't know, but I've no intention of dying so would you please shut up about it."

A year or so later I found a letter hidden away. It was from my consultant and it was clear that John had written to him asking for a prognosis. The letter said that my illness was serious and he could not rule out my dying, either from the illness or the effects of the chemotherapy, but that I was doing well and he remained hopeful that I would survive. So John had had some reason for his pessimism. Perhaps he, too, was frightened. Perhaps we should have talked. But my only way was the positive way and I simply *would not* allow myself to contemplate the alternative.

At last, at long last, my chemotherapy ended and when ensuing blood tests remained clear month after month, the day I had longed for arrived and I heard the magic words, "you are cured". In fact the doctor prefaced this with "only time will tell, but for the moment I think we can say that...", but I disregarded this. Like my daughter before me, I had been restored to health by cutting-edge medicine. My body might be battered, my energy exhausted, but six long years after that first strange virus had almost certainly triggered off the cancer, I had finally made it. I had a life, I had a future and my children had a mother. It felt like a miracle. It was a miracle.

The end of my illness brought relief for all the family, not least my daughters. However, Victoria was having a difficult time on a different front. She had never been truly happy at King Edwards School but had now become the victim of a group of girls whose constant spite and bullying were making her life hell. Their tactics became so extreme that, in a hugely anxious state, she was admitted to the sanatorium. John and I were summoned to the school and, having seen our pale, weepy daughter, went to talk to the doctor.

"I'm very worried about Victoria," he said, "she's in such a state of stress that she's hyperventilating. I really do advise you to take her away right now."

I was appalled and as we hurried down the corridor towards our next appointment with Miss Swift, the school's 'senior mistress', I said to John:

"Why don't you go and talk to her whilst I get Torla's things packed up?"

"Get her things packed? What for? She's not going anywhere until I find out what's *really* going on," and into the presence of the hard-hearted, hated Miss Swift he swept, exuding charm. It soon became clear that she and John were of one mind; that it would be wrong to remove Victoria from the school. My wishes were ignored.

"No, no," said Miss Swift, as I put my point of view, "your husband's quite right, Mrs Watson – she must tough it out, it's character building."

Character building? Hadn't she had enough character building when she was left behind in Hong Kong? Hadn't coping with my illness been enough to toughen her and her sister up? Driving home, sick with worry, I had one last stab at changing his mind.

"Why can't she leave and do her 'A' levels at the local comprehensive?" I asked. But he was adamant.

A couple of weeks later a pale, drawn girl came home for the weekend.

"No wonder you're worried, Barbara, the poor child looks dreadful," said her grandmother as we prepared the lunch, "Its high time she left that place. I can't understand why John's so set on her staying. Look, I've had an idea. Supposing I offer to pay for her to go to a secretarial college, do you think he'd go along with that?"

'Pay for' – I knew at once that that phrase would be a deal-maker and hurried off to find him. Unsurprisingly, he agreed and when we told Victoria she fell into my arms, weeping with relief. Her hated school days were over. By any standards, she had done well. She had a string of 'O' levels under her belt, was now an accomplished pianist, oboe player and guitarist, and had even won a coveted part-time place at the Guildhall School of Music & Drama to continue her singing studies. But she had felt imprisoned. Now the cage door had opened and, like a little bird, she spread her wings and flew. At St James's secretarial college in London's fashionable Grosvenor Gardens, she found new friends, light-hearted, kind girls a world away from the malicious little gang who had made her life so miserable. Soon she was a normal happy teenager, partying, giggling over boys, yearning over popstars, begging for a new Laura Ashley dress, even while she acquired office skills and studied at the Guildhall. For me, the contentment was in having one of my girls at home again.

Mary-Louise was now in the Sixth Form and Head of her House and, with 'A' levels imminent, she was thinking about her future. A very clever, academic girl, she was drawn to speech and language therapy as a career but this was an unusual profession at the time with only two centres of learning. It was also an expensive training. She therefore had to think again and decided that she would like to be a teacher. She applied to a very good college in Oxford and was accepted. We were so proud of her but when her father realised that he would have to contribute towards the cost of her training he immediately changed his mind and announced that she could not go. His mother then stepped into the fray, objecting strongly to Lou-Lou's ambition to become a teacher. Whilst I was not surprised by my notoriously tight-fisted husband's attitude, I found it bizarre that Audrey Watson, a very successful woman, a brilliant teacher, did not want her own granddaughter to follow in her footsteps. I remembered her dismissal of my own qualifications and came to believe that, deep in her psyche, was someone who, despite her achievements, had a hang-up about her own lack of academic credentials.

I begged John to change his mind, I cajoled, I shouted. But, with his mother's backing, he would not be swayed. Finally, a compromise was reached; if Mary-Louise took a year out, she could go to college when she returned. Reluctantly, inwardly hurt and angry, she agreed.

Scouring the advertisements in The Lady magazine, we spotted a Swiss family looking for an au pair. I made enquiries, spoke to the couple on the telephone several times and felt confident that they would look after my daughter and treat her well. Shortly afterwards she left for Zurich. I know she doesn't want to go, I thought as I waved goodbye, but this is going to be a real adventure.

And so it proved to be, but not the sort I had envisaged, for the job was a disaster. Not only was she housed in a rented room some distance from the family but two weeks after she arrived she caught chicken pox from the children and was left alone to look after herself. What was more she found the father, in his sinister black-leather Nazi-style clothes, cold and intimidating. Even worse, she suspected him of taking his little girls down to the basement and beating them. She hated him, she hated the job and she wanted to come home.

"Oh no she's not," said John, "it's character building. I had to tough it out on the lower deck, let her tough it out there."

The poor girl did indeed tough it out, finding a new job after just two months, this time looking after a doctor's four children. This family were kind to her but even so, my intellectual daughter soon became bored with kids, housework and being a general dogsbody, and could not wait to return to England and college. Then one night she went to a party and met a handsome young Dutchman. His name was Diederik Hoebee, her future husband. Thus does Fate turn her mysterious wheel.

When Lou-Lou returned at the end of her year in exile, her father made an announcement which was as much news to me as it was to her - she could not go to college after all because he could not afford it. Even though the modest parental contribution was well within our reach and despite my pleading, he would not change his mind. Instead, she was offered a secretarial course, which, like her sister's, would be paid for by her grandmother.

She was enrolled at a smart secretarial college in Regents Park which, not surprisingly, she hated, finding the subjects insultingly easy. Her solution was to play hooky as often as possible, her friend Imogen impersonating me when ringing the college time after time to report Lou-Lou's puzzlingly constant run of ill health.

Throughout her year in England, I was filled with an overwhelming guilt that I had failed to change John's mind from effectively tricking our daughter out of her chance of higher education. At the same time, it was a wonderful period with both girls at home and even amidst the growing turmoil of my marriage, we achieved a semblance of normal family life. But at last the course ended and she left immediately for Amsterdam where Diederik awaited her as well as a very good job with British Airways. The following summer Dick, as he was known, came to stay. He was a clever young man who was studying for a degree in mechanical engineering. He was exceedingly tall, exceedingly thin, exceedingly handsome and charmed Lou-Lou's grandmother out of her socks. He got on very well with John and Victoria, too, but decided – almost on sight, so it seemed – that he didn't like me. Perhaps he saw me as a potential mother-in-law and, as such, the enemy. But he and Mary-Louise were clearly so in love that it truly did not matter.

By the time 1976 dawned, John had only two more opportunities for promotion and when his name did not appear in the first list of the year, he took the face-saving course of handing in his resignation in case his final chance also came to nothing. He had spent 22 years in the Navy, it was the only life he knew, but now the unimaginable, the unplanned for, had happened and he found himself in 'civvy street' - a fish who was literally out of water.

As though to emphasis the end of his adventurous life, he decided to become an accountant and found a firm of chartered accountants who took him on as a trainee. It seemed to me like the most unsuitable job in the world. Now his life stretched before him, boring and predictable, pounding the same old treadmill until he retired. No wonder, then, that along with this huge and unwelcome change came an equally huge increase in his drinking. Now and then he would disappear, returning after a couple of days, dirty, dishevelled and hung-over, offering no explanation as to where he had been. He spent most weekend mornings in the pub, moving neatly on to the Cricket Club where he could continue to drink, coming home for a snack and a nap before returning to the pub for the evening session. Once, when having Sunday lunch with his mother, he fell asleep mid-mouthful and his face dropped into his roast beef.

"Oh dear," she said when this happened, "my poor boy's ill. I *thought* he wasn't looking quite right."

"Your poor boy's not *ill* he's *drunk*," I retorted, pulling him to his feet and dragging him next door to our house, where I pushed him upstairs and threw him on the bed, guiltily hoping he would choke on his own vomit. Unsurprisingly, he often had 'flu' on Mondays!

What I had not heard when we first became Audrey Watson's neighbours, was the sound of a lock clicking behind me, the key pocketed by her. For, whilst she was a brilliant teacher, a kind and generous mother and grandmother, she was also a control freak. Hand in hand with living next door to her came her growing insistence that she know and be involved in every aspect of our lives. Nothing escaped her scrutiny and if it did not please her, a big chill ensued.

Our after-school chat soon became set in stone and if I failed to go in I would be met the next day with an icy:

"Oh, how *nice* of you to pop in. Unfortunately, I don't have time to sit gossiping like some people." And back home I'd creep, uneasy and irritated but knowing I just *had* to be there the next day on the stroke of four.

If I ventured out without telling her, she'd say: "I saw you walking past the house this morning. Where were you going?"

"To Kingston."

"Rather a shame you didn't think to ask me if there was anything I needed, but there you are, why should you bother about me?"

She clearly kept watch on the comings and goings next door and if she had not been told about visitors, I would get:

"Am I right in thinking you had people to supper last night?"

"Yes, the Bennetts."

"The Bennetts? Well, I *do* hope you had a pleasant evening. It would have been nice to be asked in for a drink before dinner, but who wants an old woman spoiling the party?"

One day I committed a truly heinous crime, which resulted in cold shoulder pie for days on end:

"Barbara, I hear you went to Mrs Straight's (one of her teachers) at the weekend, is this correct? It is? Well, I simply will *not* have you socialising with members of staff without my being informed."

It all sounds, and was, so petty, but her sulks could last for days, her 'we are not amused' face and silences worse than any tirade. This was a woman who ran her successful little empire by controlling every last detail. She was used to being obeyed and her jurisdiction now extended next door to us.

As the months and years passed, I began to feel the stranglehold of Audrey Watson's dictatorship tighten, but when the son on whom she doted left the Navy, things deteriorated further. Despite her difficult ways, I had always looked on her as a friend, but now I detected a veiled hostility. Why was she like this, I asked myself, what had happened to change her? Then one day it dawned on me – I had become her rival and she was jealous. She had no idea of the tensions within our marriage and so resented the apparent domestic harmony next door. We were now in competition. She wanted her son to herself. She was not only determined to get him, she was out to get me.

It also became clear that John enjoyed this new game of ganging up against Barbara. He seemed to spend more time in her house than ours. One day I found them holed up in the dining room clearly in the midst of a deep discussion. As I entered, they both looked up, expressionless.

"Yes?" asked his mother.

226

"Er, I just wondered if John was coming in for lunch."

"As you can see we're busy? He'll come in when we've finished," and they both stared at me silently until I crept humbly away.

"What on earth have you been talking about?" I asked when he returned.

"Oh," he said airily, "Mother's very worried about her Will. She doesn't want you to get anything when she dies so we're trying to work out how we can bypass you. So if she's left her money to me and then I die before you, it goes straight to the girls, not you, d'you see? But it's very tricky."

"Bypass me? What on earth do you mean?"

"Well, you're not one of the family so why should you get any of the money?"

"Not one of the family? But I've been married to you for twenty years! Honestly, I feel so hurt..."

"Hurt? For God's sake, woman, you're so damn mercenary and...oh, there you go again, crying, you're always crying."

He was right; I seemed to cry more and more these days. As time passed I felt increasingly intimidated and undermined, and my nerves twanged like an old banjo. I wanted to hit back but felt too demoralised to even try. This isn't the real me, I'd think, what's happened to the brave woman I used to be, the feisty woman, the fighter? What's happened to my life? Germaine Greer and the women's libbers were battling for change; my sister was marching on Greenham Common. And me? I was a powerless nobody. What had I got to look forward to? Nothing. My mother-in-law was now someone I could not bear and, as for my husband, I hated him. I longed to leave him but still had no idea how to break away or what to do if I did.

For the moment, I decided to try and make something of my hollow life. One of the Grantchester House teachers was a member of the Samaritans and the more she told me about the organisation the more I felt drawn to it. I applied for their next training course and knew at once that I could do this, knew I wanted to be there when desperate souls rang, knew I could throw out a lifeline.

All went well for a couple of weeks until one day my mother-in-law called me into the dining room. Now what, I wondered, looking at her icy face.

"I understand from Mrs Clarke that you have joined the Samaritans. Is this correct?" she asked.

"Yes," I said.

"And I've been told nothing about it? How *dare* you arrange things behind my back, without my knowledge and in collaboration with a member of *my* staff. I will not have it, do you understand? You are to stop at once."

You vile, manipulative woman, I thought, I'm damned if you're going to prevent me from doing this.

"Well, I'm sorry," I said, "but I won't stop. I want to do this and I know I'm going to be good at it." Then, pleased with myself that I had stood up to her, I walked out.

That should have been that, but it wasn't. She now treated me with a frigid politeness, enlisting John to convey her mounting fury at my disobedience. He in turn nagged me constantly, joining his mother in the campaign to prevent me from becoming a Samaritan.

"Look, for heaven's sake stop this," he said, "you can see how much trouble you're causing and how much it's upsetting Mother. Why on earth you want to go and listen to a load of suicidal drunks babbling down the phone, I don't know."

"Well, you'd know all about drunks," I snapped back.

My nerves, already frazzled, began to unravel further. At last I could bear the tension no longer and on an evening when I was supposed to go to training, I rang to say I could not make it.

"Why not?" asked the pleasant woman who was my group leader. And suddenly I found myself sobbing and spluttering down the line as I tried to explain what had happened, what was going on in my life, what had gone on before, why I was now feeling so desperate.

"Well," she said kindly, "it sounds as though you have enough to cope with at the moment without listening to other people's problems. So why don't you give this a break and come back when your life is more settled? And meanwhile, ring us at any time if you feel you want to talk about it."

Oh my God, I thought, I wanted to become a Samaritan and all I've done is call on them myself.

Shortly after this, John announced, not surprisingly, that he loathed accountancy and wanted to study law, which I could see would suit his intellect and personality so much better. However, when he said he wanted me to return to teaching full time to help fund his studies at the College of Law, I felt nothing but dismay as the trap tightened around me.

Victoria now had a job with an advertising agency and commuted

228

daily to London. Her presence, her love, were my only consolation as I grew thinner and thinner, more and more nervous and increasingly depressed. I was in emotional meltdown.

One day in the autumn of 1977, Audrey, John and I were invited to a dinner and dance, organised by the Grantchester House parents.

"What's the dress code," I asked my mother-in-law, for she had the invitation card.

"Oh very casual,' she said, "your green cotton kaftan would be fine."

"My kaftan? Are you sure? It's the sort of thing I wear to barbecues."

Yes, she assured me, it was the perfect combination, long but not too formal.

On the night of the dinner, I watched from the back seat of the car as John escorted his mother down her garden path. I could hardly believe my eyes, for far from being informally dressed, she was wearing an exquisite black evening gown, glittering with jet beads, new and clearly very expensive. Her pure white hair was swept up into an elegant chignon. She looked regal. She looked magnificent. With a curt 'good evening' to me, she eased herself into the front seat and we drove off, the two of them chatting happily away to each other whilst I sat in the back, ignored. I was stunned.

"You bitch," I thought, "you did this on purpose, you've *tricked* me."

And at that moment I realised that, however many times I'd said it before, this truly was the end. In the short time it took to drive to Esher, my life seemed to flash before me. There was so much that had been good and wonderful, but at this moment it was only the saddest things that sprang to mind: my mother's death, the pain of which never quite left me; the loss of my brother; the casual cruelty and draining of my confidence during Daphne's reign; the years of watching my precious daughter's health deteriorate; my own suffering. And what about John? The drinking and the women were hard enough to bear but his shortcomings as a father to his two beautiful daughters, his total lack of interest in them, his desertion of all three of us whenever we needed him most, they were what really counted in this horrible balance sheet. And now what? Had I really survived a long, near-fatal illness just to live under the petty tyranny of a woman who was the ultimate control freak, opinionated, unpredictable, temperamental, narrow-minded and snobbish? She, who had once been my staunchest

229

friend and ally, steadfast and wonderful in the worst of times, but who now treated me with contempt.

I could also see the sort of person I had become - a nervous, anxious wreck, constantly worrying about what she would think, what she'd say, bracing myself for John's next drunken bout, the next woman to claim his attentions. Inwardly I raged, outwardly I was a weakling. I could see that I had become perfect victim material, allowing them to get away with their behaviour simply because I had never stood up to them. Was this really the sort of person I wanted to be, was this really the life I'd dreamed of when I lay in hospital, fighting with every ounce of my being to stay alive?

We arrived, and as my mother-in-law walked in on her son's arm, everyone rose and broke into applause for the revered Mrs Watson. And, of course, every woman was dressed to kill. I, on the other hand, looked so utterly out of place that all I needed was a mop and bucket to complete my ensemble. As I trailed miserably round behind them like a poor relation, I struggled not to cry, not because of my fashion faux pas but because Audrey Watson could have planned this spiteful trick so clearly meant to humiliate me. But as the evening wore on, I gradually stopped feeling sorry for myself and an icy rage filled my heart. I had no idea where I'd go or how I'd manage, but I was leaving. And what's more, I thought grimly, I'm going to be the first person in history to divorce both her husband and her mother-in-law.

By the next morning, I was beginning to waver, wondering where I would live, what I could do to earn a living when I knew I was no longer strong enough, physically or emotionally, to go back to full-time teaching. But the seed had been planted and began to germinate.

I told Victoria, now aged 18, what had happened. She had witnessed my wobbly decline and, in any case, was as familiar with – and as much a victim of - her father's drunkenness as I was.

"You've got to go, Mummy," she said.

Then suddenly, like a bolt of lightning, she told me something which was so shocking, so appalling that I could hardly believe what I was hearing. It was about my return to Hong Kong following my illness when Victoria had left her foster home and was back with her father in our apartment, awaiting my arrival. Unbeknown to them, our flight was delayed and so she had awoken early, excited that the day she'd longed for had arrived. Mummy was coming home! She went into her father's bedroom and what should she see but someone in bed with him, someone with auburn hair like mine. Oh, she thought, she's come back in the night!

"Mummy! Mummy!" she cried, running to the bed.

The woman awoke and turned towards her. It was not me. My valiant daughter had kept this terrible secret from me for seven years.

Mary-Louise, who was still working for British Airways and was now assistant to their Amsterdam Sales Manager, had also been getting increasingly worried about the situation and flew home several times to try and help. She could see my mental state deteriorating and when I told her I wanted to leave, she too agreed that it was time to go.

Now I had to steel myself to speak to my husband and mother-in-law. Too cowardly to tell them of my real intention I said – with perfect truth - that I felt on the edge of a nervous breakdown and needed to get away. They both looked astonished.

"Nervous breakdown? Why on earth would you be having a nervous breakdown?"

It was easy then to burst into tears and say I didn't know but that, "I want to stay with my father and Tiggy for a while until I feel better."

To my surprise, there was no further argument. I rang my father who was shocked to hear my news but who nevertheless arranged to come and collect me the following week.

And so at last I left. Twenty years had passed since the sailor and his girl set out on their voyage, so happy, so full of hope, the boy to sail the seven seas, the girl to keep the fragile cockleshell of family life afloat. But now our life together was over and I departed, leaving behind the shining love of our youth, the tarnished wreckage of our marriage. It was the end.

There is no joy in leaving
For I have failed.
Pale flame of love extinguished
So dies the dream.
Though my heart fears the journey
What lies ahead?
One thing I know: tomorrow
I   will   be   free.

F I F T E E N

FOR WEEKS I LANGUISHED. I had thought my departure would bring instant relief and happiness. Instead I was drowning in a quagmire of depression, weeping and despairing both for the past and the future. My dear, long-suffering parents were initially mystified by the collapse of my marriage for, with misplaced loyalty, I had never once indicated that there was anything amiss. Perhaps a long-ago echo of my father's warning of sailors 'with a wife in every port' still lingered somewhere in my mind. Perhaps I could not bear to tell him that he had been right. Now, faced with the truth, they were shaken and outraged by my often sordid tale.

"Why didn't you tell me years ago?" asked my father, "perhaps I could have talked some sense into him."

Gradually I grew calmer until the day came when I knew I could no longer put off what I had been dreading most – I had to tell John that I was not coming back. That evening I rang him. His emotions moved swiftly from astonishment and disbelief to outrage, finally exploding into an incandescent and terrifying rage. I put the phone down, shuddering and shaking, yet relieved. I'd done it. The worst was over. Now I could move on. But I was wrong. He began to bombard me with phone calls, each more drunken and threatening than the last, culminating on the evening when he screamed:

"I'm going to hang your daughter", before slamming down the phone.

Oh my God, I thought, what have I done, what on earth have I done? For, in making my plans to leave, I had made one disastrous mistake - I had forgotten all about Victoria. Now she was stuck with a man who was a useless father at the best of times but who was now out of control. Once again, as in Hong Kong, she had been left behind to cope as best she could. I was distraught. How *could* I have let this happen?

Things were every bit as bad as I feared, her father's behaviour so appalling that she eventually went to stay in someone's virtually derelict house in London. Then one weekend she decided to return home, only to find that the locks had been changed and she couldn't get in. She had a sweet boyfriend who took her home to his wealthy parents' house and they, a warm and loving family, welcomed her into their midst and into their hearts.

Mary-Louise continued to fly back as often as she could, this time to support her father who was devastated by what had happened, unable to believe that I had done what I had so often threatened to do, and left him.

"Why don't you stay with us?" asked my parents one evening when we were discussing my future, "you know we'd love it. You could get a little job in locally and we'd all be so happy together."

But much though I loved them, I knew I had to move on. I rang my sister and asked if I could come and stay with her whilst I looked for a job. The day after I told John I was leaving him, he closed our joint bank account, so I now had nothing. My father, not a rich man, gave me £100 as my 'start again fund' and off I went to London.

Patricia and her family lived in a sprawling flat in Muswell Hill. She knew all about the misery of marriage breakdown as her own had ended in 1975, leaving her with four children to bring up. As well as Lydia, her eldest, there were teenagers Adam and Mark, and Ben who, at eleven, was still not too old to cuddle his auntie. Patricia had started a ballet school some years earlier and this was the mainstay of the family's income. Even so, her life was tough as she struggled to make ends meet.

It was a lively, rowdy, bohemian household; bikes in the hall, tutus hanging from picture frames with miles more fabric trailing from the sewing machine, a cello propped up by the piano, a euphonium on the kitchen table, a half-finished canvas on the paint-splattered easel, books, sheet music, school satchels, all overseen by a pride of beautiful tabby cats.

Here, with my sweet nephews and niece showing me how to live in the here and now, and with my sister's love and understanding, the real me began to re-emerge.

I started making plans. I rang Irene, the naval wife who had lived next to us in Emsworth. She too was on her own, her husband having left her and her three children for a woman with five children, the youngest just a few months old. When this happened, Irene had tried to commit suicide

233

and if I had not found her unconscious and rung for an ambulance, her attempt would have been successful. We had been good friends as well as neighbours, happy in good times, supporting each other through our respective husbands' infidelities and, in her case, through the shadow of death. Now I asked her if she would like to share a flat with me and she readily agreed.   I was forty years old. I knew it was going to be hard.

S I X T E E N

WHAT ON EARTH POSSESSED us to take the flat above the betting shop I will never know. Stupidity springs to mind. It was certainly cheap but we soon realised it was not the best residence in the world for two middle-aged women on their own. It was in a short cul-de-sac at the poorest end of Epsom. A few other run-down shops lined each side of the street: a butcher selling lurid cuts of meat; a second-hand furniture dealer, his junk spilling out over the pavement; a corner store with half-empty shelves; a shop selling reconditioned electrical goods; a green grocers and a seedy launderette. The rest of the shops were closed, their fronts boarded up and plastered with posters for wrestling matches, obscure bands and prostitutes' calling cards.

The flat was reached through a dark and dripping archway at the side of the betting shop, which led to a door at the back. This in turn opened onto a narrow flight of stairs covered in cracked linoleum. There was a big sitting room at the front, its hideous furnishings garishly lit by strips of neon light. Thin, unlined curtains in a poisonous shade of green hung at the windows and the floor was covered with a threadbare carpet from which the pattern had long since disappeared. In one corner was a narrow bed, which Irene decided should be hers.

An unusual feature of the flat was the greyhound and horse racing commentaries that wafted up through the floorboards. On particularly noisy Saturdays we used to speculate that this might perhaps lead to our becoming experts, able to nip downstairs and put a tenner on a rank outsider. Our nag would romp home and we'd win fists-full of grubby money which would restore our fortunes.

On our first night we were awoken by the thud of feet, bumps and bangs and muffled voices emanating from the electrical shop next door.

The next morning we discovered that the shop had been 'done' and half the stock of tatty old televisions stolen. On commiserating with the owner we also discovered we were the only occupants of the flats above the shops. In other words, no-one else lived in the street. We hired a telly from him, which he carried up to our flat and got going. He, like the butcher on the other side, clearly thought he was in with a chance with the two single women who had moved in, goodness knows why, as my daughters say we looked like two worn out bag ladies at the time. They began to besiege us, one with over-frequent checks on the television set, the other bearing gifts - a couple of nice chump chops or half a pound of best mince. We got a bit worried, so the next time they came a-calling I stationed myself by the door and pressed a coin of the realm into their palms as they left, thanking them in a condescending voice for their assistance and assuring them we would ask if we needed their help again. It worked. Even so, these kind men continued to look out for us.

Still emotionally wobbly, I had ruled out teaching as a career and decided instead to return to office work, practicing my shorthand and typing whilst staying with my parents. I soon managed to get temping work but it was hard and poorly paid. Added to this were the frightening gaps between work when my income plunged towards zero. I had also underestimated the effects of my illness, and the long working days, the travelling, the crowded commuter trains, left me exhausted. One dark, freezing evening as I waited for my train, another one pulled in first and I saw that it was going to Hinchley Wood. I stood at its open doors and knew that I all I had to do was step in and within an hour I could be home again. Something even told me that John and his mother would welcome me back. I was so tired, hungry too, and knew I had just a few coins in my purse which had to last 'til Friday. But the moment passed and the train pulled out. It would have been so easy but I knew there could be no turning back.

At last I managed to get a permanent job with an import-export company in nearby Sutton. There were only four of us in the gloomy offices above a bank - the boss, so nondescript that I can remember nothing about him, Olive, the book-keeper, Melanie, a dim, giraffe-like teenager who manned the switchboard, and me. It was a mind-numbingly dull job but there was only a short commute, it was not particularly tiring work and I earned more money. All-in-all an improvement. Even so, it was with a sinking heart that I returned at the end of each day to the horrid flat above the betting shop.

My bedroom was so small that there was just space for a bed

shoved up against the wall, a chair and a chest of drawers. Like the kitchen, it was at the back of the flat and looked out over a desolate wasteland of burnt-out cars, dumped fridges, filthy mattresses, old prams and mounds of decaying rubbish, beyond which lay a railway shunting yard. It was always cold and no matter how many layers I piled on the bed, despite clutching a hot water bottle, wearing socks and a cardigan over my nightie, I just could not get warm. Even my sheepskin jacket on top of the duvet did not help. Night after night I lay huddled up and shivering before I eventually dropped into a fitful sleep.

One night I had a nightmare. In it, I dreamt that someone was pulling me out of bed by my ankles. A few nights later, I had the same dream. The following week it happened again until soon the same nightmare had awoken me, my heart pounding, for five nights in a row. I dreaded going to bed but didn't tell Irene as I didn't want to scare her, but she seemed quite happy to sit up later and later each night, watching silly films until bedtime could no longer be put off.

Then came the moment when the nightmare took on a new and terrifying form. I had fallen asleep in the freezing bed and, inevitably, the bad dream was waiting to pounce. Suddenly I found myself wide awake and an unseen, evil something had me by the ankles and was actually pulling me out of bed. I landed on the floor with a thump and lay there too frightened to move, waiting for the blow, the knife, or the hands around my throat, which would finish me off. But whatever 'it' was had gone and after a moment or two I crept in to Irene. When I told her what had happened, she clapped her hands to her face.

"Oh, Barbara," she said, "I've been having the same dream, we've got to get out of here."

The next day was Saturday. Irene had arranged to visit her mother and I decided to spend the morning cleaning the place. I changed the sheets in what I now knew was a haunted room and then dragged the bed away from the wall to vacuum behind it, something I had not done before. And there, in the winter light shining thinly through the window, I saw something which filled me with horror - below the level of the bed, splattered across the wallpaper and the carpet, was a large reddish-brown stain. There was no mistaking what it was - blood. I ran out of the room, grabbed my coat and fled.

Later, sitting in a little café in the town centre, I sipped a cup of coffee and tried to think calmly and rationally about what might have happened in that horrible place. I felt sure it had something to do with the

237

previous occupants, a gay couple. How easy, I thought, for one man to have murdered the other, dragging his body down the stairs at dead of night, out across the wasteland at the back to drive it away and dump it heaven knows where. There were no neighbours to hear the screams or see a corpse being hauled out. Had the murderer then returned to clean up the scene of his crime, coolly stayed for a few more weeks, spreading the word (so the butcher told us) that his friend had gone to Australia, before disappearing himself?

And what was the explanation for the nightmare that became so horribly real? Were we two women so vulnerable at that point in our lives that we were open to the haunting and the evil spirit that pervaded the place? Who knows? But that evening when Irene returned I showed her the stain without comment and she, too, knew at once that it was blood. One thing was very clear - we had to go. But first we had to save enough money for the deposit on a new flat.

Olive the bookkeeper's parents had unknowingly named her with pinpoint accuracy, for she was a tiny woman whose drab complexion was indeed a shade of olive. Her most prized possession was clearly her knitting machine on which she had made a series of identical dresses, each more lurid than the last. What would she wear today, one wondered, orange, turquoise, mauve, yellow, emerald green? But what she lacked in fashion know-how she made up for in heart. When, on the Monday after the haunting, I told her what had happened and about our lack of money for a deposit, she patted my shoulder and said "leave it to me" before darting into the boss's office. Within minutes she had secured an advance on my salary which meant that shortly afterwards we moved into a beautiful, sunny apartment at the top of an old Edwardian house. Below us lived a happy family, and the sound of children's laughter filled the air.

Irene and I decided to consult a fortune teller who had been recommended to her. Now that luck seemed to be turning our way, perhaps he could tell us what other areas of our lives were about to get better? We wound our way to Croydon on a bus and found him in a seedy bungalow which stank of chip fat and stale cigarettes. His ancient mother ushered us into the presence and there, faintly illuminated by green fairy lights, sat a lizard-like man. Wisps of smoke curled upwards from the cigarette hanging from his lower lip and his shabby oriental jacket was splattered with ash. After we had handed over our hard-earned cash, he stubbed out his fag in an overflowing ashtray and got down to work. He stared earnestly into a crystal ball for a while then began to sway and moan, writhe and mutter until, with a groan, he sank back in his chair, apparently unconscious. Just as I was wondering if we could creep away unnoticed he 'came to' and, in a few swift sentences, confidently predicted the same thing for us both, namely that we would cross a wide stretch of water where we would meet a wealthy stranger and – oh joy! - live happily ever after. I, it seemed, would receive an airmail letter within a few days, which would see the start of this happy adventure. Codswallop!

Victoria took over, escorting me to a soothsayer in the Barbican who had a smart office and a client list of prosperous city gents. She was assisted in her findings by a large cat – John Wesley – on whom she would call for confirmation as she consulted her cards:

"We've got a definite 'yes' coming through, haven't we John Wesley?"

She was not a charlatan but neither was she my cup of tea and I left feeling none the wiser. We gave up the crystal gazing for a long time after that until Victoria told me of a very special lady she had been to see. Her name was Mrs Reid and she lived somewhere in South East London. She was a clairvoyant psychometrist who was able to pick up information about a person from an object they wore frequently. We found her in a red brick Victorian housing estate, her little flat small, spotless, threadbare. She was a tall, angular woman, a hard life writ large on her lined face. She had just come in from her 'day job' and looked tired.

"I won't be long," she said, showing us into a tiny sitting room, "I'm just going to make meself a cuppa soup."

After a while she returned and I handed her my watch. Almost immediately, her eyes filled with tears:

"I'm picking up so much sadness here," she said, "grief, betrayal, illness... You've been thwarted at every turn, never realising your ambitions, never truly able to be yourself..."

And so she went on, outlining my life as though she had known me personally for years. Finally she said:

"But all that is coming to an end. You are going to have all the opportunities you've missed and you are going to be surrounded with love for the rest of your life."

Then she described a man I would one day meet. He would be tall, slim, with light brown hair, blue eyes, a beard, a high forehead... When we left I felt suddenly happy. The dark days were over. From now on things could only get better.

Although I had stupidly thought I could disappear without trace, John eventually contacted me and later, when we moved to Sutton, we met several times for a drink. Despite all that had happened, the tiniest flicker of our original love was still there. He was at his best, charming, witty, interesting and interested, and when he began to suggest we try again, I found myself tempted. However, I told him that if we were ever to live together again there would have to be changes. The first was that we move away from Hinchley Wood and his mother, the second that he seek help with his drinking. He said he would think about both and, meanwhile, suggested we have a holiday together. The next time we met he told me that he was not willing to leave Hinchley Wood but assured me that all would be well because he and his mother were both prepared to forgive me. *They'd* forgive *me*? I knew then there could be no going back.

A little while later I met someone else. His name was Dan and he had come into my dreary Sutton office for some reason and, on leaving, had asked me for a piece of paper, scribbled something on it and handed it back. It said: 'If you would like to have lunch with me, write down your telephone number'. So I did.

We got on immediately although careful scrutiny showed that he did not match Mrs Reid's description of Mr Right. He was shortish, his eyes were indeed blue but his hair was a greying shade of blond. However, he was a pleasant looking man, indeed he liked to point out that he bore a passing resemblance to Robert Redford, and this was true. He was a successful public relations consultant and his tales of clients, campaigns, press conferences and glamorous events fascinated me. It all sounded a world away from my mundane life. We soon became 'an item' and I began to care for this complicated man who was unromantic, generous, pragmatic, a bit of a gourmet, energetic, hyper, given to sudden anger but also very kind. Under his influence, my life slowly began to change. Firstly, he nagged me to get a better job, insisting that I was worth more than my current dead-end one and suggesting a secretarial agency that specialised in the top end of the market. Within weeks I was shortlisted for a job as P.A. to the chairman of an old established firm of stockbrokers based at the Stock Exchange in the City of London.

"Well", said Miss Human Resources at the end of my second interview, "I'm sure the Chairman would like to meet you. I'll go and get him."

After a few moments the door opened. Enter Henry Moss, fading movie-star. He was probably in his early sixties and still a very handsome man, slim and fair with Arctic blue eyes and a short, aristocratic nose. He was exquisitely dressed and, as he advanced towards me on a subtle cloud of expensive aftershave, I noticed his manicured nails and the gleam of a gold watch chain looped across his waistcoat. He exuded charm.

"*Mrs* Watson," he said in the cut glass tones of society's upper echelons, "*what* a pleasure to meet you. Now *do* tell me *everything* about yourself."

We talked for a while and then he left. Shortly afterwards Miss Human Resources returned to tell me that the job was mine.

I walked to the underground in a daze. Could I really be PA to the chairman of one of the City's oldest stockbrokers? How absolutely amazing! I'd got this prestigious job against stiff opposition, I'd earn a lot more money, I'd be working at the hub of the financial world and as for my boss - oh, what a perfectly heavenly man Mr Moss was! I could hardly believe this change in my fortunes and could hardly wait to start work.

A couple of weeks later, wearing a smart new suit, I sat at my desk high up in the Stock Exchange building, nervously awaiting the first call to action. My telephone tinkled.

"Good morning, *would* you come in," said my new boss.

I picked up my notebook and scuttled nervously along the thickly carpeted corridor to his office, praying my shorthand would be up to the financial terminology awaiting me.

Henry Moss was sitting behind his desk but had swung his chair round towards the huge windows overlooking the panorama of London stretching away into the distance. He did not look at me as I entered and after a clipped 'good morning' started to dictate. Here we go, I thought. For what seemed an eternity he gave me letters to his tailor, his interior decorator, his vintners, his friends - not a thing about stocks and shares. He spoke extremely quickly and at one point I asked him to repeat what he'd said.

"Don't *dare* interrupt when I'm dictating, do you hear me?" he snapped irritably, swinging round and fixing me with an icy glare, "now where was I? Oh, how *utterly* infuriating, I've completely lost my train of thought. Read it back, for heaven's sake."

I was astonished. Where was the charming man who had interviewed me? Later, as I typed the letters, I hoped he was just having an off day and felt sure Mr Nice Guy would return. But as the weeks went by I began to see that he was actually rather an unpleasant person. Whilst he was charm personified when he needed to be, and always to those he considered his social equals, I definitely did not warrant courtesy or consideration. In his eyes, I was just another lackey, no better than the maids and valets, grooms and gardeners who had served him throughout his life, and as such I was treated accordingly. Each day I felt more and more depressed and began to wonder how long I could, or should, put up with the situation. Dan, now an important presence in my life, agreed. After all, he said, if I could get a job like this, I could find another one just as good.

There was one member of his entourage, however, whom he did respect and that was his chauffeur Fred, custodian of the claret coloured Bentley. Fred had been in his service for years and was a dear man who used to perch on the side of my desk, swigging tea and entertaining me with endless behind-the-scenes gossip. I loved him.

"You alright, darlin'?" he asked one day when I met him in the lift. "Every time I sees you, you looks more'n more fed up. Isn't the boss treatin' you right?"

"No he's not. He's being absolutely vile and quite honestly Fred, if it goes on like this I'm leaving."

"Right then," he said, "I'd better 'ave a word wiv 'im, 'adn't I luv?"

"Oh no, no, *please* don't do that," I gasped, "he'll be even nastier if you say anything."

But he just gave me a wink and stepped out of the lift.

"Leave it to me, darlin'," he said before the doors shut.

I felt even more miserable after our conversation, convinced that dear old Fred, for all his good intentions, would only make matters worse. On the way home I bought an evening paper and scanned the Situations Vacant. And next morning when Mr Moss rang with his usual "*will* you come in", I was ready for the worst. But a charming smile greeted me.

"How *are* you today, Mrs Watson? Well I trust. And *what* a charming frock if I may say so..."

I was staggered. Whatever Fred had said to 'the boss' had done the trick. Later that week, he put his head round my office door.

"Well?" he asked.

"Fred, whatever did you say?"

"Say? I said 'e'd better pull 'is bleedin' socks up or 'e'd lose the best PA e's ever bleedin' 'ad. That's what I said. Now, where's me cuppa?"

242

I got up and gave him a hug.

From then on things changed. Whilst the chairman was still irascible, he was no longer so downright horrible. And even though I somehow felt this change was not truly genuine at least it allowed our working relationship to find a balance.

Although about a third of my job did include broking matters, largely concerned with the trust funds of the mega-rich, the rest of my day was spent on Mr Moss's personal and social affairs, and in arranging the directors' lunches. These took place on the top floor of the Stock Exchange building, where our firm had two dining rooms. Every day guests would be invited who were usually prominent figures from the world of finance and government. Each morning I liaised with the cook to work out the menus, discussed suitable wines with one of the senior directors, typed out and circulated menus and table plans, organised flowers and so on. Whilst the Chairman and senior directors always ate upstairs, there was insufficient space for more junior men, so soup and sandwiches were provided for them to eat in the 'sandwich room'. Clearly, lunching upstairs was far more prestigious, quite apart from the star quality food, and it was my task to rotate names so that everyone had their turn. This, I soon realised, gave me a certain amount of power and junior directors who incurred my displeasure sometimes found themselves banished to the sandwich room for weeks at a time. One by one they'd come creeping round my office door, making small talk whilst I waited for them to cut to the chase:

"...oh, by the way, Barbara, I've been in the sandwich room for over a month now. Any chance of lunch upstairs?"

"Over a month," I'd ask in a concerned voice, "are you sure? Let me check my lists. Oh dear, so you have. Look, leave it with me and I'll make sure you're upstairs next week."

Tee hee!

Another thing I quickly grasped was that, whilst Henry Moss had to be handled with kid gloves in the mornings, after lunch it was a different matter. He would re-appear at about three, face flushed, words slightly slurred and it was then one was able to get a rise out of him.

"Did you enjoy lunch?" I'd ask, meeting him in the corridor, "how was the pheasant?"

"The *pheasant*? My dear madam, the *pheasant* was so *tough* it must have been run over by an *ambulance* in the *First World War.*"

"Oh, Mr Moss, you are too funny for words! Eddy," I'd call, hailing a passing broker, "do ask Mr Moss if he enjoyed his lunch!"

243

And all afternoon one would faintly hear his voice repeating this witticism as he tottered round the offices. In all fairness, he was an extremely witty man.

He mixed with the cream of society and frequently figured in the social diary columns of the glossiest magazines - 'The Hon Mrs Frightfully Riche and her lovely daughter Araminta, pictured with Mr Henry Moss and the Earl of Asprey'. He was a frequent guest at Clarence House where the Queen Mother must have adored his wit and charm.

His male friends all had nicknames more usually associated with labradors: 'Dear, Dear Buffy,' he'd write, 'There's a dearth of grouse on the moors this year so Tucker, Bongo and I are repairing to Hampshire for the pheasant. Dicky therefore summons you to Broadlands this coming Friday for dressing-gown supper at eight. Do, I pray you, join us.'

He had never married and I could not make up my mind whether he was a camp 'walker' or merely irresistible to well-bred women of a certain age. Certainly, countless ladies rang to speak to him,

"Hellya," said one voice after another, "put me through to Mr Moss."

Victoria loved me to regale her with these tales of the high and mighty, and in our lunch hours we rang each other from our respective offices to practise 'the voice'.

"Hellya,"

"Hell*ya, hell*ya.*"

"Hell*ya, hell*ya, hell*YA!*"

We never tired of the joke.

A Board meeting was in progress one day and, as usual on these occasions, my instructions were that they were on no account to be disturbed. My telephone rang:

"Hellyah," shrieked a voice.

Ha, good try Torla, I thought, but I can do better.

"HellYA, hellYA," I shrieked back.

"Who *is* thet?" demanded the voice irritably.

Whoops.

"Er, Mr Moss's secretary," I said, pulling myself together, "can I help you?"

"This is Countess Fitzgower, put me through to Mr Moss *immediately.*"

"I'm afraid he's in a Board Meeting until lunchtime and can't be disturbed. Can I give him a ...?"

"My dear good woman, this is an emergency, there's been a death - put me through to him at *once*."

"Oh my goodness, I'm so sorry." I gasped, "his phone's switched off but I'll go in and tell him. What shall I say?"

"Tell him," she said, her voice breaking, "tell him the dealer's dead."

I raced to the boardroom, knocked on the door and walked in. Ten faces turned and glared at me.

"What is it?" barked the Chairman from the head of the table, "I've *told* you never to...."

"Yes I know, but I have an urgent message from Countess Fitzgower. There's been a death."

The room went quiet.

"A death?" he said, "who's dead?"

"I'm afraid it's the dealer."

"The Dealer?" he snapped, "oh for heaven's sake, it's only our racehorse. Say I'll call her later."

'Only our racehorse' eh? I thought, as I walked back to my office, that shows just what a cold fish you really are.

There were big changes in my private life. My divorce was now going ahead which, much to my surprise, had been initiated by John. I had heard from the girls that he was dating a lady whose children had not only gone to Grantchester House School but whom I had taught. Presumably they wanted to get married and I felt happy for them.

After trying one or two disastrous solicitors, neither of whom were a match for John's legal team, Dan suggested someone else. His name was Peter Grose-Hodge and he was a divorce lawyer based in one of the Inns of Court. After we had discussed the case on my first visit, he asked me about my financial position. How much did I earn? I told him. Did I have any savings? No Stocks and shares? No. Any other investments? No. Did I own any property? No. Did I have any jewellery or works of art? Nope. But despite this obvious lack of assets, he took me on.

"So you're travelling light," he said, "we'll just have to see what we can do for you. At the least, you need a home of your own."

He proved to be not just an equal to John's lawyer but also my friend. Strangely, although John had asked for the divorce, he categorically denied every reason put to him, including adultery. Indeed, he insisted that, instead of an amicable divorce on the ground of irreconcilable differences, he would 'see us in court'. Big Piggy, as I came to call Peter Grose-Hodge, would write saying: '....your husband has now taken complete leave of his senses....' However, John eventually capitulated and our marriage ended quietly and without fuss. My final bill from Big Piggy, whose services only the wealthy could normally afford, was for less than £200.

By now Irene and I had left our leafy flat in Sutton, she to work abroad and me to move into central London so as to be nearer my work. I had found a large bed-sitting room just off Sloane Square. Although a fashionable address, this was the only thing that could be said in its favour. It was a huge room decorated in migraine-inducing shades of scarlet and turquoise, and was at the front of a large, shabby, once beautiful flat owned by a divorced woman with four small children. I loved children and missed their company since I'd stopped teaching but this quartet proved to be quite the most unpleasant little mob I'd ever met. One of their nastier traits was to lie in wait until I had gone into the bathroom designated as mine, then pound on the door, shouting at me to come out because they wanted to 'go'.

"But why does she have to live here?" they'd whine as their mother tried to pry their fingers from the door knob.

"I'm sorry, darling," she'd reply, not bothering to lower her voice, "we have to have her here to help pay the school fees. We'll get rid of her soon, I promise."

Don't worry, you horrible lot, I'd think to myself, I'll be out of here the first moment I can. For the fact was that, with my divorce settlement finalised, I was now in a position to buy a home of my own.

The excitement of the search for property soon wore off when every flat I went to see had either just been sold or was unsuitable. One day, a couple of months after my quest had begun, I trailed reluctantly down the Fulham Road to look at a place which sounded on paper like a DIY disaster zone. But the moment I walked in I knew it was for me. What had originally been one side of a corner shop had been transformed into the most stunningly innovative living space. Designed by an award-winning architect, it had even featured in a glossy magazine. Half an hour later I agreed to buy it. When I told Henry Moss I was moving to Fulham he clicked his fingers and frowned in concentration:

"Fulham, Fulham, Fulham? Now let me see. Ah yes, I know - that's where all the *common* people live'"

What a joy it was to have a home again, something I had longed for, not just for myself but for my daughters. Lou-Lou still lived in Amsterdam but Victoria was nearby, sharing a house with girlfriends in Battersea. At weekends we would wander up the Fulham Road, window shopping, sipping coffee, trying on clothes, testing make-up, having our hair done, treating ourselves to little lunches. She had a boyfriend with a restaurant on the Kings Road where we often dined, free of charge and with extra pampering from the owner and the waiters. How lovely it was to be light-hearted.

In 1979 came the news that Mary-Louise and Dick Hoebee were getting married, something we had hoped for and expected. The wedding was to take place in Amsterdam on the 13th of August. Victoria and I bought gorgeous outfits and shoes with killer heels then, with mounting excitement, flew to Holland for the great day.

Behind the scenes, however, there were tensions. John and Natalie Fancey had married just six weeks earlier and he wanted his new wife to come to the wedding. But Lou-Lou, in deference to my feelings, vetoed this. He was furious but eventually relented, agreeing to come alone. It would be the first time we had seen each other for over two years and it was a daunting prospect. However, this paled to nothing compared with my apprehension at meeting my ex-mother-in-law again. Oh dear, I thought, what if she's still radiating ice-cold hatred in my direction? Equally, I knew I was far from the brow-beaten woman I used to be and told myself that whatever she was like I could and would handle it, for absolutely nothing could be allowed to spoil my daughter's wedding day.

There was also another problem. When Dick's rather difficult mother heard that John and I were getting divorced, she was horrified. Her son, marrying the daughter of *divorcees*? How simply *appalling*. Nobody must ever find out because if her family and friends got to hear of this, the disgrace would be insupportable. Now, with the wedding day approaching, she announced that John and I must pretend we were still married. Okay, I thought, I can do that. I just hoped John could too.

Victoria and I arrived at Lou-Lou and Dick's apartment to find the bride-to-be painting a pair of red shoes white.

"Oh," she said airily, setting them to dry on the windowsill, "I couldn't find white ones I liked and the shape of these is perfect."

Then came the moment I had been dreading - the arrival of John and his mother. Dick had given me a glass of brandy to calm my nerves but even so I was shaking inwardly when the doorbell rang. I need not

247

have worried for John, with his usual easy charm, put everyone at ease. Then the champagne was uncorked and we toasted the young couple as they stood on the threshold of their new life.

Audrey edged over to me. "We've missed you at Grantchester House, Barbara," she said, "but I hope you are happy in your new life."

Then, before I could reply, she added in a near whisper:

"Tell me, was I in any way responsible for you leaving John?"

I looked at her face, older now, a touch vulnerable.

"Of course not," I lied.

No wedding could have been more beautiful, Mary-Louise exquisite in her gown of cream silk and lace, Dick, tall and dashing in a cream suit.

John and I did not let them (or Dick's mother) down and, for the next two days, throughout the rehearsal, the eve-of-wedding dinner, the Town Hall ceremony, the church ceremony and the wedding reception, nobody would have known that we were not married. We put on a convincing performance and of course, because we had known each other since our teenage years, had been married for so long and had two children together, it was not at all difficult. All the acrimony had disappeared and we truly enjoyed each other's company. At the same time, I knew I much preferred my new life and would never want to turn back the clock. I asked him about his new wife and he loyally reported that she 'did not have a kind bone in her body.' One day he would find out that nothing could be further from the truth when, like an avenging angel, Natalie would step in to help him during a time of terrible suffering. But for now, I knew this was just John being – well – John and that he would no doubt report back to his new wife that I was as awful as I had always been.

The moment our flight took off for the return journey we flew into turbulence and the nearer we got to Heathrow the more violent this became. The plane bucked and rolled, juddered and shook whilst from the windows we could see the white tops of the waves far below. Victoria and I were terrified, our fear not eased when, on the final approach to Heathrow, we noticed two air hostesses strapped into their seats, gripping each other's hands, white faced with terror.

It was not until we arrived home that we discovered that this freak storm had been the cause of the worst-ever yachting disaster. Over three hundred yachts had set off from Cowes for the Fastnet Race – climax of the Admiral's Cup series - and, caught by the violent and unexpected force eleven winds, 115 of them had foundered, been blown off course or were severely damaged. Fifteen yachtsmen drowned whilst many more were injured. It was a tragic note on which to end what, for our family, had been a time of happiness and rejoicing.

Dick Hoebee had landed a very good job with Shell and not long after their wedding, he and Mary-Louise left for their first posting in Oman, a life which she would find strangely difficult.

Not surprisingly, Victoria did not enjoy the secretarial work she was doing. Her true love was, and always would be, music. One day she announced that she was giving up office work forever. She had drifted away from classical music and had now became a singer and songwriter. She got an agent and soon along came her first handsomely paid assignment, which was to perform in a nightclub in the newly-independent African state of Zimbabwe which, up until April, 1980, had been the British colony of Rhodesia. Victoria was the first 'foreign' artiste to perform in the capital, Salisbury (now Harare) following independence. At that time the country was still peaceful, its people basking in their new-found freedom, and the ten weeks she spent there were an exciting and fascinating experience. Most of her work was abroad and included a return to Singapore where she had spent such happy years as a child. She became popular in Portugal and I would sometimes fly out to join her there as her so-called wardrobe mistress. It was fun watching her performances, but backstage I felt – and no doubt looked – as out of place as a nun amongst the showgirls, acrobats, strong men and magicians. This was the start of Victoria's musical career, which, as it unfolded, would see her move away from the world of pop and cabaret as she found her own style, her own unique sound, her own music.

Not long after moving to where 'the common people live', I had some more news for Henry Moss - I was leaving. Unbelievably, Dan had offered me a job. He had told me that the Department of Energy was planning a national competition for schools and that he planned to pitch for it. This was the late 1970's and, since the energy crisis in 1973/4 when the world had felt the effects of OPEC embargos, people were beginning to realise that fossil fuel supplies could - and one day would - run out. Alternative sources of energy needed to be found, energy efficiency needed a radical rethink and people had to learn to switch off more than they switched on. The competition would invite children to come up with their own energy saving ideas.

I was inspired by this and spent the following weekend with my school teacher's hat on, writing a blue print for how the competition might be organised. I gave it to Dan next time we met and the following morning he rang me. He was delighted and said he no longer needed to write a proposal as what I had done was perfect. His next call was even more exciting; the pitch to the Department had been successful and he wanted me to join his consultancy and work specifically on this project.

And so I entered the endlessly varied, always fascinating world of public relations. Oh my goodness, I said to myself on my first morning as I walked out of Green Park station swinging a new burgundy leather briefcase embossed with my initials, I'm a *consultant*! How important I felt.

In public relations terms, Dan was an ideas man, pouring out new ideas like money from a fruit machine. He was genuinely charming and got on with people from every walk of life. He was a front man, a persuader, able to convince people of his plans, the one who pulled in the new accounts. Behind the scenes he was totally disorganised, bringing a whole new meaning to the word 'untidy'. His desk was piled six inches high with papers which overflowed onto every nearby surface. Nobody was allowed to touch them as he declared he needed them all and knew where each important document was. So he may have done, but when he went on holiday and I skimmed off the bottom half and threw it away, he never noticed!

How different my life now was. I quickly got used to Dan's lavish lifestyle; our offices were in Dover Street, Mayfair, and clients were entertained at the then hugely fashionable Langan's restaurant or taken to tea at Brown's Hotel just up the road, whilst a drink after work meant a cocktail at the Ritz. We travelled round London by taxi. Indeed my daughters noticed that I had developed 'taxi arm' for, if we were standing at a bus stop and a cab hove into sight, I simply had to hail it!

The 1970's were a dark time for the country with Britain derisively labelled 'the sick man of Europe'. Now, towards the end of the decade, strikes swept the country as workers protested against the Government's tough wage restraints. Lorry drivers, oil tanker drivers, ambulance men, and nurses, walked out. Dustmen stopped work, leaving streets piled high with vermin-ridden rubbish; even gravediggers downed tools in a couple of cities. By contrast, this was a period of renaissance for me, a time of new and exciting opportunities, and so, when I walked into the Department of Energy for the first time and looked down Millbank to where, a short distance away, lay the hospital that had saved my life, I knew that I was

250

incredibly lucky.

After months of work, liaising with the Department, finding sponsors for the prizes, contacting schools all over the country, and working with the Science Museum (which was to house an exhibition of winning work) the entries began to roll in. We searched through them for interesting ideas that might be used for publicity. One that caught my eye came from three ten-year-old boys who had come up with an idea for boiling eggs in an energy efficient way (place in cold water to cover, put lid on the saucepan, bring to the boil, turn off heat and leave for seven minutes). I contacted Dr Magnus Pike, an eccentric scientist whose science-related television programmes had made him a star, and asked if he would like to witness a demonstration. He agreed. Then I went to see Anton Mossiman, head chef at the Dorchester Hotel, and asked him if the boys could give the demonstration in his kitchens, to which this kind and charming man immediately agreed. I sent out a press release headed 'Egghead meets the Eggsperts', finalised all the arrangement then crossed my fingers and hoped for the best. I was worried because Dan had been against the idea from the start, moaning incessantly that it would be a damp squib and, when the day came, complaining about this waste of his valuable time. But to my delight, the Press turned out in force and, even better, a couple of television crews arrived as well. It was my first big publicity coup and the thrill of it sent adrenalin pumping through my veins. On the way back to the office, Dan leaned back in the taxi and sighed happily:

"Ah," he said, "that was one of my better ideas."

One evening, Dan and I were sitting in a fashionable restaurant in Jermyn Street having supper. We were talking non-stop, as we always did, arguing, joking, re-living the day, planning strategies, throwing ideas back and forth, fizzing, when he suddenly said:

"I've got something to tell you."

"What?" I asked, expecting news of our latest campaign.

He opened his wallet, took out a photograph and pushed it across the table. It was a picture of an exquisite woman lying on a poolside recliner, her perfect body slim and tanned in a bikini, her hair falling in shining waves around her shoulders.

"I'm married," he said.

I stared from the photograph to him, aghast, unable to believe what I'd just heard.

"But you can't be," I stammered, "you would have told me, you..."

251

"No," he interrupted, "just think back a minute, when did I ever say I *wasn't* married?"

"But if you're married, why did you say we could never meet at weekends because that's when you see your daughters? I assumed..."

"...you *assumed* I was divorced? But have I ever *said* I was divorced? No. Anyway, it's true, weekends are when I spend every minute I can with my girls, but that doesn't mean to say I don't see them the rest of the week."

"But we're out two or three nights a week, late meetings, having dinner, concerts... We go on business trips together. And we were away for three days at the Three Choirs Festival. I mean, how do you explain that to your wife? I just don't understand."

He began to talk. How he had known the moment he walked down the aisle that he'd made a terrible mistake. How unhappy and incompatible he and his wife had always been. How she was a Roman Catholic and they could therefore never be divorced. How the only thing that mattered to him was his daughters and so he would never, ever leave his wife because it would mean losing them.

As he spoke I began to cry and, to my horror, simply could not stop. I couldn't manage a few pathetic tears into a lace-edged hanky. No, this was projectile sobbing, wet and loud and ugly and embarrassing, bringing conversation at the surrounding tables to a halt.

"I'd better get you home," muttered Dan, paying the bill as quickly as he could before hustling me out, hailing a black cab and – I'm sure with a sigh of relief – helping me into the back. As the taxi wound its way to Fulham with me slumped in the back trying to stifle my sobs, I wondered what he was doing. Had he caught the tube back to West London, walked through his front door and called out:

"Hi, honey, sorry I'm late, my meeting ran on and on..."

I lay in bed next morning, exhausted after a sleepless night of tears, disbelief and shock, and reflected on the bombshell that had hit me. It really was a double whammy because I had lost not just my man but my job. Now I was on my own again, a lonely forty-something with the added burden of a mortgage to pay. I felt drained of emotion; it was too much to take in, too painful to contemplate, so I pulled the duvet over my head and tried to black it all out.

I must have dozed off because the telephone woke me. I reached for the receiver and muttered 'hello'.

"Where the hell are you, woman?"

252

It was Dan and he was his normal exasperated, exasperating self.
"What's happened? It's ten o'clock and we've got the Department team coming in at twelve, and you choose today to have a lie-in – *honestly*!"

"But, but..." I stammered, "after last night, I thought you wouldn't want me to work for you."

"Wouldn't want you to work for me? Oh for God's sake don't be so stupid. Look, get up here fast. We'll talk about all that later."

Bang, and he had gone. Feverishly, I bathed and dressed, grabbed my briefcase and ran for the Tube. Red-eyed, haggard I may have been but I was no longer downcast. In fact I felt exhilarated, certain that if I was going back to work all would soon be well between us.

Where was my head? Why wasn't I seething with rage, seeing through his deception, realising how devious he had been, capitalising on my naivety and allowing me, by default, to believe he was divorced? Why didn't I rage at the unfairness of it all both to me and his poor wife? Why didn't an insistent voice in my brain remind me that only three percent of married men leave their wives for the 'other woman'? Which is what I now was, 'the other woman', me, who for so many years had suffered the role of the aggrieved wife. But no, I rushed into the office, apologising for being late, joining in the preparations for the meeting and knowing from the way Dan smiled at me that all would be well. I couldn't help noticing, though, that today he was wearing a wedding ring.

As the days went by and guilt inevitably rose again and again to dance before my eyes, I simply disowned responsibility and blanked it out. Poor Dan, I thought, his wife truly doesn't understand him (ha, that old chestnut) and one day when his girls have grown up I'm sure we will then have the chance to be together. For the moment, it was business as usual.

One of my strangest and most demanding assignments came when the Home Office commissioned our consultancy to carry out an attitude survey in ten prisons. They wanted to cut back on energy bills and a huge engineering survey was underway. However, the human factor was the weak link because, whilst it is relatively easy to change people's opinions, it is much harder to change actual behaviour. Our task was to establish to what extent prison staff were, or could be, motivated to save energy. I drew the short straw and a freezing February morning found me knocking on the Judas gate of Strangeways Prison in Manchester, where I spent the day scribbling down the thoughts of a cross section of people from the Governor to the lowliest prison officer. The echoing din, the metallic clash of doors slamming and keys turning, the smells, the heavy male energy, the underlying tension – it was a hostile environment but one I got used to as my work continued in the months ahead. However, on that first day I learned a valuable lesson. The prison, like all similar Victorian jails, was of the 'five spoke' design where each wing radiated out from a central hub. I followed a prison officer up a spiral metal staircase from the ground floor to the first floor of this circular hub. As we walked to the centre I heard laughter and the sound of running footsteps beneath me. I glanced down and there, through the open iron lattice floor, was a group of grinning prisoners, all looking upwards.

"Right," said my guide, "first rule for a lady when visiting a prison – never wear a skirt.

I went to jails all over the country. On one wing in Wandsworth Prison I was shown into a cell much larger than the others, currently used as a shop where prisoners could buy toothpaste, cigarettes, sweets and so on. Behind the counter there was another, closed door.

"Why is this cell so much bigger than the rest?" I asked.

The two officers looked at each other.

"Shall we tell her?" asked one.

"Go on then," said the second.

This had once been the condemned cell, he told me, and the second door led to the gallows. The last person to be executed here was Hendrick Neimasz, a murderer, who was hanged in 1961. Until that moment, I had never before felt a chill run up my spine.

My visit to an industrial prison in the West Midlands in March 1982 was particularly auspicious but not because of what I saw or learned. In fact, I found it particularly sad because the inmates were heartbreakingly young. No, it was a day forever imprinted on my memory because, back in London, Mary-Louise was in labour. Because of her medical history it had been decided that she should return from Oman so that the birth could be supervised by a cardiac specialist. The last place I therefore wished to be was several hundred miles away, and in a prison of all places. Throughout the day I kept excusing myself to 'ring my office' whilst in fact calling the hospital to check on her progress. It was not until late afternoon that a baby boy was born, safely and with no medical emergencies. Lou-Lou and Dick named him Diederick Michael and from that moment on he was not only their precious son but the light of his doting grandmother Bebe's life. In fact, the feeling was mutual, as he made clear one day when he was three. I had just returned from a business trip and, seeing him playing outside, hurried out to say hello. Michael raced down the garden, leapt into my arms and flung his own plump little arms round my neck.

"I love oo so much, f****** old Bebe," he murmured.

I mean, how proud can one get? Not only did my grandson adore me but he already had a precocious, if inexplicable, grasp of Anglo-Saxon epithets.

My final visit was to Lewes prison, a small establishment where long-term prisoners were often sent to serve out the last part of their sentences. As it was in a charming old town in the beautiful county of East Sussex, it was also very popular with prison officers. Thus, the atmosphere was the most relaxed of all the jails I visited. I was shown round the prison kitchen, a hive of activity as lunchtime approached

"Are all these men long-term prisoners?" I asked the officer in charge.

"Oh yes," he said, "there's seventeen men working in here and they're all murderers..."

I saw an elderly man walking towards me, white haired and gentle faced. He was carrying a large platter of meat in one hand and a carving knife in the other.

"...oh, and he's a double murderer," continued the officer cheerfully, "he was convicted of murdering his first wife, served his time, got married again as soon as he was released and then killed her too."

Gulp.

As to whether prison staff were interested in, or could be motivated to save energy, the answer in the long report I submitted to the Home Office could have been written on the back of a postcard - they couldn't have cared less. They had so many other grievances, all of which acted as disincentives, that they simply were not interested in what seemed to them like a minor consideration.

However, as a result of this survey a great deal more work came into the consultancy mainly from the Architects Departments of County Councils. Now considered quite experienced, I was asked to write a major report on the subject and, when it was finished ten months later, it was published by the Oxford Business Press. Dan and I were on a train heading north for yet another meeting when he pulled the proofs out of his briefcase and handed them to me.

"There you are," he said, "your first book. I hope you feel proud."

Well I did for about five seconds until I noticed that my name was nowhere to be seen. The ensuing row went on until we reached

255

Birmingham by which time I'd threatened to sue him if, as the author, my name did not appear on the front cover. He countered by saying that as I had been paid to write it he need not include my name. But I won and the most boring tome ever published was eventually launched at the House of Lords. I was asked to give a speech and enjoyed starting it, probably predictably, by saying:

"Ladies and gentlemen, how nice it is to be in the House of Lords this morning instead of in prison..."

One morning, two years after we had started working together, Dan walked into the office. He was late and uncharacteristically quiet.

"Barbara," he said, "I need to speak to you in the conference room."

I followed him in and sat down. I noticed that he looked tired, his eyes red-rimmed.

"Well," he said, "I won't beat about the bush. My wife has found out about us."

Someone had seen us having dinner together and had told her. Now she was making a stand, insisting that unless he dismissed me from the company and swore not to see me again, she would force him to leave their home and, although she would never divorce him, she would make it as difficult as possible for him to see their daughters.

"So I'm afraid that's that. I simply cannot risk doing anything that will ruin my girls' lives. I'm sorry but you're going to have to pack up and leave right now."

He reached across the table and took my hand.

"Look," he said, "we've had the most wonderful time together, the best of my life. I've seen you grow from that timid, too eager to please woman, to the person you are now – confident and clever, the true Barbara. Now you have to go and live your life, do other things, meet new people, be happy. But I must stay and do what is right by my family."

And that was that. Half an hour later I was out on the street, devastated but somehow not surprised. And in a strange way it was almost a relief that this subterfuge had ended. The guilt I had suppressed for so long now stabbed me. I knew all too well the pain of being deceived and so I understood exactly how Dan's wife must be feeling. Now it was payback time and here I was being sent home in disgrace – and quite right too.

As the weeks passed, I gradually began to get over the loss of someone who had been my friend, a man who, like a catalyst, saw my potential, forced me out of the old mould, restored my confidence and, through impatience, bloody mindedness and the sheer force of his personality, helped me achieve more than I had ever thought possible. I could also see that he was not, and never would have been, my 'forever man'. Maybe there would be someone else, maybe not. For the moment I was on my own.

Finding work was not a problem as, when it became known that I was available, a public relations acquaintance with offices in Old Bond Street asked me to join him as a senior consultant. I was delighted because his company specialised in charity work, organising huge, nationwide fundraising campaigns whilst at the same time raising public awareness of the cause through publicity of every kind. Whilst I had enjoyed my work with Dan, it had never really moved me, but now I could throw myself into projects which truly touched my heart.

I started off with three accounts: the National Deaf, Blind and Rubella Handicapped Association, the Royal British Legion's annual Poppy Appeal and the Motor Neurone Disease Association.

The latter was a very sad charity as this disease has no known cure and therefore there could be no hope. In fact, it proved a difficult cause to promote until we heard the news that the film star David Niven had just died of MND. His death was all the more poignant because Niven had spent his last days in his Swiss home, alone except for a couple of nurses, his alcoholic wife Hjordis having returned to her native Sweden. We now had a tragic yet newsworthy hook on which to hang our campaign. By the end of his life he was paralysed, only able to move his thumb. We therefore decided to call our appeal 'The David Niven Thumbs Up Appeal'. We contacted his Hollywood friends and soon some of the greatest stars in movie history were lending their names to the campaign, with Douglas Fairbanks, Junior and Elizabeth Taylor heading the list. And so this actor whose films had given enjoyment to millions was, through the manner of his death, pivotal in raising huge amounts of money for research into this terrible disease.

The National Deaf, Blind and Rubella Handicapped Association – what a mouthful! Fancy saying that when you answer the phone! Our first task, therefore, was to change the name and I still feel rather proud that it was me who came up with the title 'Sense', which the charity is known by to this day. Of all the organisations I worked with, Sense was closest to my heart. The thought of anyone, let alone babies, who could neither see nor hear was almost too awful to contemplate. And yet this amazing group of people had set up a special centre where mothers could bring their babies and learn ways of communicating with them. They did not confine their help to children, offering all sorts of help and opportunities to deaf-blind people of every age. It was inspiring, it was moving and I wanted to do everything I could to raise millions for them. We set to work. There were patrons and supporters to be recruited, fundraising ideas to be thought out, appeal brochures to write, advertisements to be placed, press releases to be sent out, special events to be dreamed up plus television and radio appeals to be arranged. This was such a moving cause that finding big names to support it was easy. Cilla Black agreed to make a radio appeal and I wrote a script incorporating the words of 'Liverpool Lullaby', one of her greatest hits: 'Oh you are a mucky kid,' went the lyrics, 'dirty as a dustbin lid, when he finds out what you did, you'll gerra belt from yer Dad.' She conveyed so movingly the fact that deaf-blind kids can't go out to play and get mucky that within minutes, thousands and thousands of pounds had been pledged. We went on to help Sense raise a great deal of money and represented the charity for a number of years.

Complacency is something one cannot afford in public relations, which is a job where attention to the tiniest detail is paramount. I almost lost the Sense account when, in planning a big fundraising evening, I overlooked a small but vital detail. The venue was to be a ship on the Thames. Everything was in hand – printing, catering, drinks, flowers, live music – and several hundred guests were expected. We had found sponsors to cover the cost of the evening, businesses and wealthy donors to give valuable raffle prizes, and were expecting a stellar turnout of celebrities. These included Esther Rantzen, a very popular figure at the time thanks to her television consumer show 'That's Life', and Anthony Andrews who had recently found stardom as Sebastian Flyte in the iconic television series 'Brideshead Revisited'. Victoria had enlisted three of her pretty girlfriends to help her sell raffle tickets and on the morning of the event, I put on my coat to go and buy the books of tickets. "Oh, you've got so much to do, I'll go for you," said one of my colleagues kindly.

Come the evening and everything was going perfectly. Perfectly, that is, until the time came for the draw. Esther Rantzen pulled the first raffle ticket out of the hat:

"Now then," she called, "who's the lucky person who's won this bottle of Dom Perignon? Blue 55!"

To my horror, up trotted not one but four guests, each clutching a winning ticket, for instead of buying them in four different colours, my well-intentioned colleague had bought four books of tickets, all of which were blue. Fatally, I had not noticed this and now an unholy mess ensured when every number called brought forth four claimants.

"Right," said Esther gamely, "let's narrow this down; anyone wearing red knickers is eliminated..."

The following morning I was hauled before my boss and listened shamefaced as he lambasted me for almost ruining the evening.

"But, it wasn't me who bought the raffle tickets," I protested feebly, "it was..."

"No," he interrupted, "it was *your* show – the buck stopped with you."

It was a lesson I never forgot, but my boss must have forgiven me because shortly afterwards he proposed me for membership of the Institute of Public Relations.

Famous people played an important part in fundraising. – and I'm sure they always will. Movie stars, actors, opera singers, ballerinas, athletes, soap stars, pop singers, comedians - I met so many and was always touched that they were so generous of their time whilst remaining helpful, charming and approachable. Now and then, however, I'd run into people whose fame had gone to their heads. Ernie Wise, now on his own following Eric Morecombe's death, hogged the cameras, droned on about himself instead of the charity and then, as a final insult, insisted on being paid for his appearance. And a very famous - and presumably wealthy - comedienne not only demanded a fee but also leant from her cab as it was about to depart, twiddling her long red talons at me and snapping: "taxi fare, taxi fare." However, the honours for arrogance and appallingly bad manners go equally to Lauren Bacall, the ageing movie star and widow of Humphrey Bogart, and Kingsley Amis, novelist father of Martin Amis. They were quite the most unpleasant people I have ever met.

I had only been with the new consultancy a matter of weeks when a daunting project was lobbed my way. The Royal British Legion was already a client but now we were charged with helping to boost the income from their annual Poppy Appeal by generating as much publicity as possible in the run-up to Poppy Day.

"I want you to think up some sort of road show," said my boss one morning, "take it all round the country, let people know where their money goes when they buy a poppy, come up with some good ideas that will grab the media's attention because we want lots of coverage – oh, and the Legion have only just agreed to this so you've got just three weeks to organise it. Okay?"

I felt far from okay, for I hadn't a clue what to do or how to do it. Our first Poppy Tour was a simple affair; just me, a spokesman from the Legion's national executive, a remarkably pretty former Bluebell showgirl with legs a mile long, and a five-foot high pole on the top of which perched a gigantic poppy. For two weeks we criss-crossed the country by train, wedging the wretched poppy into luggage racks, leaving it in hotels, getting it caught in revolving doors, side-swiping unsuspecting passersby - oh, how I grew to hate that poppy! But we attracted quite a lot of publicity and the Poppy Day takings started to creep up.

By the following year we had come up with a much more interesting plan. As well as recruiting a star for each city we would visit, we decided to form a three-girl pop group which would, predictably, be called The Poppies and, with a new-found nepotism, I recruited Victoria as the lead singer. The other two were what were known as 'publicity girls', although they preferred to be known as models. They were very pretty, extremely stupid and they couldn't sing, but as they only had to mime, this did not matter. A Parisian friend made a beautiful scarlet costume for Victoria and little ra-ra skirts for the girls. Then I had another idea. David Shilling was a well-known milliner at the time whose own annual publicity stunt was to design a bizarre hat for his mother Gertrude to wear at Royal Ascot – a giraffe, a wedding cake, the Eiffel Tower – each year's hat more outlandish than the last. However, David's hats also appeared on the catwalks and graced the heads of society's leading ladies. So I went to see him, handed him a bag of petals from the Legion's famous poppy factory, and cheekily asked if he'd make a hat for Victoria to wear on the tour. The dear man agreed and produced a tiny, utterly exquisite creation. She, meanwhile, had written a song, which was as poignant as it was beautiful, as appropriate as it was catchy:

Wear your poppy with pride,
For those who have died
For a cause they believed in.
Keep the memory alive
For those who survive,
For they still need you.

As we climbed aboard our minibus and headed off on a bright October day, I prayed my plan would work – the celebrities and The Poppies would hook the Press and the speaker would move them with his eloquence. Southampton, Exeter, Plymouth, Bristol, Cardiff, Belfast, Birmingham, Manchester, Leeds, Newcastle and Norwich, here we come!

On that second tour the Legion spokesman was a man called Jimmy Hughes, a university lecturer in Belfast who had reached the rank of Colonel during World War II. He was a very special man, an orator, the power of whose words never failed to move me.

"War," he said, "is an abomination. Some people think the Legion glorifies war but nothing could be further from the truth. Of course we honour the memory of our fallen comrades, but we also exist to support ex-service men and women and their families who suffer as a result of war."

He often finished his speech by quoting the words carved on the memorial commemorating the allied troops who fell during the Battle of Kohima, words which always made my eyes fill with tears:

'When you go home, tell them of us and say,
For your tomorrow, we gave our today.'

The novel idea of a pop group supporting what were seen by some as the Legion's old fuddy duddies worked. Their beauty, Victoria's lovely voice and, of course, the tiny miniskirts, all helped and after every performance, press photographers surrounded them, reporters pushed forward with their notebooks or shoved microphones under their noses. For me, however, the Holy Grail was the arrival of television cameras, meaning that we would hit the local news that evening. We usually did.

The tour was meant to support the work of local Legion groups and for the most part our efforts were welcomed. But in one or two places our presence caused deep resentment. These old soldiers dared not voice their irritation to 'the man from head office' and so I became the focus of their wrath. Like a pack of aggressive terriers, they went for the throat – how *dare* I interfere, this was *their* patch and they didn't want some snooty woman from London trying to muscle in on the act.

"But you've known we were coming for months," I'd say, "and anyway, we're not here to interfere but to help you. The more publicity you get, the more people will give."

But they didn't want to know. Now, with The Poppies fronting the show, they had something they could really get their teeth into.

"It's dis*gust*ing," they roared to the attendant press.

"MINISKIRTED POP GROUP OUTRAGE LEGION MEMBERS" announced the headlines.

"Oh dear, that's torn it," said Jimmy Hughes as we headed for a radio station the following morning.

"Leave it to me," I said.

Next morning, in yet another city, I was on the phone early, asking television, radio stations, and local newspapers, whether they would be covering our event.

"Well," was the usual answer, "it's on the diary but we won't make up our mind until after the morning meeting."

"Well, I won't blame you if you decide not to come," I'd say innocently, "because our pop group has been causing great offence to some Legion members – the tiny skirts and everything you know..."

"Oh really? Tell me more..."

Got yer! The media turned out in force, busily interviewing people in the crowd, doing their best to rustle up a bit of controversy. One radio reporter buttonholed an old lady at the front of the crowd:

"Girls in miniskirts, pop songs – isn't it rather disrespectful to our veterans and our war dead?" he asked.

The old soul, relishing her moment in the spotlight, seized the microphone and cried: "On no, I think they're r-e-a-l-l-y, r-e-a-l-l-y, l-o-o-o-v-e-l-y!".

How lucky I was to be involved in work that I knew truly made a difference. Perhaps 'lucky' is not the right word, perhaps I should say 'honoured'.

Back in early 1980, my evenings were dull after the fever pitch of life with Dan. One night a friend invited me to a party given by a dating agency, so I went along, hating to find myself one of the desperate middle-aged singles all looking for that special someone.

"No," I thought as I left, breathing a sigh of relief to have escaped, "what I need is some time on my own. I definitely do *not* need a man."

I decided to join an Adult Literacy group as a teacher. It was here, in a grotty building near Hammersmith Hospital, that I met Nellie. A short, sturdy little lady in her late forties, she had worked in the hospital's laundry since the age of 14, just a stone's throw from the grim street where she had been born and had lived all her life. She could neither read nor write and, try though I might, all the usual methods of teaching her just did not work. For weeks we made no headway. Perhaps I'm a hopeless teacher, I thought, or perhaps she's someone who will never learn to read. Then one day I had an idea. On a piece of paper I wrote the word 'LAUNDRY'.

"What does that say?" I asked, holding it up.

"Laundry," she said at once.

I wrote another word.

"Physiotherapy," she said

I wrote another and another and another...

"Accident & Emergency, Ante-Natal, Cardiology," she chanted, her voice growing louder and louder with each new word, "Intensive Care, Gynaecology, Haematology, Orthopaedics..."

"Nellie!" I exclaimed, "YOU CAN READ!"

"I CAN READ! I CAN READ!" she cried.

We jumped up from the table and flung our arms round each other. The supervisor put his head round the door.

"What's going on?" he asked.

"I CAN READ!" Nellie shouted, her face aglow.

I held up each word and she read them out proudly.

"My goodness, Nellie," he said, "d'you realise what this means? If you know all these really long, complicated words, everything else is going to be a piece of cake!"

This dowdy, downtrodden, forgotten little lady blossomed from that moment on, becoming ever more confident as her literacy slowly took wings. Then came the day when she told me she had a boyfriend. Oh, Adult Literacy is about so much more than reading!

I always had a car from my local minicab company to take me to Hammersmith for these classes, as I did not feel happy using public transport at night. And so it was that, on a November evening in 1980, my doorbell rang. I pressed my intercom.

"Your car, madam," said a pleasant voice.

"Coming," I said and, picking up my bag, walked into the hall and opened the front door.

A man stood there. For a timeless moment we stared at each other, unable to move or speak. All the sounds of the city seemed to fall silent. The world itself seemed to disappear. Then he stepped backwards, stumbling over the steps, and that broke the spell. I followed the stranger out into the street. He opened the door of his car. I climbed into the back. Then together we drove away into the night.

I did not know that this was Nicholas John Ridley Swanson, co-owner of the cab company, born of the same lineage as Bishop Nicholas Ridley, the great English martyr, and great-grandson of a Swedish Count. I did not know that this was the moment when the clairvoyant's prophesy would come true   I could not have guessed that here was the man with whom I would share my life, that he was the one who would truly honour me, as I him.   Unknown too were the adventures we would share, the struggles, the disasters, the joys that lay ahead.   Here was the man with whom I would both laugh and cry.   He would care for me, nursing me in sickness, shouldering every burden.   We would support each other through the best and worst of times.   Here at last was the man who would, as was foretold, 'surround me with love for the rest of my life', and who, nearly thirty years later, is still my one and only, my shining star.

Nick & Barbara after a service to celebrate their 25th anniversary
in December, 2005

A F T E R W O R D

In 1984 NICHOLAS sold his cab company and opened an antique shop just off the Kings Road in London, initially under the guidance of his younger brother, already an experienced dealer. I later left my job in public relations to join him, and - apart from a three-year idyll in rural France - we worked for the next 22 years as dealers specialising in English oak and country furniture, spending the last fourteen years before we retired living in and working from our Tudor house in the medieval town of Petworth, West Sussex – an antiques Mecca which attracts visitors from all over the world. Hodgkins Disease never returned to haunt me but both colon cancer and breast cancer did. Why I have been spared again and again, I do not know. What I do know is that I am truly blessed.

When her son was old enough, Mary-Louise (who now uses her middle name, GRACE) became a very successful business woman and then, in order to achieve her childhood ambition, went to university where she gained a first class honours degree in Linguistics and Language Pathology. She is now a Principal Speech and Language Therapist working for Solent Healthcare NHS Trust.

In 1985 VICTORIA (now known as AEONE) represented the United Kingdom in the Eurovision Song Contest in Gothenberg where her co-written song 'Love Is' came a worthy fourth. She later moved to Los Angeles to pursue her musical career and married a music producer, engineer and writer, Jeff Silverman. Their work together produced a huge catalogue of songs covered by many well-known artists such as Rick Springfield and has been used in numerous hit television shows. Although the marriage ended they continue to work together in different ways. Now a recognised artiste and composer, her work has featured in hundreds of films, television programmes and trailers, and her four albums have met with critical acclaim. www.aeone.com

My sister PATRICIA went on to study aromatherapy and to open her very successful London School of Aromatherapy. In 1988 her book 'Aromatherapy - an A-Z' was published. It has been translated into twelve languages and is not only the world's best-selling book on the subject but has been described as 'the most comprehensive guide to aromatherapy ever published'. She has written four other books: Subtle Aromatherapy, A Change for the Better, Astrological Aromatherapy and Angels in our Time. She moved to Totnes, Devon, in 1989 and was inspired to change her name to Ishvara D'Angelo. Now aged 79, she continues to work as an artist, astrologer, sculptor and writer, and has recently been taking cello lessons. www.angelart.me.uk

My father, CHARLES died in 1985 aged 82. He was suffering from heart failure and was tired, unwell and ready to go.
"Oh, I wish I could die," he would sigh.
"If you die I'll kill you," I'd joke.
And then he did.

My stepmother ELLEN (TIGGY) died four years later during a visit to France, where Nick and I were then living. She was describing her childhood and the wonderful puddings her mother used to make when she paused and a half-smiling, faraway look crept over her face. Then, felled by a heart attack, she collapsed, dying in my arms on the way to hospital.

Life as the wife of an army chaplain meant that my sister-in-law SARAH and brother-in-law PETER WHITE, and their children, spent a number of years moving from one military base to another, including Belgium, Wales and Surrey. When Peter left the army he became a parish priest in several different places. However, he eventually became Vicar of Barming, a pretty village in the heart of Kent, where they lived until his retirement and where Sarah was as pivotal as her husband in their commitment to, and running of, the parish.

My mother-in-law, AUDREY, soldiered on at Grantchester House School until her health began to fail, first taking a part-time role and then selling up – well over thirty years after she first opened its doors in 1948. She

267

eventually moved to Kent to be near Sarah and the family, where she died in 1987 aged 79. I am glad to say that Victoria effected a reconciliation between Audrey and I, and that we once again became friends.

JOHN became a very successful barrister. However, his marriage to Natalie ended in divorce and he went on to marry for a third time, a relationship which was to prove disastrous. In 1991 he was diagnosed with an inoperable brain tumour. Natalie, who had had no contact with him since their divorce, awoke one day with the strong feeling that she should call, only to discover that he was in hospital having an exploratory operation on his brain. Realising that his third wife simply did not care about him and the awful illness which had beset him, she stepped in, taking him into her own home and looking after him for the rest of his life. In his last days John gave to his daughters the gift they had always wanted – they came to know that, in his own way, he loved them, and always had. As the end approached, his towering courage was extraordinary to behold. Shedding his worldliness, he became again the pure, spiritual soul of his youth. Around him was a radiance. He died, aged 55, with his two daughters and his second wife by his side. I came to his bedside moments later. Then we four women who had all played our part in his life, bade his spirit farewell as it rose up into the light of God.

A C K N O W L E D G E M E N T S

WRITING THIS BOOK has been a long, always rewarding, often difficult task which would not have been possible without the help of the following people:

Very special thanks are due to my son-in-law, NEIL LAWSON BAKER, who not only took the beautiful photograph of a swan on the cover but also designed the cover himself. In addition, he spent endless hours working meticulously on the preparation, scanning and insertion of photographs, as well as guiding me through other 'techy' aspects of the production process. He also has my love and gratitude for all he has brought into our lives. www.neillawsonbaker.com

My most grateful thanks to my sister, ISHVARA D'ANGELO, who helped me with the painstaking task of proof-reading my manuscript and was also able to tell me things about our mother and our family which I did not know. I thank her too for being the best of sisters who was a true light amidst the often-sad days of our childhood. www. angelart.me.uk

To ANDREW CORK, Managing Director of Print on Demand–Worldwide, and PAULINE TEBBUTT, Publishing Services Advisor, my thanks not only for their professionalism but for their kindness and patience in helping me through the complications of the publishing process.

Thanks also to my sister-in-law SARAH WHITE, who has been immensely helpful in filling in background details about the Watson family and, of course, for her steadfast love and friendship down all the years.

I am touched and honoured that KATIE HOEBEE used the wartime part of my manuscript as the basis for history projects with the primary school children she teaches.

Where would I have been without feedback and encouragement from those who read sample chapters? Firstly, four people who are very precious to me: my grandson, MICHAEL HOEBEE, my stepchildren, KARA and BEN SWANSON, and Ben's partner, LISA LYNCH. Also, the following dear friends: TERESA and the late AUGUST WEDDEPOHL, JENNI and IAN WARREN, MARY and PHILIP IDE-SMITH, TONY PHILLIMORE and MIKE GRIFFITHS. My thanks to you all.

To my daughters, GRACE LAWSON BAKER and AEONE WATSON - who, like a silver thread down the winding pathway of the years, have illuminated my life - my deep love and thanks not only for encouraging me to continue down the writing road but also for their understanding that I have written about the father they loved in a way which may be as painful for them to read as it was for me to write.

Finally, my deep and abiding love, and thanks to my husband, NICHOLAS, who has had to live with me during the gestation of this book, putting up with my frustration and occasional despair that it would ever be finished, whilst continuing to help, encourage and urge me on.

West Ashling,
West Sussex, June, 2010

Visit the author on www.facebook.com